The German Revolution of 1989

A united Germany is now the major economic and political force of Europe. Prior to the autumn of 1989 no one thought unification possible, and even now there is much uninformed speculation about this new and powerful nation. Clearly a better understanding of the causes and consequences of what could be called 'the most successful revolution in German history' is needed. The contributors to this volume, among them East German scholars bringing their valuable insider knowledge, examine the unique combination of 'real socialism' in the country previously considered the most reliable member of the Soviet bloc.

Gert-Joachim Glaeßner is Professor of Political Science at the Humboldt University and the Institute for Social Science Research in Berlin and **Ian Wallace** is Professor of German at the University of Bath.

The German Revolution of 1989

Causes and Consequences

Edited by
Gert-Joachim Glaeβner and Ian Wallace

BERG

Oxford / Providence

First published in 1992 by
Berg Publishers Limited
Editorial offices:
165 Taber Avenue, Providence, RI 02906, USA
150 Cowley Road, Oxford, OX4 1JJ, UK

Library of Congress Cataloging-in-Publication Data
The German Revolution of 1989 : causes and consequences / edited by
Gert-Joachim Glaessner and Ian Wallace.
  p. cm.
  Includes bibliographical references and index.
  ISBN 0–85496–785–0
  1. Germany (East) –Politics and government—1989–1990.
Germany—History—Unification, 1990.   3. World politics—1989–
I. Glaessner, Gert-Joachim, 1944–   II. Wallace, Ian.
DD289.G46   1990
943.1087′9—dc20   91–37778
                                                            CIP

British Library Cataloguing in Publication Data
Glaessner, Gert-Joachim
  The German revolution of 1989: causes and
  consequences.
  I. Title   II. Wallace, Ian
  943.087

  ISBN 0–85496–785–0

Printed in Great Britain by
Billing & Sons Ltd, Worcester

Contents

Contents

List of Tables

Foreword

The year 1989 marks a turning point in history. Two hundred years after the French Revolution an empire collapsed, the roots of which stretch back into the nineteenth century. Socialism had set out to make real what the French Revolution had promised – freedom, equality, fraternity. The theoreticians of socialism wanted social justice based on individual freedoms. Socialism of the Soviet type, which came into being in October 1917 and established itself after the Second World War as an alternative model to the western democracies, always subordinated these individual freedoms to what it termed social rights. In essence, it represented a model by which Soviet and, later, Chinese and other societies might achieve the modernisation they lacked. It was only in such societies that revolutions after the Soviet pattern took place.

After 1945 'occupation regimes' (Samuel Huntington) were established in central and eastern Europe. The Soviet Union emerged from the Second World War as a world power. The system of Yalta, which sought to establish zones of influence, led to the division of the world and of Europe into two antagonistic blocs, the most visible expression of which was the division of Germany and in particular of Berlin. This appeared both inevitable and lasting and seemed even to promote the maintenance of stability in Europe – as long as the Soviet Union was prepared and in a position to live up to its role as a world power.

After determining the post-war order in Europe for forty years, this constellation began to undergo dramatic transformation after 1985. The Soviet leadership under Mikhail Gorbachev came to realise that it could not guarantee the continued existence of its empire by use of force. Glasnost and perestroika gave rise to radical change in the ossified socialist states of central and eastern Europe – much more so even than in the Soviet Union itself. According to Gorbachev, glasnost and perestroika were intended to unleash a revolution in the Soviet Union; in fact, they led to a 'reverse revolution' in Central Europe. The peoples won back their freedom and their right to self-determination. They toppled the old regime, although it is not always clear what this will eventually lead to. It is an open question whether democracy can be achieved. Whatever the outcome, however, these countries have now returned to Europe.

The radical changes in the German Democratic Republic are part and parcel of this historical process, which has changed the map of Europe and led to a new geopolitical constellation. Whether the Germans and their neighbours like it or not, a united Germany is now the major economic and political power at the heart of Europe. Until 1989, both German states and societies, the Federal Republic and the GDR, thought of themselves in terms of their peripheral situation. Both were outposts of mutually hostile systems. Throughout the GDR's existence, its political culture was marked by the conflict between, on the one hand, the officially prescribed political and ideological orientation towards the east and, on the other, the attraction exercised by the western way of life. The Federal Republic was the first really 'western' society in Germany; she was the 'European Germany' which the writer Thomas Mann had called for after the Second World War.

Without the assistance of its western part, Germany has become a new nation-state. Prior to the autumn of 1989 no-one had believed that this would happen in the twentieth century. Since all politicians and experts had proceeded on the assumption that the unity of Germany could only be achieved as part of a post-national European peace, nobody has yet worked out how Germany can best fulfil its new political role under radically altered circumstances.

After the war two very different societies developed in Germany, and these must now grow together. During the 1990s Germany will be preoccupied with efforts to make the much-invoked 'unity of the nation' a tangible reality. 'Nation-building' means removing or modifying social cleavages, dealing with cultural differences, and developing common values and patterns of behaviour. At the same time Germany is faced by expectations which it can scarcely fulfil. These come from central and eastern Europe, which will become increasingly significant at a time when Germany must redefine its role as a major economic power, as a medium-sized power within a new Europe, and as a political culture subscribing to western ideas of individual human rights and a free democracy.

This constellation of factors provides the background against which to raise the question of the causes and consequences of the

'German revolution' of 1989. Until just before its collapse the GDR was regarded as a relatively stable factor within the Soviet system. The implosion (rather than explosion) of the political system could not have been predicted. There are numerous indications that a unique combination of destabilising factors coincided to bring about the end of 'real socialism': the Soviet Union's decision not to defend its empire by force, as in 1953, 1956 and 1968 (Mazowieski's non-communist government in Poland was the proof of this); the opening of the borders in Hungary and the mass exodus which it unleashed (this signified a large-scale renunciation of loyalty to the state, especially by young people); the cultural transformation of the GDR which, over the years, led to increasing similarity to cultural values in developed western societies; the loss of the communist goal-culture, particularly among a younger generation which no longer believed the promises of the political leadership and withdrew from the ideological embrace of the Party; and, finally, the increasingly obvious signs of economic and ecological crisis. Attempts by the political leadership to use the means available to an authoritarian welfare state in order to secure loyalty collided with the limits of growth.

The contributors to this volume – four from the United Kingdom, three from West Berlin, two from East Berlin, and one from North America – hope to contribute to an understanding of the processes which we have here been able to do no more than adumbrate. They do so from a variety of backgrounds and perspectives, and in the knowledge that the causes and consequences of the most successful revolution in German history will continue to intrigue the Germans themselves, their immediate neighbours and the world community for years to come.

Gert-Joachim Glaeβner
Ian Wallace

-

PART I

Political, Social and
Economic Change

–1–

Political Structures in Transition

Gert-Joachim Glaeßner

Revolution or Counter-Revolution –
Some Considerations

War and revolution would, thought Lenin, dictate the course of the twentieth century. This century has indeed witnessed two world wars, a Cold War, and what was seen as the advent of a new epoch in 1917 – an epoch which began with civil war and terror and which after seventy years seems now to have come to an end.

Revolutions have generally been dictated by violence, and those of the twentieth century have been so on an unprecedented scale. In her book *On Revolution* Hannah Arendt wrote:

> The . . . differences between war and revolution (the fact that war is inspired by necessity and revolution by freedom, that the focus of world events is increasingly shifting away from war and towards revolution) should not obscure the fact that we are dealing with phenomena which historically have been closely interrelated. Their common link is violence, and the role played by violence should be all the more important to us *because* it appears to disqualify war and revolution as political phenomena. (Arendt 1974: 4)

With the possible exception of Romania the revolutions of 1989 appear to have broken this causal link.

In the case of the GDR it can be asked if, in view of the collapse of the political system, the events of 1989/90 did constitute a revolution. For the old elites who had always feared that their social experiment would end this way the events were a counter-revolution, that is, the restoration of the old capitalist order. The first freely elected Prime Minister of the GDR, Lothar de Maizière, stated on taking office that radical change in the GDR was 'part of a revolutionary process of renewal in eastern Europe which is at the same time a Europe-wide and world process'. He went on to say that although 'some may believe that the GDR witnessed a counter-revolution it was a law of necessity that after seventy years "real socialism" had to be *countered* with something. Those for whom socialism constituted a brutal party dictatorship, conformism, economic étatism and centralized command economics had committed such a fundamental error that now only unequivocal opposition is possible' (*Neues Deutschland*, 20.4.90).

As recently as November 1989 the *éminence grise* of the GDR social sciences, Jürgen Kuczynski, spoke of a conservative revolution, that is one which preserved and renewed society. Events have proved him wrong. Similarly, those including the writers Christa Wolf and Stefan Heym who on 4 November 1989 addressed a demonstration of more than half a million people on the Alexanderplatz in East Berlin placed their hopes in a revolutionary renewal of socialism.

If revolution is taken as the fundamental, not necessarily violent overthrow of the political, economic and social structures of society then the events in the GDR seem to have been a revolution. In my view the revolutionary change of 1989 in the socialist countries bade the final farewell to a secular utopia which had aimed to establish a just social order of equals and which ended with the loss of the bourgeois freedoms and civil society which had since 1776 and 1789 been painstakingly, albeit only partially, accomplished.

The toppling of the SED (Sozialistische Einheitspartei Deutschlands – Socialist Unity Party of Germany) leadership marked at the same time the end of a social experiment which had been imposed by an external agency (the occupying forces) and which did not in any way reflect the economic, social and cultural conditions of such an industrially developed, if war-ravaged, country as the former Soviet Zone of Occupation. The Soviet model of compensatory development implemented in central Europe after 1945 began to impede, not enhance, modernisation in the developed countries without however entirely preventing it, notably in the cultural sphere. The revolutions which took place in central Europe and in the GDR were in the first place not of a conservative, but of a compensatory nature: they restored the conditions of a liberal bourgeois order. In the GDR this became known as an 'abrogated revolution' in view of the specific national conditions which resulted in the process of an adaptation of the GDR model and its incorporation into the Federal Republic.

The Structural Defects of 'Real Socialism'

The implosion of a political and social system which had hitherto been considered invincible demonstrated that the collapse of the GDR resulted not from specific or accumulated errors but from structural defects within the system. The system was based on the belief that a modern, industrial society could be planned and regulated from the centre and that the Marxist–Leninist party exercised a monopoly of the scientific understanding of the laws of society. This belief contained the more fundamental reason for the emergence of authoritarian political and social structures which were neither flexible nor responsive to change. These structures could make only a belated and half-hearted response (if any) to the need for change and modernisation.

This system has been termed 'structural Stalinism'. It represents a political conception which can be characterised as the following: the SED conceived the political system as a homogeneous entity moulded, directed and controlled by the Party. Within this nexus the independence of specific spheres of policy or a division of powers was not tolerated. Only a centralised policy based on standardised principles could, in its view, accomplish the social objectives of the Party: the building of socialism/communism. Everything was subordinate to this goal. Only within this uniform complex of Party, state and society could a division of tasks between specific institutions and organisations be envisaged. Executive, legislature, judiciary and all the state institutions and 'social organisations' could not question the leading role of the Party. This Marxist-Leninist Party defined itself as the 'political and organisational centre of society'. The state was its 'principal instrument' in the formation of a socialist society (Glaeßner 1989: 90–105). The mass organisations (the unions, youth and women's leagues) and the fraternal parties were of their own free will to subordinate their interests to the leading role of the SED. Any suggestion of the independence of individual spheres of the political system or even of a division of powers would be regarded as a general attack on the basic premises of the state and the social order. All components of the political system were to pursue the same aims and function according to the same principles. This implied above all the recog-

-5-

nition of 'democratic centralism' as the regulatory principle of the whole social order. Both the structure and the function of the political system of Soviet-type socialism clearly demonstrate that 'democratic centralism' as a regulatory principle assisted in securing the hegemony of the Party in all spheres of society. Its removal would have meant depriving the Party of its influence on the recruitment of new political cadres, specific mechanisms of instruction and control and the parallel structure of Party apparatus, state administration bureaucracy and state security.

The right of the Party-state to subordinate all spheres of society to its direction and regulation prevented the pursuit of pragmatic and responsive policies and produced an artificial politicisation of everyday life. The inherited centralism and authoritarianism, notwithstanding the signs of corruption and neo-feudal privileges, acted as a major impediment to the development of society and to the resolution of the economic, social and cultural problems with which the GDR and the other socialist states had long been confronted. The key fact that society and political life were wholly subordinate to the Party precluded any successful process of modernisation or adaptation and resulted ultimately in the collapse of the old system.

Socialism of the Soviet type failed to display its superiority to capitalism. It proved unable to cast off the chains of Stalinism and to create a modern, working socialist society in its place. If anything, only a radical modernisation of the system could have salvaged elements of the ideas which spawned the socialist movement. This historic opportunity has now been squandered, and not only in the GDR.

In a paper which is part of a research project entitled 'Philosophical questions on the elaboration of a view of modern socialism' undertaken at the Humboldt University in East Berlin (project researchers had enacted a pivotal role in anticipating the events of October and November 1989) the deep-seated reasons for the crisis are described:

> The growing indications that the situation will deteriorate or worse still explode, coupled with the difficulties encountered in resolving it in a constructive fashion, derive from the growing sense of powerlessness amongst the people who are confronted with existing social structures. Socialisation of the means of production has assumed almost exclusively the forms of economic étatism. The provision for certain human needs as determined by the state on the one hand and the use of repressive

measures to quell pressure for change in major societal structures are mutually determinant. There is little room for independent action, for taking responsibility for one's own actions and there is great reluctance to take risks which together form the guiding values of the generations of today. Priority is given to fulfilling what is prescribed by the state. (Bresch and Goyke 1989: 107–8)

This mechanism prevented real change and the adaptation of both the political and the social system to changing circumstances. As in other Soviet-type socialist countries the GDR would have required a root-and-branch modernisation and restructuring which, in order to be successful, would have had to cast off the chains of the socio-economic, political and cultural structures of society and the political system. This was the basic prerequisite for the successful modernisation of the political, economic and social system.

The advent of perestroika in the Soviet Union presented the GDR with arguably its last opportunity to initiate such a regulated process of transformation. It was an opportunity lost. The SED and its notion of party-centralised planning and rule failed to grasp the complexity of the new problems. It failed to realise that since the 1960s social, cultural and political changes had occurred in the GDR which affected every political sphere. Neither the normative regulations in place nor existing institutional system and state doctrine could cope with the new difficulties faced. 'Real socialism' as the derivative of Stalinist rule had proved to be a political and socio-economic system unequal to the demands of a modern society. It has failed once and for all and the 'GDR model' has collapsed in its wake (Thomas 1972).

The Failure of a Historical Experiment

In the analysis of historical revolutions the social sciences have emphasised that revolution is not necessarily defined by violence and sudden change. A number of factors must coincide: a change in the political elite, the overthrow of the normative and juridical basis of a society and fundamental change in the structure of political and social relations. Three more deep-seated dimensions merit our attention, however.

Firstly, the changes in central Europe marked the end both of chiliastic utopianism and of nineteenth-century secular evolutionary thought. Until very recently the twentieth century had been characterised by ideological argument about views of society which sought to reduce the complexities of modern societies to simple arithmetic. For the first time this century history is again open and not obfuscated by ideological artefact.

Secondly, since the former socialist countries are not – until now anyway – transforming into repressive regimes it is possible to examine the repercussions of such a social experiment which prevented the development of a bourgeois society in the Soviet Union and destroyed it in the countries of eastern and central Europe by supplanting diversity with an ideological, political and cultural monism and deliberately demarcated itself from the development of the 'World Revolution of Westernization' (cf. von Laue 1987).

Thirdly, one of the many examples of creative graffiti to be seen on the Berlin Wall in 1990 read 'I am Cain and Abel'. The former socialist countries eschew the diametrically opposed attempts at explanation launched from the outside and in the GDR as a reaction to the past. Such attempts obscure the view of the complicated nexus of relations between rule and obedience, conformism and resistance, relative social justice and glaring inequality in the political sphere, between the system and the private domain. The structures of authority and society were interwoven in diverse ways. Only if this is borne in mind can the durability of acquired modes of behaviour and attitudes even after the fall of the old political order be properly understood.

In the midst of the unfolding crisis in the socialist countries of central and eastern Europe the GDR was considered by many observers to be an island of relative peace and stability. While it became increasingly clear that the political leadership no longer read the signs of the times observers outside the GDR did not show sufficient historical and sociological awareness to forecast a scenario which would broadly identify what was to happen in the late summer and autumn of 1989.

Everything appeared to be part of socialist normality. The fortieth anniversary celebrations of the GDR were designed to prove that it was a stable socialist republic and an esteemed member of the international community. However, inadvertently, the bombastic self-congratulation of the Honecker leadership operated as a catalyst for a popular uprising. The fortieth anniversary festivities degenerated into an embarrassing funeral oration of a political and social system which had proved unable either to adapt or to reform and of a ruling phalanx which, remote from any reality, believed in its own proclamations of success.

Nevertheless, the situation had only a few years earlier presented an entirely different picture. At the beginning of the 1980s, with the Cold War at its height, the GDR leadership secured recognition because it had adhered to a relatively independent line from the Soviet Union under Brezhnev. In autumn 1987 Erich Honecker was received in Bonn with full honours as the representative of the second German state. However, shortly thereafter regression – at first barely discernible to Western observers – set in which was within two years to lead to the collapse of real socialism.

Only on 11 October 1989, after tens of thousands had left the GDR, did the politburo of the SED begin to grasp the situation. A declaration admitted that problems existed and pledged political concessions – only too late, as subsequent events have shown. The removal of Honecker from office on 18 October could no longer arrest the collapse of the old regime. The mass exodus of young East Germans in particular continued unabated, oppositional groups made further inroads and the belief spread amongst broad sections of the population that radical reform alone would not be enough to prevent the collapse of the GDR.

Increasing numbers of people took to the streets chanting 'Wir sind das Volk' ('We are the people'). On 7 November, three days after the major demonstration in East Berlin buoyed up by the hope of a fundamental and new beginning, the government of Prime Minister Willi Stoph resigned; a day later a new politburo was appointed and on 9 November the borders were opened. On 13 November Hans Modrow (SED) was appointed the new Prime Minister by the *Volkskammer* (People's Chamber).

This development would have been impossible had several factors not come together to precipitate the collapse of the old order. The thousands of young people alone could have achieved no more than the few hundred courageous members of the opposition groups or indeed the reformers within the ranks of the SED and its allied parties. The opening of the frontier between Austria and Hungary created for the first time since 1961 a situation in which the people could escape the constraints of life under the SED. This meant the loss of the very foundations on which their authority rested, namely that no-one could escape their power apparatus and had therefore to conform one way or another. The confluence of these factors produced the necessary volatile mixture, facilitated the implosion of the political system and blew away the old structures.

The GDR was not alone in this regard. In 1989 the old regimes in

Poland, Czechoslovakia and Romania collapsed, while the Chinese leadership held on to power by means of a massacre. The deeper underlying causes of the crisis in the system now merit our attention.

The social and political crisis of the GDR was part of a general crisis of socialism in those countries upon which, after the war, the socio-economic and political system of the Soviet Union had been imposed. *Prima facie*, it can be considered a crisis of a political and social order also beset by inefficient economic performance, even if economic decline did precipitate the political and social crisis. Seen in the wider context, however, it is the crisis of a pre-modern political and social system.

The ruling communist parties aimed to standardise the societies they ruled and to create in their image a new socialist (wo)man. The reality in both the GDR and the other socialist countries was somewhat different: societies had successfully opposed the uniformity advocated by the leadership. In addition, the previous twenty years had seen a process of cultural and social change not dissimilar to that of modern industrial societies: there was a differentiation in social structure and the old class conflict lost its importance; new 'cleavages' emerged; new values and modes of behaviour came into view; the influences of international culture and civilisation could no longer be held at bay as had been possible in the early 1960s when the ruling SED attempted to prohibit western television viewing. However, the Berlin Wall and closed borders prevented the population from participating actively in these developments. There was a growing sense of imprisonment which fuelled discontent. The SED response was either non-existent or insufficient.

On top of this another factor not without its dangers for orthodox circles came into play after 1985: glasnost and perestroika in the Soviet Union. A process unique in world history and without recourse to war took place – the transformation from a dictatorship and its claims to hegemony to an enlightened authoritarianism with elements of democracy. The countries of the erstwhile socialist bloc could not remain unaffected; 1989 became the year of the collapse and overthrow of real socialism in central and eastern Europe.

The Collapse of the State Party

Individual groups within the state party, the SED, had long attempted to stimulate a thoroughgoing reform process. After

Gorbachev's accession to power in the Soviet Union pressure mounted on the Party hierarchy to initiate wide-ranging reform along Soviet lines. For a number of reasons debate never went beyond the stage of informal discussion in small circles. Reformers made their views public for the first time in October and November 1989 and secured in the following weeks and months significant influence over the restructuring process of the political system.

At the same time grass-roots discontent mounted. It secured the replacement of the party leadership of Egon Krenz who had taken office in October. Krenz had been Honecker's 'crown prince' and had been the politburo member responsible for state security. Discontent also forced the convening of an extraordinary Party congress of the SED on 8 and 16/17 December – against the wishes of the leadership. This congress resolved to 'reform the SED as a modern socialist party' which would have to make a radical break with 'Stalinist structures'. Stalinist socialism had been unable to respond to the compelling economic, social, defence, ecological and cultural problems of civilisation. It was in fact part of these problems.

The Party congress could not, however, resolve to take the radical step of dissolving a party incriminated by history. Its new name, SED-PDS (Party of Democratic Socialism), combined two barely reconcilable political views. Despite its radical self-criticism the SED-PDS was scarcely able to lend credibility to its political transformation. Its influence on the running of the state was secured, albeit at a price: the SED-PDS forfeited much credibility even with its new, reform-minded leadership because, despite its efforts, it remained unable to shed old-style thinking and old apparatus structures and faced the accelerating changes in the political climate practically bereft of power.

Even after the Party had been renamed again as the Party of Democratic Socialism in February 1990 it could not shed its history. The series of scandals and comprehensive evidence of the complicity of leading members of the PDS in the old system could not, however, destroy the standing of the Party in the eyes of long-standing members, as is demonstrated by the remarkable success achieved in the elections of 1990. This was in large measure due to the PDS's success in attracting not only old-guard communist support but also many of those who most feared the social costs of unification with the Federal Republic – first and foremost state servants, members of the security apparatus but also a large number of intellectuals who had not yet abandoned the socialist ideal.

Gert-Joachim Glaeßner

Collapse and a New Beginning – The Citizens' Movements

The existence of political groups which appealed in the autumn of 1989 for the establishment of a liberal and socially just society in the GDR galvanised hundreds of thousands of people into taking to the streets and calling for a new beginning. However, it was only for a very brief period, if at all, that the aims of these groups coincided with popular opinion. This only emerged later because everyone was caught up in the cataclysm and there was no time in October 1989 to mount a debate which could have brought such differences to light. They quickly emerged after 9 November: the people motivated predominantly by materialist concerns who wanted to leave the GDR permanently and the revolutionaries of the citizens' movements motivated by post-material values and attitudes had little common ground, not to mention the reformist circles in the SED itself which had remained silent and had just begun the search for an alternative stance.

The oppositional and citizens' groups which briefly articulated the mood of broad sections of the population were informed by the conditions in which they emerged: they were culturally rather than power-orientated. They were grass-roots democratic movements and opposed to absolute political views. They opened society for a frank and controversial debate on the problems of the people. However, when faced with a situation in which an authority considered to be invincible had been exposed as a monolith these movements were forced to confront severe problems before they were ready. Were they to join in the struggle for power or to continue to act as the voice outside the logic of power? The opposition faced an old dilemma. Unlike its Polish counterpart, the opposition in the GDR had never succeeded in forging an alliance between the opponents of the system supported primarily by intellectuals, critical members of the Party intelligentsia, and the workers. All past attempts at reform of Party rule (in 1953, 1957 and in the years after 1963) had failed for this reason.

Months before October 1989 and galvanised by the ballot-rigging of the communal elections in May of that year, the large number of grass-roots initiatives which had found refuge under the roof of the Church had to make a decision about if and when they should initiate the necessary process of change in the GDR. The mass exodus of late summer demanded an unequivocal stance. Even in 1990 the advocates of a new political culture remained in the minority.

The citizens' movements had emerged at a time when any political activity beyond the regulated forms of 'socialist democracy' was prohibited and subject to state repression. Evidence of this is provided in the (now public) reports of the Ministry for State Security which warned the Party leadership of the growing influence of these groups among the population: their number was estimated at about 2,500. In mid-August 1989 the Church organisation known as 'Renunciation of the Practice and Principle of Separation' called for the formation of a broad movement which could stand at the next elections as an 'identifiable alternative' to the SED and its allied block parties.

It was no coincidence that in October/November 1989 New Forum had become the symbol of change and rebellion. New Forum saw itself as a broad church on the left and umbrella for the opposition, and continues to define itself as a movement which seeks to facilitate and stimulate a 'democratic dialogue' on questions affecting the whole of society. Their founding appeal stated:

> If all the contradictions in society are to be recognised, opinions and arguments heard and explored, if the general interest is to be distinguished from social interests then we need a democratic dialogue on the role to be played by the rule of law, the economy and culture. Together, across the country and publicly we must consider these questions and talk with each other . . . To this end we now form a political platform for the whole country which will enable people irrespective of occupation, party or group affiliation to participate in the discussion and work out the vitally important social problems of the GDR. For this overarching initiative we have chosen the name NEW FORUM. (Bresch and Goyke 1989: 19)

On 12 September 1989 twelve people published an 'Appeal for Involvement in Personal Affairs' (among them Ulrike Poppe, Wolfgang Ullmann and Konrad Weiß). Faced with the reluctance to reform state socialism and the ongoing crisis in the GDR they appealed for the creation of an alliance of all reform-minded people: 'We invite all those who wish to join in a dialogue about the principles of a democratic restructuring of our country.' This appeal was the first public act of the Citizens' Movement: Democracy Now. It also contained 'ideas for a democratic restructuring of the GDR' introduced by the following statement:

> The aim of our proposals is to secure peace within our country and thus

beyond our frontiers. We want to assist in the formation of a society based on solidarity and to democratise all spheres of life. At the same time we need to discover a new symbiotic relationship with our natural environment. We want to see the continued development of a new socialism distinct from the one which became bogged down in étatism. In place of the tutelage of a Party which had elevated itself to the status of conductor and pedagogue of the people we want a state founded on the basic consensus of society, which is accountable to society and thus enters the public realm, the *res publica* of responsible citizenship. Social achievements which have proven themselves as such should not be jeopardised by a reform programme. (Demokratie Jetzt 1990)

The citizens' movements which predate October 1989, such as New Forum, Democracy Now and the Initiative for Peace and Human Rights, derived great moral authority from their willingness to speak openly and their long years of involvement in the opposition movement. The citizens' groups sought to bring about social dialogue about the various problems which had accumulated in the decades of bureaucratic socialist dictatorship. This dialogue would be the *sine qua non* for the creation of a civil society.

However, the dynamic of events was overtaken by the need to set in place new, democratically legitimated institutions – first and foremost a parliament and a freely elected people's chamber (*Volkskammer*) – in order to prevent the collapse into anarchy and economic and social disintegration. This meant that the new movements were forced into making a decision before they were ready on whether to become a party or to remain a movement with corresponding forms of organisation and decision-making. They opted to remain a movement without, however, ignoring events in parliament.

It cannot be forgotten that the reluctance to constitute themselves as parties weakened the influence these groups wielded over political developments. During the so-called Round Table discussions, which took place throughout the GDR and brought together people of widely varying background and political persuasion, they exerted great influence on GDR political life – not only in the central Round Table of the government of Hans Modrow but on all levels and in many spheres of society, including the mass media and the universities. This took place, however, without their ever having to secure the broad consent of the people. Initially, when attention was focused on the removal of the rubble of the old system they could effectively articulate public interest. As the elections approached it became clearer that, despite their moral integrity, these new groups could not in themselves gain a majority. They represented minority views, especially in their desire to follow an independent 'Third Way'.

The Emergence of a New Party System

In all the information published about the GDR in the GDR it was always noted with pride that the country had a working multi-party system which had stood the test of forty years. Since the late 1940s the parties of the 'Democratic Block' – the Democratic Farmers Party (DBD), Christian Democrats (CDU), Liberal Democrats (LDPD) and National Democrats (NDPD) – had been reliable partners or, more precisely, servants of the SED. They recognised in their manifestos and statutes the leading role of the SED and endorsed SED policy in the *Volkskammer*, local people's assemblies, the National Front (the alliance of parties and mass organisations), and in the various party newspapers.

In early December 1989 these parties left the Democratic Block and in so doing preordained the collapse of the National Front as the most important political regulative in the elections to the new assemblies. The 1976 programme of the SED had referred to the National Front and the Democratic Block as part of a 'popular socialist movement which plays an important role in bolstering the steadily growing cohesion of all classes and social strata on the basis of the ideals of the working class'. In December a commentary in the Party newspaper *Neues Deutschland* referred quite rightly to a structure which was 'obsolete and in the Stalinist mould' (*Neues Deutschland*, 7.12.89).

Two months earlier the Block parties had unanimously supported the leading role of the SED. While the LDPD and the CDU succeeded in November in creating the embryo of independent policies, comparable attempts by the Democratic Farmers Party (DBD) and the National Democratic Party (NDPD) – both artificially created by the SED in 1948 – remained curiously ill-defined. The Block parties replaced their leaderships at the end of 1989, only the LDPD chairman Manfred Gerlach remaining until February 1990, and all developed new programmes which deleted their belief in socialism. All wanted to obscure the fact that they had to live with a legacy just as onerous as that of the SED.

Just as the citizens' movements had been informed by the specific

-15-

situation of the GDR, so too the formation of parties reflected these conditions. At the end of 1989 and in the early weeks of 1990 a large number of parties and similar groupings appeared and registered officially with the Ministry of the Interior. Among them were Democratic Awakening; the social democratic SDP, which changed its name to SPD in January 1990; the Greens; the Green Party in the GDR; the Green League (a non-party-political umbrella organisation); the Democratic Association GDR 40; the Progressive New Party; the Free German Union in the GDR; the Liberal-Socialist People's Party; the Party of the Centre; the Independent People's Party; the German Forum Party (an offshoot of New Forum); the European Home Party; the 'Nelken' (a Marxist party inspired by Karl Liebknecht and Rosa Luxemburg); the German Communist Party (KPD), which sought an alliance of 'all honest communists'; and in late January the German Reunification Party (DWP), which advocated the reunification of Germany in the borders of 1990. Other new parties included the German People's Party (DVP); the Christian Social Party of Germany (CSPD), which was later absorbed into the German Social Union (DSU) and the CSU-GDR; the Free German Union (FDU); and the Party of Central German National Democrats (MNP) with a clear affinity to the western neo-Nazi NPD.

In the run-up to the parliamentary elections to the *Volkskammer* the restructuring of the party system was largely determined by the West German model. Under the mounting influence of and pressure from West German interests new party groupings were formed, for example the Alliance for Germany composed – despite their differing views and internal conflict – of a coalition of CDU, German Social Union (DSU, close to the Bavarian CSU), and the citizens' movement Democratic Awakening – social + ecological, and the Alliance of Free Democrats formed by the LDPD, the FDP (Free Democratic Party) of the GDR, and the German Forum Party. By mid-January 1990 the SDP, founded formally on 7 October 1989, took the name of its West German counterpart, the SPD, and thereby affirmed that it stood in the tradition of German social democracy. However, the election campaign revealed that the attempt to transpose West German politics and structures to the GDR would not be without its problems. Repeatedly the past caught up with the old GDR parties and the SED.

The creation or reformation of parties entered a second phase in summer 1990. The Alliance for Germany – the electoral coalition of conservative parties – dissolved itself and Democratic Awakening became part of the CDU. The DSU retained its status as an independent party, the CDU absorbed the remnants of the Democratic Farmers Party, and the NDPD (National Democratic Party of Germany) joined the Free Democrats. Fusion here meant that the members, organisation and some of the assets of the four former Block parties became concentrated. Again, this is not without its difficulties for the parties in the west as they are the inheritors of wealth accumulated in the communist past.

Elections

Prevented from participating in democratic elections for over forty years the people of the GDR were called upon to do so on no fewer than four separate occasions in 1990: on 18 March for elections to the *Volkskammer* which had been brought forward from 6 May; on 6 May for the communal elections; on 14 October for elections to the regional parliaments in the newly reconstituted *Länder*, and on 2 December for the first all-German elections to the Bundestag.

The first free elections in the history of the GDR took place on 18 March 1990 with parties still in embryo which displayed similarities and differences when compared with those of the Federal Republic. In total, twenty-four parties and groupings fielded candidates; there were also five joint lists:

1. Alliance for Action Unified Left/Nelken (VL);
2. Alternative Youth List (AJL) (including the Free German Youth (FDJ));
3. Alliance 90 (New Forum, Democracy Now, Initiative for Peace and Human Rights);
4. Alliance of Free Democrats – the Liberals (German Forum Party, Liberal Democratic Party, FDP);
5. Alliance of Socialist Workers (BSA) (German Section of the Fourth International);
6. Christian Democratic Union (CDU) (joint list with DA and DSU);
7. Christian League;
8. Democratic Farmers Party of Germany (DBD);
9. Democratic Awakening – social + ecological (DA);
10. Democratic Women's Alliance of Germany (DFD);
11. German Beer Drinkers Union (DBU);
12. German Social Union (DSU);

13. Unity Now;
14. European Federalist Party – Europe Party (EFP);
15. Europe Union of the GDR (EU);
16. Green Party and Independent Women's Association;
17. Communist Party of Germany (KPD);
18. National Democratic Party of Germany (NDPD);
19. Party of Democratic Socialism (PDS, successor party of the SED);
20. Social Democratic Party of Germany (SPD);
21. Spartacist – Workers' Party of Germany (SpAD);
22. Independent Social Democratic Party (USPD);
23. Independent People's Party (UVP);
24. Association of Working Groups for Employment Law and Democracy (VVA).

Table 1.1 Results of election to the *Volkskammer*, 18 March 1990

Party or electoral alliance	Votes cast
CDU	4,710,598
SPD	2,525,534
PDS	1,892,381
DSU	727,730
Alliance of Free Democrats	608,935
Alliance 90	336,074
DBD	251,226
Green Party/Independent Women's Assoc.	226,932
Democratic Renewal	106,146
NDPD	44,292
DFD	38,192
Alliance for Action United Left/Nelken	20,342

The result of the elections to the *Volkskammer* surprised all the parties. Of the twenty four contesting parties, electoral alliances and associations twelve won the number of votes necessary to gain a seat in the *Volkskammer* (see Table 1.1). The unexpected victory of the Alliance for Germany, but above all the vote for the former Block party CDU, the poor result for the SPD – particularly in areas always considered to be its historical bastions, the relative success of the PDS which attracted double the number of votes it had in membership, and the modest showing of Alliance 90 (i.e. those without whom these free elections would never have taken place) illustrate that, firstly, voters had made a clear and unequivocal decision in favour of a speedy unification of the two German states and that, secondly, they displayed little willingness to break radically with established political forces.

One of the most salient features of these results was without question the marked regional differentiation in voting patterns. For decades the SED and its social analysts had emphasised the spiritual and cultural unity of the people. The result, however, reveals deep cleavages in GDR society: between north and south, classes and social strata, manual and clerical workers, the old and young. It shows the consequences of central state rule, of its neglect of the regions, and of a privileged capital city. All these aspects are echoed in the voting patterns of the population.

Most observers believed at the time that it was not yet possible to deduce party preference from these voting patterns. The results of elections to the regional parliaments on 14 October 1990 and the first all-German elections to the Bundestag only partially bore out this hypothesis. While continuity in voter behaviour was clearly visible there were also instructive changes (see Tables 1.2 and 1.3).

Table 1.2 Results of election to the *Bundestag* on 2 December 1990 in Eastern and Western Germany

Party	Eastern Germany (%)	Western Germany* (%)
CDU	43.4	35
CSU	—	9.1
SPD	23.6	35.9
FDP	13.4	10.6
Greens	—	4.7
Alliance 90/Greens	5.9	—
PDS	9.9	0.3

* excluding West Berlin

(*Source*: *Frankfurter Rundschau*, 4.12.90, p. 6)

A comparison of all three election results reveals, in view of the enormity of the political and social convulsions in 1990, remarkable stability in voter behaviour. The Christian Democrats remained the most powerful force. Only in Brandenburg, and even then only in elections to the regional parliaments, was the SPD the strongest party. Here, as in Saxony where the CDU gained a resounding absolute majority, the results of the elections to the regional parliaments were determined by high-profile candidates for the post of regional Prime Minister such as Manfred Stolpe in Brandenburg, a

Table 1.3 Results of elections in the five new *Länder* of the former GDR to the *Volkskammer*, regional parliaments and *Bundestag*

Party	Volkskammer (%)	Regional parliament (%)	Bundestag (%)
Mecklenburg-West Pomerania			
CDU	36.3	38.3	41.2
SPD	23.4	27.0	26.6
Left List/PDS	22.8	15.7	14.2
Alliance 90	4.4	6.4	5.9
FDP	3.6	5.5	9.1
Other*	9.5	7.1	2.9
Brandenburg			
CDU	33.6	29.4	36.3
SPD	29.9	38.2	32.9
Left List/PDS	18.3	13.4	11.0
Alliance 90	5.4	7.2	6.6
FDP	4.7	6.6	9.7
Other*	8.1	3.1	3.4
Saxony-Anhalt			
CDU	44.5	39.0	38.6
SPD	23.7	26.0	24.7
Left List/PDS	14.0	12.0	9.4
Alliance 90	4.0	5.3	5.3
FDP	7.7	13.5	19.7
Other*	6.1	4.2	2.3
Saxony			
CDU	43.4	53.8	49.5
SPD	15.1	19.4	18.2
Left List/PDS	13.6	10.2	9.0
Alliance 90	4.7	5.6	5.9
FDP	5.7	5.3	12.4
Other*	17.5	6.0	4.9
Thuringia			
CDU	52.6	45.4	45.2
SPD	17.5	22.8	21.9
Left List/PDS	11.4	9.7	8.3
Alliance 90	4.1	6.5	6.1
FDP	4.6	9.3	14.6
Other*	9.8	6.4	3.9

* includes results for the DSU

(*Source*: *Frankfurter Rundschau*, 4.12.90)

leading churchman in the GDR, and in Saxony Kurt Biedenkopf, a leading voice of the future in the CDU.

In all the *Länder* the PDS continued to lose support. Unlike the CDU and the FDP which emerged on the basis of the former Block parties, it was very clearly perceived by voters as a party which stood for the old order. This also explains its relative success in (East) Berlin where the PDS still managed to gain 23.6 per cent of the vote and several direct mandates to the Berlin regional parliament in elections held at the same time as those to the Bundestag. This compares with 30 per cent in the communal elections in May. It was even in a position to elect Party Chairman Gregor Gysi to the Bundestag on a direct mandate.

The result of the German Social Union (DSU), based on the Bavarian Christian Social Union (CSU) from which it received massive support, is also noteworthy. During the elections to the *Volkskammer* it gained 13.6 per cent of the vote in Saxony where the CSU started a massive support campaign, although securing only 5.7 per cent in Thuringia. In the other *Länder* contested its level of support remained insignificant. In the elections to the regional parliaments in October its vote in Saxony crumbled to only 3.6 per cent and in Thuringia to 3.3 per cent. In total, it lost 237,000 voters to the CDU and gained only 81,000 (*Neues Deutschland*, 16.10.90). From the 6.6 per cent the DSU won in the *Volkskammer* elections a mere one per cent remained after the elections to the Bundestag. The experiment had failed.

In conclusion, it can be said that, after four elections, there have been no dramatic changes in voter behaviour. Conditions are for the time being stable and the mood liberal–conservative.

Translated from the German by Colin B. Grant.

References

Arendt, Hannah, *Über die Revolution*, 2nd edn, Piper: Munich, 1974

Autorenkollektiv unter der Leitung von Karl Becher, *Einführung in die marxistisch-leninistische Staats- und Rechtslehre*, 2nd rev. edn, Dietz: Berlin, 1986

Bresch, Ulrike, and Goyke, Frank (eds), *Oktober 1989: Wider den Schlaf der Vernunft*, Verlag Neues Leben/Elefanten Press: Berlin, 1989

'Demokratie Jetzt. Dokumentation des Arbeitsbereichs DDR-Forschung und Archiv (zusammengestellt von Helmut Müller-Enbergs)', *Berliner Arbeitshefte zur sozialwissenschaftlichen Forschung*, Nr. 19, Berlin, January 1990, Dok. Nr. 29

Glaeßner, Gert-Joachim, *Die andere deutsche Republik. Gesellschaft und Politik*, Westdeutscher Verlag: Opladen, 1989

Kuczynski, Jürgen, 'Konservative Revolution', *Neues Deutschland*, 8.11.90

von Laue, Theodor, *The World Revolution of Westernization. The Twentieth Century in Global Perspective*, Oxford University Press: New York and Oxford, 1987

'Regierungserklärung des Ministerpräsidenten der DDR', *Neues Deutschland*, 20.4.90

Thomas, Rüdiger, *Modell DDR. Die kalkulierte Emanzipation*, 7th edn, Hanser: Munich, 1972

-2-

The Failure of 'Real Socialism'

Rolf Reißig

The crisis of the 'real socialist' system in the German Democratic Republic in 1989 increasingly permeated the economic and social order, the political system, the value system and the very existence of the state. Mechanisms within the state aimed at crisis management had long since disappeared, and it was anyway becoming increasingly clear that a thoroughgoing transformation of the system in its entirety and a radical break with the past were necessary. However, the system itself no longer offered the foundations for such transformation. Awareness of this fact grew amongst the principal actors of the convulsive changes of October 1989 only after events were under way. This general and pervasive crisis, however, was only the final product of a long process in which crisis and change, loyalty and rejection in the population, conformism and partial attempts at reform from the SED coalesced with a further increase in latent crisis potential.

The contradictory and complex process in the GDR which could still have developed in various ways explains why in both east and west the GDR had so long – albeit with certain provisos – been considered capable of change and development. As late as 1989 Zbigniev Brzezinski wrote that of all the states in the eastern bloc only the GDR displayed a degree of stability and economic power (Brzezinski 1989: 238ff.).

However, the crisis of 1989 in the GDR, as throughout real socialism, brought something new to the fore: the type of development in the societies of eastern Europe had finally and irrevocably reached its outer limits. Not only was there a failure of the so-called 'strategies for crisis resolution' deployed by the vanguard party in the past as in 1953, 1956/7, 1961 and 1970/1; there was no conception of how the real socialist system could be reformed and transformed from within without abandoning socialism. After years of decline real socialism across the world now entered its terminal phase.

Real Socialism – From Decline to Collapse

The crisis and final collapse of the GDR formed part of the crisis and collapse of all the state socialist systems in eastern and central Europe (Vogel 1990); in other countries too this crisis did not arrive suddenly but was the culmination of a long process. Its symptoms became increasingly visible in the second half of the 1980s in all these countries and underlined its general and worldwide character. The economy of the GDR was already beset by steadily worsening standards in its production forces and was massively indebted and economically dependent on the developed industrial economies. Elsewhere, the country's infrastructure was in a state of collapse, large regions were becoming wasteland, there was an absence of innovation and efficiency and acute environmental crisis.

There were major problems and crises in distribution, an erosion of real wage levels, unemployment, parasitism and growing impoverishment in large sections of the population. The political system was characterised by authoritarian rule, a lack of democracy and public openness and a continued blurring of the distinction between security apparatus, Party and state. The social organisations were reduced to the instruments of the state and people's assemblies to mere rubber stamps; widespread political disorientation was compounded by resurgent nationalism and increased ethnic conflict, and the Party continued to act as the sole repository of reality, suppressing any thought critical of the system and placing the social sciences at the service of the state.

The ruling communist parties could no longer exercise political and ideological hegemony: their authority rapidly declined. Ideological legitimacy also swiftly declined and was not replaced. Leadership crises in the ruling communist parties intensified across eastern Europe at this time. The opposition, whose development and identity differed from country to country, seized the initiative in most countries. There was no debate between the communist parties and their peoples on the symptoms of this crisis, on the growing contradictions it demonstrated, on its causes, or on possible reform: on the contrary, such debate was usually consciously repressed. Quite clearly there was no sign of a political alternative with an eastern or central European dimension, at least in the Soviet Union and eastern Europe.

Neither the restructuring process in the Soviet Union nor reform in Poland and Hungary achieved the desired effect. Instead, the problems grew even more serious. Perestroika had obviously come too late and was, at least at first, haphazardly implemented.

The Crisis of the System – A Different Socialism or Different System?

The crisis of socialism which first emerged as a crisis of the Stalinist model and elicited calls for change from communist and socialist reformers had now widened to such a degree that the system itself was under threat. Reform of the system became the first priority. The open outbreak of the crisis in world socialism in the autumn of 1989 altered the course of developments away from reform of the system and towards its abolition. In the GDR too it became clear in 1989 that fundamental restructuring, and a radical new departure, could no longer be sought from within the system and its apparatus.

The factors which ultimately brought about the collapse of the GDR did not lie in the political errors of the SED leadership or an arthritic politburo (although both were contributory factors) but in the contradictions of an administrative socialism based on bureaucratic centralism.

A critical analysis of the development of socialism in the twentieth century is required because the end of the GDR and thus of state socialism in Germany coincides with the end of post-war history and a distinct history, theory and practice of revolution which had lasted almost 75 years. This paper does not propose to do this, especially since such analysis cannot be conducted in terms of the result – the collapse of the socialist system – but must involve an examination of the way in which the communist parties, caught up in the broader sweep of history, functioned with their crises, structural defects and opportunities for change and conformism.

'What we need is a rigorous self-criticism of those on the socialist left – one which assesses both historical practice and socialist theory' (Thierse 1990: 40), and to eschew the self-delusion of the belief that only the 'old, corrupt leaderships' bore the guilt for the demise of real socialism and that basically a good and correct view had simply 'not been properly translated into practice'. This is reflected in the still widely used method of perceiving the root of evil in Stalinism alone and in the thesis that this was not true socialism anyway. The key points of the system and its structure are automatically ignored. Of course, the systems of central and eastern Europe did not remotely correspond to the idea held by socialists and others on the left. But as a political and economic system there was and is no other socialism than that which existed in the Soviet Union, central and eastern Europe and in China.

Over and above such various approaches (which also demonstrate that these societies have not even begun to be sociologically examined) one indisputable fact remains: the real socialist systems of the 1980s had lost any hope of survival. Why?

The Decline of 'Real Socialism'

The socialist countries of eastern Europe were unable to transform themselves into modern, open societies. They remained closed industrial societies with monopolistic and centralised structures, riven by antagonism and with a social structure which was largely levelled and ossified. They possessed little social mobility, achievement was rarely rewarded, while the basis of a civil society was largely non-existent: they were therefore incapable of reform and qualitative change.

Ultimately, closed societies never have any prospect for survival. Although the real socialist countries severed themselves from world developments they could indeed have survived longer, but this situation itself underwent fundamental change in the 1970s and 1980s and compelled the socialist countries to open up and modernise in the form of the Conference on Security and Co-operation in Europe (CSCE), international division of labour and the arms race. However, a thoroughgoing modernisation of existing structures was, despite ambitious plans, no longer possible.

In the end the socialist states did not embody any *alternative* direction for the development of society. They represented instead a social order in which the original idea of socialism (according to which people would create a socially just, democratic and caring society) was not only not recuperated but was negated. Democracy was replaced by the dictatorship of a leadership phalanx; communal ownership and the socialisation of the means of production was replaced by economic étatism; the producer was separated from property and product; a command economy was established rather than a socially just system based on solidarity, one which encouraged feudalistic dependency, not the free development of the personality; individuality was levelled and bound by prescribed norms. Increasingly socialism came to be directed and decreed from above and not by a broad popular movement from below. Clearly, a social system dies not only when it has reached the limits of its development potential but also when it has lost acceptance from within, when the majority voluntarily rejects it and is disillusioned because the avowed aims and claims of the system are not being realised.

The demise and eventual collapse of real socialism was preordained by the reversal of the socialist ideal: dictatorship, not democracy, state, not social ownership, a centralised command economy which denied competition. This was predated by a long, differentiated and troubled history in which there were for a time various opportunities. The various crises of the system in the GDR (1953, 1956, 1960/1, 1968, 1970/1, 1980, 1989) did not stimulate fundamental change but were 'resolved' according to the same precepts each time: by criticism of 'subjectivism', by direct appeal to the masses for change, partial reform and attempts at accommodation with new situations. At the same time the system maintained the basic structures of this type of socialism. As a result stagnatory tendencies re-emerged and penetrated more deeply a growing number of social spheres and eventually expanded into a new crisis. There were other more serious attempts at reform in the history of the SED, but only in 1953 with the so-called New Course, the early 1960s (New Economic System of Planning and Direction [NöSPL]) and the early 1970s under the watchword of 'unity of economic and social policy'. They all failed as they did in all real socialist countries because they were inconsistently applied, followed a narrow technocratic approach and either failed to transform the party monopoly or were sabotaged. Often, they would fall prey to factional in-fighting and the victory of conservative over reform-minded groups, or to armed suppression in the form of the 'fraternal aid' of the Warsaw Treaty states in their invasion of Czechoslovakia in 1968.

The opportunity to develop a sustainable form of socialism – although slender – was gambled away. The crises multiplied while retaining a certain potential for change. This situation changed fundamentally and irrevocably in the 1980s. Administrative and centralistic socialism reached the point beyond which it could not develop. Its final crisis loomed. The roots for repeated crisis are to be found in administrative-centralistic socialism itself. The system was based on a two-way process: on the one hand, all key productive forces and property and all important positions of power in society were concentrated in the state and the Party, while on the other hand the working people continued to be expropriated. This process only served to deprive them of such functions, positions and forces (Brie 1990:17).

The essential components of the development of a modern society, such as self-interest, initiative, responsibility for one's own actions, had been destroyed for years to come. The dynamic forces of modern societies – the market, money, gain (not to be confused with profit), openness, the rule of law, and democracy – were comprehensively eliminated, even liquidated. The release of these forces – economic efficiency, democratic discourse, and the scientific truth which the subsystems require – did not materialise.

As a result of this bureaucratic-administrative planned economy the almost total state control of production, centralised price-setting, the monopolistic structures across the whole economy precluded or constrained genuine economic competition, innovation at grass-roots level, independent and creative action in industry and in the individual. The effectiveness of the laws of value and the economy was undermined. The fact that people were generally disorientated, would not assume responsibility and merely awaited the decree from above flows directly from this expropriation of people at grass-roots level and from the elimination of the subsystems of a modern society. In competition with the modern, capitalist economic systems the real socialist states fell further behind and in the 1980s actually reached the point where they were economically and financially dependent on the western industrialised states. The impact of the pronounced consumerist values of the west grew appreciably in eastern Europe from year to year.

The deepening of the symptoms of crisis in the development of the real socialist state can be largely traced back to the way in which the various political systems were either structured or functioned. Despite a number of differences from country to country these systems were universally characterised by a centralised leadership and power apparatus concentrated in the hands of, in the GDR, an SED leadership phalanx and of the state it dominated. A genuine democratic control over power by means of a division of power, openness and civic participation was non-existent in the real socialist countries: civil society was in effect amputated. The control of power by society was replaced by the prescribed adulation and trust of the people for their leaders. The range of interests, needs and motivation did not meet with a corresponding diversity in opportunities or structures. The basic tenets and values of a peaceful and democratic polity, such as a democratic discourse, conflict and tolerance, the search for consensus, majority rule and respect for minority rights were eliminated. 'Democratic centralism' – the all-pervasive organisational principle – was diametrically opposed to this and resulted instead in hierarchical decision-making and the suppression of democratic activities. Those in power were guided by a deeply ingrained belief in the universal efficacy of firm central-isation and an administrative system of direction. But how could a modern, complex and differentiated economy and society be directed and led by an incompetent and bureaucratic centre?

It was the realisation of this aim which was, however, the basic premise of the ideology of the ruling communists. How could a party, let alone politburo, possibly possess the creative energy necessary to replace or at best pool the initiative, the knowledge of millions of people or the discourse of society? The task was simply impossible, even admitting the best intentions of the powers that be. A form of 'modifying', of making the system and the structures of direction more responsive in various socialist countries could never, as was the intention, be accomplished through democratic centralism. The result was instead the consolidation of a bureau-cratic system based on command and directive. Socialism in all the countries of eastern Europe suffered from the fact that it had been imposed, directed from above, officially extolled and had not re-sulted from a popular mass movement.

Although this economic and social system of the Soviet type may have enabled the compensatory industrialisation of the slower growing agro-industrial countries, it was at the same time a model wholly inappropriate for the formation of a modern society with an efficient economy, quality of life, pluralistic openness and demo-cratic civic participation. For eastern Germany and Czechoslova-kia, which had previously been economically and culturally de-veloped, it was impossible to regard the imposition of this econ-omic and social model as progress. Marxism-Leninism, shorn of Marx's critical analysis of society, became the ideology of the state of this inchoate authoritarian socialism. Its key function lay in providing the ideological legitimation of political practice.

The history and end results of the processes of development in the real socialist countries confirm that its conflict, stagnation, crisis and the ultimate collapse were produced from within the system itself. There were and still are, of course, external factors which influenced and continue to affect the decline of the socialist societies. The Cold War, the east–west conflict, the division of

Europe, the external threat and trade embargoes slowed economic change and impeded political reform. The polarisation of political forces in Europe also signalled the disintegration of the coalitions forged in the Second World War around anti-fascism, democracy and progress. The symbols of hope for post-war Europe ended up by confronting each other as implacable enemies.

In the socialist countries a 'fortress and defence' mentality emerged which increasingly became the keystone of official policy. The notion of stability was reduced almost exclusively to its military and security meaning while the quest for domestic consensus and the struggle for ideological hegemony were forced into the background. Western 'influences' were examined for the sole purpose of refuting them. This 'new' society was to be wholly independent and opposed to the rest of the world. The economy and the evolving eastern European market were to be separated from the international market. The worldwide recessions since 1975 affected the socialist countries with varying degrees of severity, but all were unprepared. Accordingly, they were unable to play any economic role in the search for a progressive way to resolve the global change. This in turn further eroded their political influence in the solution of world problems. Despite the new policies of peace and détente heralded by Gorbachev, the 1980s witnessed the rapid loss of the political authority and influence of the states of the 'socialist community'.

Stalinism contra Leninism?

As the first historical variant of administrative and centralistic socialism Stalinism may be seen as having exaggerated its economic, political and social model by perfecting it into a brutal regime of terror. The liquidation of the land-owners, of the critical intelligentsia, of the army leadership, long-standing Bolsheviks and all enemies – real or imagined – inside the Party was ultimately the consequence of this political model and not merely the actions of one despotic megalomaniac. However, not all real socialist systems experienced such extreme forms as the liquidation of the grass roots and the complete suppression of individual self-interest and of the dynamic forces of modern society. The GDR similarly combined the expropriation and oppression of the grass roots with attempts at their partial stimulation and development. This distinction should be borne in mind when undertaking a concrete analysis of real socialist systems, their similarities and differences. At the same time, we are dealing with one common type. It was an essentially identical model of socialism which was dominant in all real socialist systems, and which is now collapsing and being replaced.

Whereas as a social system Stalinism completely deformed and irredeemably compounded the problems of socialism, it is not the sole cause of crisis. This aspect needs much more detailed examination. The inescapable question must be: are Stalinism and Leninism one and the same? Hermann Weber, a great authority on communism, writes:

> It is certainly true that under Stalin a distinct order and ideology did evolve which in many ways went against the principles of Leninism . . . Even if Stalin attempted to reconcile the practice of Stalinism with a belief in Leninism this could not disguise major differences. The new privileges of a new all-powerful bureaucracy, the elimination of party democracy, enforced collectivisation, the oppression of non-Russian nationalities and the absolute power of the secret police are amongst the key differences. Stalinism was born of Leninism but it meant the negation of many of Lenin's principles. (Weber 1988: 65f.)

Now more than ever we need a critical analysis of Lenin, of his theoretical positions and practical policies. This requires firstly placing Lenin in the context of the feudalism of Czarist Russia. In addition, we should distinguish between the diverse and contradictory approaches to be found in Lenin's writings in the various periods of his work (1902–1914/15, 1916–1918, 1919–1921, 1922/3). For instance, there is the Lenin who opposed bureaucratisation, who called for the participation of the masses and adhered to the old revolutionary ideals of equality, and there is the Lenin who believed in the absolute power of the political elite, who more than suggests voluntarism, for whom the goal of exercising and maintaining power is paramount and who at the Tenth Party Congress pushed through a ban on Party factions and advocated the use of violence.

Moreover, Lenin's New Economic Policy (NEP) of 1922/3 clearly contained serious corrections of earlier positions and endorsed greater latitude for private initiative, measures which would integrate the Soviet economy into the international economy, peaceful trade, and steps towards coexistence with the capitalist states. This notwithstanding, Lenin's ideas contained the seeds of their own deformation and the eventual failure of real socialism. In my view these seeds lie above all in his conception of the party, democracy, and the revolution and its practice.

A party which defines itself as preordained vanguard, which claims to have a monopoly of truth, which acts in order to forge the consciousness of the masses, which within the party prohibits the process which would allow the formation of democratic will and decision-making, which after seizing power abolishes the role of the elected councils and which goes as far as to exempt itself from democratic control – a party theory and practice of this type is not so much the basis for a democratic socialism as for the development of a dictatorship.

Lenin's attitude towards democracy must be seen as one of the vulnerable points in his ideas, in particular his almost total negation of the achievements of 'bourgeois democracy'. His view that 'socialist democracy' represented a total break with 'bourgeois democracy' was to have the grave consequences which are now plain for all to see. However, Hermann Weber legitimately points out that it would be to exaggerate the influence of theoretical positions if they were to be seen as the chief cause for the developments in the Soviet Union in the subsequent decades of Stalinism. The realities of the time in Russia, the inhuman feudalism, the isolation of the revolution and the incipient bureaucratisation of life characterised the practice of Leninism and further deepened the divide between the aims and the results of the revolution. Reality imposed itself on Lenin's policies.

Beyond a Failed Historical Experiment – Five Theses

Although a thoroughgoing analysis of the development of socialism in the twentieth century has still to be undertaken, with hindsight we may draw the following conclusions.

Firstly, the formation of an administrative-bureaucratic, dictatorial socialism, its demise and eventual collapse may not be clearly contained in theory. The basic emancipatory core and other beliefs and ideas in Marx contradict this (above all in his view of history and man, for example). In Lenin, however, the contradictions in his theoretical stance are more fundamental while in his conception of democracy, the party and revolution there is clear potential for deformation, stagnation and the collapse of socialism. For this reason alone the argument that it was only a good theory 'badly implemented' and that therefore Stalinism *alone* should be subjected to criticism is unconvincing and distracts from the overall critical view required. But it is not theoretical positions in themselves which constitute the main reason for the development of this type of socialism in the Soviet Union and the other eastern European countries. As an official state ideology which prevented any critical social analysis and precluded both theoretical and practical alternatives Marxism-Leninism is itself both the product of the deformation of socialism and the ideological basis of its demise, disintegration and collapse.

Secondly, the more the variant of the administrative-centralistic form of socialism succeeded or was imposed (firstly in the Soviet Union and after 1945 in the other countries of eastern and central Europe) and the various alternatives and attempts at reform foundered and democratic socialist opposition movements suppressed, the more inevitable the historical defeat of socialism became. This also applies to the fact that there had been historical opportunities for change (the last being Czechoslovakia in 1968), fundamental reform, democratisation and radical restructuring. But these alternatives had been thwarted by Soviet hegemony and the ruling politbureaucracies of the Warsaw Pact states. Gorbachev's step-by-step implementation of perestroika came too late to engineer a fundamental conversion to democratic socialism. Although conceived as a reform and renewal of socialism, perestroika itself contributed to the abolition of the socialist community.

The crisis of real socialism is not an isolated phenomenon. It is no longer possible to effect a direct transition from administrative-bureaucratic socialism to democratic socialism, however ill-defined. It is the real socialist system itself which has utterly failed, not its administration or its practical realisation. Overcoming it is the basis of any future progress. The construction of a massive apparatus of repression and observation, the wide-scale use of violence and terror, corruption, abuse of office, embezzlement by leading personalities has meant that the founding tenet of socialism as an emancipatory and liberating movement has been discredited for decades to come.

Thirdly, we need to examine more closely the way in which the problems of socialism have developed in the course of the twentieth century. The conditions for overcoming capitalism and replacing it with socialism were neither ripe in Russia (very definitely because of economic and cultural underdevelopment) nor anywhere else for that matter. Capitalism, which intensified social antagonism by crisis, war and expansionism and for a time sowed revolution amongst the masses (1917/18), was not – as became clear – in the throes of death and decay as Lenin had thought. A sequence of victorious revolutions in Europe did not materialise. The development potential of capitalism was far from exhausted: the attempt to 'outwit' history had failed.

Fourthly, the precise nature of the transition to socialism cannot be restricted to a question of timing alone. It is not a question of a *premature* revolution: historical progress is not achieved by breaking with 'capitalist society' or by changing the system by violent overthrow of the old order or the introduction of socialism by an external agency. Rather, it is achieved as an organic development on the basis of the dynamic energies fundamental to modern societies, through continuity and change.

By these means alone can there be a fundamental reform and democratisation of the economic and social order.

Only such a modern conception of development based on a unified and pluralistic workers' democratic movement could have wrought change in the direction of society. However, subjective and objective factors prevented this. We must now therefore disabuse ourselves of past illusions, *system thinking*, belief in progress and socialist models of all kinds. History is once again to be seen as that which it always was, namely a concrete political and social process involving various agents; history is open-ended.

Fifthly, the end of the real socialist system cannot be equated with the end of history *per se*. Its demise should be seen instead as the necessary precondition for confronting both the old and new challenges which face humankind. The end of the Cold War in Europe, the end of its division into enemy blocs can release the energies which can resolve the central issues of today. This requires a fundamental change in the criteria and structures of development in our social system for what is a long-term, complex and evolutionary process. This means in essence a change in our understanding of the quality of progress and the systematic elaboration of a new understanding of civilisation and development for the world.

We must exchange international confrontation, expansion, military force and deterrence for a lasting world peace for all peoples on the basis of co-operation and solidarity. We must stop unchecked economic growth and the degradation it causes to the planet for future generations (the ecological catastrophe is not a nightmare vision of the future, it is with us now). We must seek symbiosis with nature and the restoration of the ecological balance. We must depart from the concentration of wealth in the hands of a few industrialised nations and the increasing exploitation and underdevelopment of the countries of the Third and Fourth Worlds and embrace instead a new, just and co-operative world economic order. Social marginalisation in the industrial countries should be resolved by a genuine social democracy with more social justice. Patriarchal rule, thinking and modes of behaviour must give way to the equality of the sexes. We should replace the type of democracy that has a pronounced bias towards parliamentary form and institutions with one which brings together representative, direct and economic democracy.

While eastern Europe stands on the threshold of an uncertain transition to modern society, the bourgeois societies themselves need to be modernised. When set against the collapse of the state bureaucratic models of socialism, the bourgeois societies of the present have proved that they are modern and open, with a capacity for innovation. They represent a contradictory complex of a modern quality of life in capitalist form. The inviolable preconditions for adaptable and open societies lie in democracy, the rule of law, division of powers, openness, competition, and the innovatory potential of the economy. However, new global challenges and the need to change the principles and structures according to which we develop confront these modern bourgeois societies with the need to discover a new model of development. Change does not mean the abolition of the modern quality mentioned above but it does involve the realisation of new principles and structures of political and cultural regulation. This would enable us to address the greening of the economy, full social democracy, the equality of the sexes and the global problems of humankind. The principle of welfare could be developed as a positive alternative to the principle of capital (cf. Klein 1990: 69). This cannot occur in a vacuum. Such reform, transformation and social and ecological progress demand social and democratic movements, the cultivation of informed and critical public debate.

Change in the GDR and the Unification of Germany

The radical change which took place in the GDR in October and November 1989 was the direct result of a worsening economic, social and political crisis, mounting and widespread popular discontent with the long-endured realities of real socialism and the revolt of the citizens' movements against the hegemony of the SED. However, the potential for crisis in 'real socialism' was inherent in the way in which the system functioned, in the adoption of the Stalinist-Soviet model of socialism (albeit in modified form) and in the fact that the establishment and existence of the GDR were inextricably interwoven with and dependent upon the Soviet Union. Similarly, the GDR developed as part of one nation, and was always confronted with the influence of the larger, more powerful and ultimately more attractive Federal Republic. Such potential was also inherent in the dysfunctions of centralised, administrative and inflexible economic planning and in the contradiction between an inchoate civil society and a political system dominated by one party. However, only after awareness grew and other factors precipitated crisis could this latent crisis potential ripen into the conditions for the revolution of autumn 1989.

Notwithstanding such latent tension, the development of the GDR was not an uninterrupted history of crisis and error. No state could have survived for forty years on this basis. But the latent potential for crisis did make the development of the GDR imponderable in other ways. Since this potential for crisis was never defused, since there was never any attempt at fundamental renewal and democratisation and a reconciliation of socialism and German identity, it exploded all the more violently in the autumn of 1989. In so doing it not only swept away socialism but also the GDR in its wake. A historical experiment had failed.

Revolution or Restoration?

How can the nature and essence of the changes in the GDR and the developments elsewhere in eastern Europe be characterised? On this question Ralf Dahrendorf makes the following observation: 'We possess no theory which could help us either to bring about the transition from socialism to the open society or to understand it' (Dahrendorf 1990). Indeed, only limited use can be made of classical theories of revolution in the analysis of current events. The changes in eastern Europe must clearly also be subject to international comparative analysis. This in turn will require a quite specific focus and theoretical approach. For the moment we shall confine ourselves to the GDR. Jürgen Habermas has undertaken the first attempt to systematise the various approaches and interpretations of the revolutions in eastern Europe (Habermas 1990: 181ff.). I share the view of many authors that change in the GDR began in October 1989 and developed initially as a *democratic revolution* which underwent a number of different stages.

The first stage was a pre-revolutionary stage and lasted from summer until October 1989, in which a crisis affecting both rulers and ruled matured. The second was the revolutionary stage, the period of the actual democratic uprising between 6/7 October and November with the active public demonstration of the citizens' movements, the emergence of new political groups and parties, the break with established power structures, the eclipse of the hegemony of the SED, the Round Table, and the calls for a democratic renewal of the GDR. The post-revolutionary third stage started on 9 November but involved several phases: elections to the *Volkskammer*, the economic and currency union and accession to the Federal Republic. In addition, the West German economic and social model was adopted and the various parties and groups were realigned.

If one accepts the definition of a revolution as the overthrow of the ruling strategic elites and the replacement of old forms of rule with new forms in addition to a social convulsion, then the events of both the GDR and elsewhere in eastern Europe were indeed a revolution. It was a revolution because these political, social and cultural changes – at least in October and November 1989 – were secured by pressure from below, from a mass popular movement. It was conspicuous by its peaceful nature. At the same time it was part of a wider eastern European revolution based on the developments in the Soviet Union, and it also precipitated change in Czechoslovakia, Bulgaria and Romania.

The revolution in the GDR also amounted to a *recovery* (Jürgen Habermas) of lost ground. With it the GDR recovered democracy and the rule of law, a pluralistic political system and market economy, and re-entered Europe and the modern age. However, Habermas' view that such recovery was characterised by the almost total absence of innovative and forward-looking ideas does not in my view hold for the first two stages of the revolution. While it did not produce a new type of society this was not preordained. The opposition in the then GDR, the citizens' movements, new political groups and parties and reformist circles within the SED did not at first simply support the GDR, but one radically renewed, democratised, open, pluralistic and based on the rule of law – in other words, in the form of a democratic, humane socialism. The Berlin Wall was to be gradually removed and both states were to come together slowly through closer co-operation in Europe.

This path would have been the better option for the GDR since it was in the interests of both German states and their European neighbours. Not least, it would have given the people of the GDR more time in which to come to terms with their past. However, this democratic revolution was interrupted. On 9 November it entered a new phase with the adoption of the economic, political and social system of the Federal Republic. Even in this post-revolutionary phase it was not only a question of recovery but of renewal, of which the Round Table – particularly the draft constitution and social charter – but also the role of the citizens' movements and the emergence of civil society are good examples.

The Revolution Reformed

The first signs of a change in popular mood were beginning to emerge in November and December 1989. The slogan which precipitated the downfall of the SED regime, 'Wir sind das Volk' ('We are the People'), became more frequently 'Wir sind *ein* Volk' ('We are *one* people'). Moreover, the call for a 'new GDR' was replaced with the calls of the major political groupings for 'Deutschland – einig Vaterland' ('Germany – united fatherland'). Why did this change take place? Some claim that there was 'manipulation' or 'external interference'. Undoubtedly this was the case. After the breaching of the Berlin Wall the West German parties (already buoyant in the GDR) performed a new role: they could now enter the fray directly on the territory of the GDR and campaign there. This direct involvement by West German parties limited the scope for independent development in the GDR. The fact that a majority wanted the Deutschmark as quickly as possible was understandable. But the decisive reasons for this change were more deep-seated and lay in the GDR itself. Not only did the revolution remove a post-Stalinist rule; it also wrought the collapse of the entire system, of a whole social order and system of values. An identity crisis followed bringing with it a social vacuum. People were beginning to look for a way out of this vacuum and the worsening economic crisis when the Wall was suddenly opened on 9 November. What amounted to unification from below was under way and reunited millions in a short space of time. For those seeking escape from the GDR the Federal Republic seemed to offer the perfect haven: a proven economic and social model which would obviate the need for another experiment in socialism (even if it was to be pluralistic and democratic). People were attracted by the promises of Chancellor Kohl and others to save them from the abyss.

The prospect of a new socialist beginning was anathema to the people who had first-hand experience of socialism in the GDR. And there was also no other *workable* socialist model in Europe: the crisis of perestroika was plain for all to see. At the same time there had been media exposure of Stalinist crimes, the machinations of the State Security Police (Stasi), corruption, embezzlement and the privileges of the SED leadership. The legitimacy crisis of the system reached its apogee. Moreover, no clear and credible political force had emerged to take charge of the helm and steer the GDR in an independent direction. even the civil rights groups and other new political groups would have failed. The masses had had enough of radical democracy and a renewed GDR and rejected both the citizens' movements and the socialist reformers. There would be no new GDR and definitely no socialist experiments: they wanted instead unification with the Federal Republic.

For a Future Germany

Little has remained of the original idea that the two German states should converge naturally. The forced pace of unification and the profound crisis of the former GDR paved the way for its accession to the Federal Republic and the almost total adoption of the West German model. Germany is now unified although economic, cultural and social unity will take considerably longer – possibly between eight and twelve years.

A process unique in history, the direct convergence of two diametrically opposed social systems and the immediate transition from a command to a market economy, has produced new conflicts. Large sectors of the economy and agriculture have collapsed, unemployment is rising quickly, qualifications have become worthless; a fundamental change in lifestyle and in social structures is taking place. Eastern Germany is now undergoing a difficult period in the transition to a market economy. Eastern and western German industry are far from compatible. A long-term structural plan must supplement transitional measures as a matter of urgency (although it is not yet in evidence). However, in the medium and longer term we can expect considerable economic upturn and social consolidation.

The transition from dictatorship to democracy will not be smooth. Above all we must avoid suppressing the history of the GDR: it must be critically examined. This is just as urgent for the whole country as it is for each individual and there remains much work to be done. There is a widespread feeling among the people that dependency on the SED is merely being replaced by a new dependency in a reunited Germany. In this sentiment lie the seeds of any future economic, social and cultural conflict. The problem is not so much that such conflict will actually exist but rather how we will cope with it. We need integration through co-operation, not one-sided absorption.

It should be emphasised that eastern Germany can bring new ideas into a united Germany, notably the experience of the citizens' movements, of a democratic popular movement, of the Round Table of all parties and movements, autonomous forms of democracy, a working draft constitution and a range of social rights. However, at present the new ideas and innovations from the embryonic phase of the democratic revolution in the GDR are being suppressed and marginalised. It remains to be seen what exactly will survive. Their recovery will be largely contingent on the strength of the citizens' movements, and the development of an informed political culture. Whichever course future developments may take, much will remain of the revolution in the GDR: the overthrow of an old social order long bereft of innovative potential, liberation from a dictatorship, the struggle for democracy, human rights and the encouragement of economic efficiency and new attitudes.

The question often asked today is: what will the future Germany be? The answer affects not only the Germans because the German question is also a European question. The unification process of 1989 had a different point of departure from that of 1871 and should therefore yield a more progressive result both in Germany and for her neighbours. It remains to be hoped that Germans in both East and West use this opportunity to fashion a new Germany.

The Federal Republic by virtue of its economy, rule of law, political culture and role in the world market forms the basis for the future Germany, and justifiably so because these are the foundation stones of modern society. Bourgeois society has proved itself to be modern, innovative and open, all the more so when set against the collapse of state bureaucratic socialism. However, the future Germany should not be an enlarged Federal Republic. No state in history has ever dissolved without its impact being felt elsewhere. But here we are dealing with two states belonging to one nation. The Federal Republic will also have to change in response to the process of unification even if this does not at present appear likely. The problems arising from unification are of a different nature to those in the old Federal Republic. There will be no linear continuation of the successes of the past. Social and democratic questions new and old remain. The priority is social justice not only in terms of distribution (reward according to performance), but also in the opportunities for education, employment, health, individual development and the social protection of future generations. We need self-determination in a society in which policy is not merely decreed from above but flows from the full participation of the people. The interests of the individual should stand above those of the group. We need a polity in which the state is no longer a social authority which rules society but which serves the people, social groups and the individual, in which social organisations are endowed with sufficient rights. We require the development of a civil society.

The modern bourgeois societies of western Europe in particular face new global challenges. As an economically powerful country Germany should face them head on. It should help to achieve a breakthrough of a new rationale for the progress of humanity as a priority in Europe. Germany should play an active part in steps to ensure disarmament and the creation of a new European security order. It could and should harness its economic potential and use its geographical position to play an active role in ensuring the integration and modernisation of eastern Europe. It should actively support the establishment of comprehensive social welfare, democratic freedoms and environmental responsibility across the continent. We need not a German Europe but a European Germany. The unified Germany cannot be allowed to prosper at the expense of the Third World but must advocate a new, equitable world economic order and help the people of the Third World to help themselves. The new Germany should be a peace-loving, federal, socially and environmentally responsible state; it should be a bridge between east and west, north and south.

These challenges can be met only by means of the democratic participation of the people, democratic movements and political parties. Germans in east and west should seize this opportunity: Europe and the world will judge them accordingly.

Translated from the German by Colin B. Grant.

References

Brie, Michael, 'Die allgemeine Krise des administrativ-zentralistischen Sozialismus. Eine reproduktionstheoretische Skizze', *Initial* (Berlin), 1, 1990

Brzezinski, Zbigniev, *Das gescheiterte Experiment Der Untergang der kommunistischen Systeme*, Ueberreuter: Vienna, 1989

Dahrendorf, Ralf, 'Die offene Gesellschaft und ihre Ängste. Rede auf dem 25. Deutschen Soziologentag', *Frankfurter Rundschau*, 13.10.90, p. 7

Habermas, Jürgen, *Die nachholende Revolution*, Suhrkamp: Frankfurt a.M., 1990

Klein, Dieter, 'Die bürgerliche Gesellschaft vor der Reform zur überlebensfähigen Gesellschaft', *Utopie konkret.* (Berlin), 2, 1990

Thierse, Wolfgang, 'Zögernde Bemerkungen zum "Demokratischen Sozialismus"', *Zeitschrift für Sozialistische Politik und Wirtschaft* (Kiel/Cologne), January 1990

Vogel, Heinrich (ed.), *Umbruch in Osteuropa*, Bundesinstitut für ostwissenschaftliche und internationale Studien: Cologne, January 1990

Weber, Hermann, *Kommunistische Bewegung und realsozialistischer Staat*, Bund-Verlag: Cologne, 1988

−3−

From Stagnation to Transformation: The Sociology of the 'GDR Revolution'

Manfred Lötsch

No state in history has ever got into a crisis in such a ridiculous way as the GDR. There was no reformer pronouncing new theories, no general riding into the capital at the head of his tanks; no, the emergency occurred because the people left; instead of strikes and demonstrations they occupied embassy buildings; instead of clashes with the police they left for Hungary. They left behind a party without any direction, a multitude of grasping official bodies, the media with their incessant trumpeting of official phrases, and at the head of all of this a government which had no more face to lose because it had long since lost it. (Heym 1990: 271)

This is a fairly accurate description of the phase immediately preceding the end of the GDR. Even in the way it was articulated and took shape the crisis in the GDR differed from that in other socialist countries. A system which had appeared so permanent and deeply entrenched was eliminated in a way which hardly merits the term 'revolution'. As in the fairy-tale about the Emperor's new clothes where an innocent child simply put into words what others saw (namely that the Emperor had nothing on), the regime was toppled because the people simply ignored the dangers and staged a revolution for which there are few historical parallels − a revolution in which the most striking weapon was not the people's anger but their wit.

And the real problem starts here. It is easy to find the reasons for this widespread social unrest. In short, they consist of the wide gulf in technology and the direct results and manifestations of this in everyday life, the striking and permanently increasing difference in living standards compared to the other Germany. The sensitive subject of the motor car was only just the tip of the iceberg, with the Trabant acting as a symbol of the GDR economy as a whole. Ironically, the ban on travelling which affected the whole population apart from the small, privileged group of so-called *Reisekader* and the pensioners had the totally opposite effect to what was intended. Instead of keeping the idea of affluent western society away from the people in the GDR, which was its real purpose, it gave rise to fanciful dreams and illusions. Since it had become normal not to believe a word of official propaganda, in the end no-one believed it even when it was saying what was true. Social unease and divisions, new poverty and crime, homelessness and other forms of alienation in the west were more or less dismissed as SED propaganda. In this context, it is quite telling and by no means simply chance that the main voting tendency in the south of the GDR was for the Christian Democrats (CDU). Here state propaganda produced a remarkable dialectical effect by essentially cancelling itself out. This was because in these areas reception of West German television was not possible for technical reasons, which is why the Dresden region was known as the 'the valley of the ignorant'. Since the western media failed to get through with their corrective influence ('corrective' in the sense that they dealt with real problems), ordinary people rejected the message of GDR television and simply believed the opposite to be true. Just as the opposite of a mistake is always a mistake, so too the opposite of a cliché is always a cliché.

Theoretical Concepts of Legitimation

When a state collapses along with its whole social system, it is essential to look at the causes and reasons behind such a chain of events. We can return to this later – the more interesting and pertinent question is really quite a different one altogether: what kept this system together for so many years? No gift for prophecy is needed to predict the usual response when this question is asked today. It was (as current cliché explanations would have it) the State Security Police and other repressive mechanisms which stabilised 'the system' against 'the people' and ensured its survival.

This explanation is not completely wrong but, as with all clichés, it is also not entirely adequate. For the sake of honesty and justice it is still worth pointing out an unusual fact, even if no-one from the former GDR wants to hear or accept it. There was a time when the GDR's socialist constitution was not only accepted by the majority of the people but was actively supported by them too. Nothing could be more inaccurate in terms of history and sociology than to describe the whole of GDR history in sweeping terms as an unbroken chain of oppression (incidentally, the cliché of the 'SED ruling against the will of the people' plainly ignores the fact that, at the end, nearly one in five adults in the GDR was a member of the SED).

Of course this is not the crux of the matter. We get a bit closer to it if we take a brief look at the country's economic and social development in a period of relative stability and prosperity. Such periods of development did indeed occur, even if in less spectacular fashion than in the Federal Republic. Significant developments occurred in the late 1940s which were still quite evident in the 1950s, and, although they slackened off in the 1960s, they can quite clearly be regarded as evidence of 'social and economic progress'. This was true, for example, in areas such as housing, availability of foodstuffs and technical consumer goods, incomes, and living standards as a whole. What is defined as 'social security' may well have been relatively modest (as regards lower incomes and minimum pensions, for example), but there was still 'social security of a special kind'. There were indeed poor people in the GDR, but this was not poverty in the sense of a widespread social phenomenon or in the sense of starvation, homelessness etc. Moderate economic growth combined with moderate social progress, the absence of the kind of open conflict in the political superstructure which might have challenged the social and political consensus – all these are factors which must be considered in trying to answer the question we asked at the start about why the system should have survived for so long.

In this context social scientists in the GDR strove to find a mode of operation which stabilised and supported the system – not for opportunistic reasons or for 'fear of repression from various organs of power' and so on, but in the earnest belief that socialism, however defective it may have been in practice, was none the less an attempt at a society which seriously pursued the goal of human equality (cf. Bloch 1977: 547–729). My colleagues and I, as the social scientists of the then GDR, identified with the basic social model which had been adopted, even if nowadays many seek to shake off this stigma.

But this is just the surface of the problem. A similar observation can be made in regard to the sociology of mass consciousness and mass behaviour. However refractory this thesis may seem at first sight, it is none the less historically true that the 'Party' (whoever that may mean) by no means ruled repressively against the people from the very beginning, but instead had their complete approval – precisely because its policies were not only ideologically legitimised but also responded to the real needs of the people, articulated them and in a certain sense even served them.

It is clear, looking at just a few examples, that the cornerstones of the 'sociopolitical programme' were far more than simple propaganda ploys. Certainly it was an illusion to proclaim a 'solution to the housing problem by 1990' (even when implemented, the concept proved to be mistaken because the attempt to solve the problem by extensive new housing development stood in stark contrast to the advancing decay of the inner-city housing stock, especially in small to medium-sized towns and major inner-city districts). None the less, hundreds of thousands of new flats were built in this way (in Berlin-Marzahn and Berlin-Hellersdorf, in Leipzig-Grünau and elsewhere) which, if these suburbs are not judged on aesthetic grounds, can quite easily be taken as evidence of a 'successful sociopolitical programme' and which were recognised generally as examples of social progress.

Or take the courting of the working class. Here it was not just a case of ideology – in the shape of a dogma, for example, which saw the working class as the leading and ruling political class. There were quite definite political considerations too. Thus, only the labour of the workers and peasants was considered as productive. This was related to a theory of productive labour pre-dating Adam Smith and David Ricardo, in which only the utility value of labour was counted as productive. Amongst other things the completely new character of scientific labour associated with the scientific and technical revolution was pressed into a concept dating from the nineteenth century. This could have been acceptable had the distinction between productive and unproductive labour been retained only in its original sense (as a means of distinguishing between them in relation to their involvement in the production or use of the surplus social product) and not used in a moralising sense – which practically boiled down to differentiating between useful and non-useful labour.

All this would not be worth mentioning if these things had only been a collection of odd theoretical disputes. But such is not at all the case. This theoretical construct concealed quite tangible social facts, problems and tensions. If only labour with a direct utility value is considered as 'productive' and any other as 'unproductive', and if this is then combined, either explicitly or implicitly, with an evaluation in moralising terms, then intellectual activity in general or scientific work in particular ultimately appears to be precisely that which it is not: a luxury to be tolerated, at best. Those carrying out this sort of work are then considered to be, at best, second-class partners of the working class (behind the peasantry) and are therefore regarded as unreliable, having a social function only within the limits set by 'the leading role of the working class' (cf. Henrich 1989). Above all, this meant that, in the final analysis, intellectuals were to have no say in state affairs. For a while such attitudes and patterns of behaviour seemed to have a good chance of surviving the 'GDR revolution'. One of the most noticeable effects of that revolution was the barely disguised hostility of the masses towards the intelligentsia. This deserves mentioning for just one reason, namely as a major factor amongst the mechanisms responsible for the lack of scientific and technological innovation in the GDR. 'The working class as the main driving force of the scientific and technological revolution' is a contradiction in itself, and, amongst the conflicts which ultimately led to the collapse of the GDR, the conflict dividing the political leadership and the intelligentsia, although it may not have been the most obvious, was ultimately the most significant.

Sociology as a Factor of Stagnation and Transformation

In the search for an apt description of the development of GDR sociology it would be fair to talk of 'a long and tortuous road of discovery'. This naturally requires some explanation.

In the social sciences the principle of 'partiality' (*Parteilichkeit*) is ambivalent, Janus-like. On the one hand, it stands as a blanket term for a certain degree of social commitment, in contrast to Max Weber's 'value freedom'. For example, those concerned with the sociology of poverty, starting with an interest in the topic itself, will normally work from the basis of a certain feeling of solidarity with the poor. Anyone working on the sociology of developing countries will probably be more concerned with the needs of such countries than with those of the rich industrial countries. 'Value-free feminist sociology' is a contradiction in terms, since it is precisely feminist sociologists (both men and women) who have practised the principle of 'partiality' to perfection. So the principle of 'partiality' is *not* the chief sin of sociology in the GDR, the failure of which is of quite a different kind. Let us be clear, however, that, in seeking to identify the characteristic features of GDR sociology, our purpose is not to justify them but, in the final analysis, to ask whether the development of GDR sociology over a number of decades and the personal fate of those bound up with it can simply be dismissed as a sort of 'zero option'.

Stefan Heym talked on one occasion of the GDR's having left no historical traces. This is both accurate and wrong. It is accurate if it is meant to imply that the effects which were intended (by ideology, 'education' etc.) quickly disappeared without much trace: within the first days of the crisis in the GDR there was little evidence of the Marxist consciousness which was supposed to be widespread in the population, especially amongst the younger generation. It is misleading, however, inasmuch as it overlooks some essential factors. In particular, it ignores the fact that the social behaviour of the average GDR citizen (whoever that might be) quite clearly reveals its origins and the impressions which have moulded it – not only in terms of the distinct dialects spoken in different parts of the country (which is a trivial example) but also in terms of basic social behaviour, for example in simply transposing hopes of salvation from one authority to another. Moreover, the lack of historical traces does not explain the radical nature of the political and social changes which swept across the GDR. Rather, these were the result of new developments clashing with patterns of behaviour which had emerged over the long period of GDR history ('long' in terms of a human life, not of history).

Whatever may have become of it, the ideal of social equality – ranging from Plato's 'everything belongs to everyone' via the utopian designs of More, Campanella, Saint-Simon and Owen, to the vision of a 'society where the free development of the individual is the condition for the free development of all' (Marx and Engels 1959: 9) – remains in essence and in terms of intellectual history one of the greatest ideas which man has ever produced for himself. The legitimation and social acceptance of actually existing socialist power structures over the years cannot be explained in anything other than such grand terms. Moreover, the scale of the disaster is directly related to the grandeur of the ideas, values and goals which collapsed with the system. In the west, on the other hand, a change of government is quite a normal event, however serious the differences between the government and opposition might be. This is precisely because the basic shape of the social system remains untouched, which could hardly be said to have been the case in the GDR. In short, it could be said that society's disillusionment stands in direct proportion to its expectations. It is easy to see that this is a completely different view from that which sees the history of 'really existing socialism' simply as unreformed Stalinism.

Against this background, critical sociological analyses were not directed at 'the system' as such either objectively or in what might be called a hidden sense. The main idea was always to remove the *defects* of the system rather than the system itself – just as the doctor seeks to cure his patients rather than bury them. In this sense sociology in the GDR was ahead of other social science disciplines in one important respect: its empirical character meant that the potential for discontent became the subject of sociological research. 'A contented body', Ernst Bloch wrote, 'has nothing to complain about . . . But the land of milk and honey only exists in the (ever instructive) fairy-tale, and in the fairy-tale of the state' (Bloch 1977: 548).

It had long been known that the wish to travel was at the top of the list of people's needs and that it could no longer be suppressed by compensating the people with other things (low rents and charges, low prices for everyday goods, etc.). Studies over the years had shown that nothing would come of the promised 'end to the housing shortage by 1990' simply because the increasing stock of new houses was matched, and more recently exceeded, by the decay of the housing stock in the inner cities. It was no secret that there was not much competitive spirit around. It was calculated that, when compared with skilled workers of the same age, most academics had made up at the earliest by their fifties the shortfall in their incomes resulting from the longer periods they had spent in education. In short, academic careers had long ceased to be financially attractive (especially since the shortfall was even greater for other graduates, particularly in the arts and social sciences). No expensive research was necessary to discover that there was a time-bomb ticking in the area of consumer goods, especially concerning prices and availability. Such potential for discontent was evident from studies dealing with other topics – and, anyway, simple common sense provided the most essential facts. All this forms the background to the sociological pattern of behaviour (I mean the behaviour of sociologists) which swung back and forth between seeing and shutting its eyes to the problem. This strategy, which involved a considerable degree of repression and which was aimed at saving face academically and safeguarding a 'bourgeois existence', is difficult or even impossible to explain to those not directly involved.

In such circumstances it is not surprising that, as regards models and theories on social structure, GDR sociology often gives a complex picture when otherwise such a pluralism of views is scarcely in evidence (Hanf 1991: 73). More recent theories would also seem to find it difficult to avoid the conceptual misunderstanding which is as old as social research itself dealing with 'social structure': namely the assumption that the right *question* has been asked when the aim is to find out what *the* structure of a given social system is and which structural model would be best suited to describe this structure and reproduce it in theoretical terms. Just like the constant battle between class and stratification theories and their various factions, the debate in the GDR failed to overcome a serious conceptual misunderstanding because it constantly revolved around the question of which was the 'best' (if not the one and only valid) structural theory.

A glance at other sciences would have been sufficient to identify the basic error in methodology. If, for example, a doctor who is searching for *the* structure of the human organism first of all asks the question 'in relation to what', before then, in the light of the answer, describing various structures (such as the anatomical, physiological, neurological etc.), then he is using a methodological concept which can be defined as a 'structure–function paradigm'. This means that describing structures only really means anything if it is done in relation to the *functions* of the system under analysis. Thus, with regard to the social reality of the GDR, widely differing descriptions of the structures emerge depending on whether the organisation of society is illustrated according to the material situation, power structures, the life opportunities in general which are available, etc. In this sense, the theoretical dispute which broke out in the GDR about what socialism actually had been in structural terms was really an attempt to answer the question before it had even been properly formulated.

To cite just one example, the term 'society of estates' (*Ständegesellschaft*) would certainly appear to have some empirical validity. It would be quite easy to discover strata and structures amazingly similar to estate structures (Hanf 1991). Yet there are at least two basic respects in which socialism differs fundamentally from a society of estates. In the first place, one of the basic features of such a society is its substantial historical longevity, and, secondly, its structures are codified and institutionalised, this being a condition of their longevity. This could hardly be said of the scale of the inequalities in socialism (using 'power' and 'privileges' as benchmarks). The definition of socialism in terms of the Asiatic Mode of Production, proposed a few years ago by the Hungarian sociologists Konrád and Szelényi, is also a bit wide of the mark (Konrád and Szelényi 1978). True, striking similarities can be found, such as the state-centralised organisation of surplus labour and redistribution of the surplus product as well as the quasi-religious (in this case ideological) mechanisms for legitimising and securing the position of the leadership. At the same time, however, the qualitative differences are so great that things cannot be reduced to one single explanation. History does not repeat itself so easily, not even in the course of three millennia.

The search for historical models seems to me totally inadequate when it comes to providing a theoretical explanation of the nature of socialism. In the first place this is because historical analogies are quite unsuited for understanding new historical phenomena, and secondly because socialism incorporated elements of *all* previous social formations, including forms of slave labour in the Gulag Archipelago, feudal structures of privileges, processes of 'original accumulation' taken from capitalist society (the anti-kulak policies of the Soviet Union in the 1920s and 1930s bear an uncanny resemblance to Marx's description of the enforced removal of the peasantry from the land in the period of original accumulation (Marx 1962: 741)), and, finally, processes of (partial) modernisation in the scientific and technological revolution of the present. All these factors prevent any definition of socialism in terms of its being a social formation in its own right – and, on the other hand, reveal too many essential, distinctive features to allow it to be equated with other types of formation. To do real justice to the matter, it is probably best not to try to fit socialism into what are, in any case, simplified schemes depicting the sequence of social formations (cf. Lehrbuch 1972: 137). Better instead to define socialism for what it really is: a conglomeration of elements from every preceding social formation. It was quite definitely not that stage in human development which Marx and Engels had anticipated, the first step on the road 'from the realm of necessity to the realm of freedom' or the first phase of an essentially classless (communist) social formation. Whether the vision of a society which can progress beyond today's more or less capitalist phase has for that reason lost all point is an entirely different question.

The Forces of Change

The GDR revolution developed in two clear phases which were different in every respect – in terms of aims, movements and dominant actors. As regards the content of both phases, the change could be regarded as the transition from a revolution driven from within to one determined by external forces. This shift was determined chiefly by a change in the respective dominant forces and the interests which they articulated. Intellectuals (in the broadest sense) were the principal actors behind the first phase. New Forum was no workers' movement, either in its social composition or its political aims and aspirations; the fact that workers joined its demonstrations is another matter altogether. If one looks for the true driving forces and the ideas which they pursued, then the intellectual nature of the first phase is quite evident. Political and intellectual matters predominated: freedom of opinion, of speech, of the press and of assembly. In short, this period was concerned with the right to articulate interests which by no means fitted in with the 'identity of fundamental interests amongst all workers' as officially asserted (cf. Henrich 1989; Bahro 1990; Knabe 1989). Amongst other reasons these were clearly typical intellectual demands because ordinary workers were already quite used to expressing their opinions in daily life (even at their work-places). Based on sociological research carried out shortly before the outbreak of the crisis, using among other things free (i.e. non-standardised) interviews, we know from our own observations that workers did not think much of the taboos which intellectuals, whatever their attitude in private, necessarily accepted or at least respected.

As always with revolutions (it is almost a law of nature) this shift in aims was accompanied by a change in the driving forces and leading actors. Now quite practical material interests shaped and determined the future course of events ('if the D-Mark comes, we'll stay – if not, we'll go to it'). In short, political and intellectual demands were replaced by demands shaped by everyday concerns and interests. This shift of emphasis, however, only applied to the *domestic* situation in the GDR. The other and ultimately decisive factor behind the revolution, the mass exodus via Hungary, was quite obviously based on material interests. At least in its basic sociological tendency this was not a case of a stampede to political freedom but of actions anticipating higher living standards.

To avoid any misunderstanding: this is not meant to sound dismissive in any way. It is quite normal for the driving forces and their guiding interests to change in the course of a revolution. It would be quite absurd to reproach everyday behaviour for reflecting everyday interests – not least because to a certain extent what we are dealing with are the after-effects of socialist development. After all, the 'basic economic law of socialism' insisted that natural law (in the sense of comprehensive 'objective' needs) entailed 'securing the greatest welfare and free all-round development of all society's members' (Lenin 1956: 40; *Lehrbuch* 1972: 141). Certainly, the question of where to draw the line between this acceptable end on the one hand and social reality on the other has a lot to do with one's necessary theoretical standpoint and is by no means an academic question in a pejorative sense. 'Anyone who strives for democratic socialism', Günter Grass wrote quite aptly, 'should, in the light of experience, reject the misleading idea of Marxism-Leninism and, in line with history, talk instead of Leninism-Stalinism' (Grass 1990: 53). Nobody knows how socialism under Marx's leadership would have looked, but it can hardly be disputed today that the decisive conceptual errors must be laid directly or indirectly at Lenin's door. Such errors included the hostility towards *any* form of private property (which largely explains the continuing malaise of Soviet agriculture even today), suppression of any form of opposition either within the party or in society as a whole, and last but not least the fatal idea of a one-party system and thus the actual abolition of the party as a political institution, since this can logically exist only in relation to other parties. It is one of the cardinal failures of Gorbachev's perestroika that it has overlooked this point.

A Tentative Conclusion

Naturally, there were other mechanisms at work beneath the surface of state relations between the two Germanies. The reason German unity was achieved under the *Anschluß* terms of the Basic Law was not, as was officially claimed, that there was no reason to alter what was said to be (with whatever justification) the world's most liberal constitution. It would have been quite possible to take this and that, if not from the GDR's old constitution, then at least from the draft constitution of the Round Table – article 34, for example, concerning the rights of the Sorbs (*Verfassungsentwurf* 1990). But this chance was thrown away when the Federal Republic's Basic Law was accepted unconditionally. This was not because the problem had been overlooked but because there was not the slightest reason for the dominant force in the process of unification to sacrifice or alter anything. It was might rather than right which ensured that unification occurred in the form of accession (not to say *Anschluß*). Why should the one state (at least in the minds of its leaders) subject itself to critical appraisal and modification when it is able simply to swallow up the remnants of the other? When wars – even if they are just cold wars – reach an end, peace is always arranged according to the maxim 'winner takes all'. It seems that even the civilised elements of present-day bourgeois society have done little to change this.

This is not just a problem of constitutional law. There is a deeper mechanism lying beneath considerations of national and constitutional law which is relevant for *sociology* for the very reason that there are no aspects of life here which have not been affected to a greater or lesser extent by the consequences of German–German developments.

On the other hand, the GDR's past has not sunk totally without trace. 'We are not equipped for living', Bobrowski said; 'We have our nature, our senses, five of them in the city, seven in the country . . . but that is not enough. A few things come to our aid: kindness and helpfulness to man in general, punishment and isolation for law-breakers, rules and regulations for officials. This is how we cope' (Hein 1990: 145). To develop this a little further, it could be said that anyone who has difficulty in finding his way through the welter of new rules and regulations will not find it easy to cope. Having been used to a state which did everything for them, GDR citizens do now have difficulty coping not just with the 'transformation of the system' but with the practical, everyday consequences. As was seen in the headier days of the revolution, the effects of this nanny state were such that long-established behaviour patterns did not disappear but were simply transferred to the new social situation. The basic pattern of behaviour has remained the same (precisely the hope for a new kind of nanny state), and all that is changing are the people (and institutions) to whom it relates. Fundamental changes in everyday behaviour patterns have certainly not followed changes of political scenery. It would be the task of a sociology/politics unit which has yet to be invented to find out how many of the demonstrators in Leipzig voted for and supported the state just a few months before the revolution. Its field of enquiry could be defined as the pathology and anomalies of mass behaviour.

Moreover, the structures and institutions transferred from the Federal Republic are hardly the best solution to every problem. The Federal Republic's social services system may well be superior to that of other western countries (the USA, for example) and it cannot be disputed that it comes off well in comparison with what was called the 'system of social security' in the GDR, but it does have failings of its own. Its transfer to 'the new federal states' will not occur without some difficulties. This will be the case, for example, where certain social security benefits are dependent on personal contributions which people from the old GDR could not possibly provide. Amongst most pensioners at least, the delight at reunification gradually has given way to fear and worry.

All in all, therefore, the social phenomena in evidence since the revolution are indications of deeper problems. Generally speaking, German unity is not so much a planned transformation of the system as a structural breakdown. There is no time to adjust to new developments either in terms of institutions or everyday sociology. Whether another form of transition (such as a step-by-step trans-formation) would have been possible and whether it would have had a greater chance of (mass) social acceptance must remain idle speculation. But it is worth thinking (and talking) about *what* these developments mean and *for whom*: obviously not in terms of the old cliché 'winners = capitalists, losers = the working class', but in a sociologically specific and differentiated way. At least one thing is certain. Both regional and social differences determine the likeli-hood of belonging to one group or the other. The prospects of 'young urban professionals' in the Federal Republic (old and new) are different from those of a forty-year-old (or, heaven knows, an even older) employee from the former GDR.

State unity is a long way from being followed by social and socio-economic unification. This will only come when, as a *conditio sine qua non* of real unification, the two German societies come together at all levels and not just in the political superstructure or where MPs' allowances are concerned. Of course, this itself will be an ambivalent process, but the market economy cannot be had without some risks. As far as social structures are concerned, one society which can be classed as specifically socialist is being trans-formed into a society with structures typical of a market economy –

that is to say a society with elites based on wealth and performance, a middle class, a lower-middle and upper-lower class, and finally an under-class which is more or less socially excluded. It is, above all, the extremes of this stratification pyramid which definitely contain the potential for social conflict. There is no reason to fear that political and social scientists will run out of work in such circumstances. Whether anyone can be found to pay for social research of this kind is quite a different matter.

Translated from the German by Gordon W. Smith.

References

Bahro, Rudolf, *Die Alternative*, Tribüne: Berlin, 1990

Bloch, Ernst, *Das Prinzip Hoffnung*, vol. 5, Suhrkamp: Frankfurt a.M., 1977 (Freiheit und Ordnung. Abriß der Sozialutopien)

Grass, Günter, *Deutscher Lastenausgleich. Wider das dumpfe Einheitsgebot – Reden und Gespräche*, Aufbau: Berlin, 1990

Hanf, Thomas, 'Modernisierung der Gesellschaft als sozialstrukturelles Problem', *Berliner Journal für Soziologie*, Sonderheft 1991, pp. 73–82

Hein Christoph, *Als Kind habe ich Stalin gesehen*, Aufbau: Berlin, 1990

Henrich, Rolf, *Der vormundschaftliche Staat*, Rowohlt: Reinbek, 1989

Heym, Stefan, *Stalin verläßt den Raum*, Reclam: Leipzig, 1990

Knabe, Hubertus (ed.), *Aufbruch in eine andere DDR. Reformer und Oppositionelle zur Zukunft ihres Landes*, Rowohlt: Reinbek, 1989

Konrád, György, and Szelényi, Ivan, *Die Intelligenz auf dem Weg zur Klassenmacht*, Suhrkamp: Frankfurt a.M., 1978

Lehrbuch der politischen Ökonomie des Sozialismus, Die Wirtschaft: Berlin, 1972

Lenin, W. I., *Werke*, vol. 6, Dietz: Berlin, 1956

Marx, Karl, *Das Kapital*, vol. 1, Dietz: Berlin, 1962

Marx, Karl, and Engels, Friedrich, 'Manifest der kommunistischen Partei', *Werke*, vol. 4, Dietz: Berlin, 1959

Sozialreport, Institut für Soziologie und Sozialpolitik der Akademie der Wissenschaften der DDR: Berlin, 1990

Verfassungsentwurf für die DDR, Staatsverlag: Berlin, 1990

−4−

'Perfecting' the Imperfect: The GDR Economy in the Honecker Era

Mike Dennis

The Development of the Administrative-Command Economic Mechanism

The Soviet zone emerged from the defeat of the Third Reich with a severely reduced economic potential, over 40 per cent of industrial capacity having been lost due to the direct and indirect consequences of war. The situation was exacerbated by Soviet dismantling operations and exaction of heavy reparation payments out of current production. An additional burden was the separation of the zone's economy from its major sources of raw materials and semi-manufactured products in the three Western zones and the subsequent reorientation of its trade towards the socialist east.

The mechanism with which the Soviet zone and later the GDR sought to rebuild its damaged economy was the Soviet-type administrative-command system. This system, though originally rejected for Germany by the German Communist Party (KPD) in its programme of June 1945, began to take root in the late 1940s and early 1950s, especially after Stalin's break with Tito in 1948. In 1950, a State Planning Commission was created as the supreme planning authority and the country's first five-year economic plan was introduced in 1951. The nationalisation of industry and the collectivisation of agriculture gathered momentum during the 1950s, particularly after Walter Ulbricht, at the Second SED Party Conference in 1952, announced the launching of the 'planned construction of socialism'.

The main characteristics of the administrative-command economic mechanism, as it evolved albeit with certain national modifications throughout the Soviet imperium in eastern Europe, were state ownership of the means of production, central planning of the economy through detailed short- and medium-term national economic plans, the administrative setting of prices and a concentration on material balances rather than on financial flows. This kind of system had some value in periods when, as in the late 1940s and early 1950s, it was necessary to mobilise resources rapidly towards specific goals such as the development of the basic materials and capital goods sectors. However, given its intrinsic flaws – a high level of wastage, partly the result of the heavy dependence on physical plan targets, the misallocation of prices and the limited assortment of goods and services – the model ultimately proved inappropriate to the running of a highly developed economy and to the promotion of innovation. Although the view is now common that such a system is irredeemably flawed, the GDR, it is generally conceded, did manage for many years to operate the system's levers with some success and to emerge in the later 1960s as a significant industrial power and the Comecon state with the highest standard of living.

The New Economic Mechanism

The SED political and economic elites made numerous efforts to 'perfect', that is streamline, the traditional economic mechanism, but only in the 1960s was a substantial modification attempted. In response to a stagnating economy in the early part of the decade and a widening gap in labour productivity with the Federal Republic, the SED leadership, with Soviet backing, launched an economic experiment in 1963. Known originally as the 'New Economic System of Planning and Management of the National Economy' (NES), it was renamed in 1967 as the 'Economic System of Socialism' (ESS). The autonomy of the nationalised enterprises was increased by reducing the number of compulsory state indicators and by giving more weight to indirect steering techniques, above all prices, profit, credits and interest.

Concerned at the difficulty in pushing through economic goals by means of indirect steering methods and anxious to promote economic modernisation, Ulbricht and his advisers introduced a structural policy in 1968. The policy gave priority to so-called 'structure-determining tasks' which were necessary for the automation and rationalisation of production processes. The emphasis on such 'tasks' soon resulted in distortions: the neglect of non-priority sectors led to supply difficulties in the priority areas, and bottlenecks became particularly acute in energy. The situation was exacerbated by unfavourable weather conditions and increasing (though modest) foreign indebtedness. Confronted by growing social unrest and management dissatisfaction with the system, NES/ESS was abandoned at a Central Committee meeting in December 1970. In truth, NES, despite the greatest role for monetary categories and a limited decentralisation, did not represent a radical departure from the traditional system. Moreover, a fundamental break with centralised mandatory planning and a movement towards a less bureaucratic and less demonetised economy was judged inexpedient by the SED at a time when the Prague Spring and unrest in Poland appeared to threaten the still vulnerable social and political order in the GDR.

Recentralisation under Honecker and the Unity of Social and Economic Policy

Honecker's accession to power in 1971 thus signalled a return to a comprehensive control hierarchy and a reinforcement of centralised resource allocation. Material balances proliferated once more: whereas 500 had been administered by central bodies in 1967, 800 were in operation in 1971–2. The State Planning Commission's role received a boost: for the first time since the introduction of NES it controlled about 300 material balances. Central control was also furthered by an increase in obligatory plan targets covering, among others, commodity production, wages, exports and imports.

The undermining of the limited autonomy of the economic units in the state system was extended into other areas by the nationalisation of semi-state and private enterprises, together accounting for 11.5 per cent of industrial production. Industrial productive artisan enterprises were nationalised, too, and the whole process was completed by June 1972. The concentration process eliminated one of the main advantages associated with the smaller units, that is their flexibility in responding to changes in demand for furniture, clothing and other consumer items. Such an outcome was not easily reconciled with another of the regime's goals, a general improvement in living standards on the basis of higher labour productivity and economic growth. The goal of a higher standard of living was incorporated into the 'Main Task' proclaimed by Honecker in 1971. This interdependence of economic and social policy was enshrined in the SED's new Party programme of 1976. The 'Main Task', a leitmotif of the Honecker era, was the foundation of the social contract which Honecker sought to establish between regime and populace. It typified the socio-economic mode of legitimation in communist states whereby in return for an acceptable standard of living the citizens tacitly, if unenthusiastically, were supposed to accept the Party's claim to be the leading force in society.

In the early 1970s, the regime's side of the bargain was to place a desperately needed housing construction programme into the centre of social policy and to uphold the principle of state subsidies for staple foodstuffs, rents and public transport fares. Material incentives and other rewards were to be used to stimulate higher productivity without widening differentials so far as to undermine a key element of the SED's legitimation strategy, that is the Party's claim to be striving for the social equality of the social classes and strata.

In retrospect, the first quinqennium of the Honecker era can be regarded as 'the best time of Honi': 400,000 new homes had been constructed and 209,000 dwellings modernised. Produced national income, according to official figures, rose by 30 per cent and the stock of consumer durables increased too. Between 1970 and 1976, ownership per hundred households of motor cars rose from 15.6 to 28.8, television sets from 69.1 to 83.6 and washing machines from 53.6 to 75.7 (*Statistisches Jahrbuch* 1977: 304).

The GDR in the World Economic Crisis, 1976–1984

While the GDR was enjoying modest prosperity, the storm clouds were gathering elsewhere. The explosion in the world market price of oil and other raw materials, first in 1973–4 and, then, much more seriously for the GDR, in 1979, together with higher charges for Soviet oil and natural gas caused a sharp deterioration in the terms of trade of the GDR, a country heavily dependent on outside supplies of cheap raw materials. Economic recession destroyed the regime's aspiration to modernise the economy by means of technological imports from the west, above all from the Federal Republic, financed by liberal credits from western banks. Net indebtedness to the west mounted rapidly from $6.7 bn (British billion) in 1977 to a peak of $11.67 bn in 1981. In the latter year, the cumulative trade deficit to the Soviet Union reached 2.3 bn transferable roubles. In 1982, the situation deteriorated further when in the wake of the rescheduling of the hard currency payments of Poland and Romania the GDR, too, from the middle of the year, was no longer able to rely on new credits from western banks (Cornelsen 1987: 52).

As part of its short-term crisis management strategy, the SED reduced imports from the west, with the significant exception of the Federal Republic, and launched a vigorous export drive based on an increase in the sale of mineral oil products. With outside supplies of raw materials and energy so costly, the production of the GDR's main domestic source of energy, the highly noxious lignite, was expanded from 258 million tonnes in 1980 to 319 million tonnes in 1988, with deleterious consequences for the environment. Between 1982 and 1984, investments were cut back sharply, which meant that much ageing plant and machinery could not be replaced.

Although consumers were obliged to tighten their belts by one or two notches, the SED leadership proceeded with the utmost caution in such a politically sensitive area. The price of basic necessities remained the same and the state poured massive subsidies into rents, public transport charges and consumer staples. These subsidies escalated from 16.9 bn marks in 1980 to 40.6 bn marks in 1985.

The readjustment of foreign trade with the OECD, excepting the Federal Republic, soon produced positive results: in 1982, at current prices, imports fell by 30 per cent and exports rose by 9.1 per cent. The net hard currency debt began to fall: from $8.7 bn in 1982 to $6.8 bn in the following year. The West German connection was vital to the whole recovery policy. Not only did intra-German trade plug some of the gaps left by the drastic reduction in GDR imports from other OECD countries but two large interest-free loans of DM 1 bn in mid-1983 and DM 950 mn one year later, both backed by the West German government, helped restore the creditworthiness of the GDR. By the end of 1984, the western credit markets were once more open to the GDR. In addition to the two credits, the GDR was able to draw upon a high annual flow of West German transfer payments. At the beginning of the 1980s, about DM 3.7 bn per annum were transmitted by the Federal Republic for the use of roads in the GDR, transit traffic to West Berlin, postal and communication services, receipts in humanitarian causes, visa fees, the minimum currency exchange requirement, and the sales carried out both through Intershops (a chain of hard-currency shops selling luxury and western goods to tourists and, from 1974, to GDR citizens) and through Genex (the state organisation set up in 1957 to co-ordinate the delivery of presents purchased in hard currency by western purchasers for East German recipients) (Michel 1987: 76–82).

A major organisational change took place during the economic crisis: the expansion throughout industry and construction of large economic units, the combines, and the elimination of the middle tier, the Associations of Nationalised Enterprises (VVBs). The number of combines rose from forty-five in 1975 to 171 in 1985. The size of a combine in industry varied from twenty to forty enterprises, enjoying similar production lines, and between 2,000 and 7,000 employees. Supplier enterprises and research centres were often located within a combine. The SED leadership, in particular the czar of the economy, Günter Mittag, envisaged major benefits such as economies of scale from the closer linkage within the combines between producers and suppliers. A fundamental disadvantage of the concentration of so much economic power in these large units soon emerged however: their monopolistic position inhibited creativity and risk-taking and thereby reinforced an intrinsic defect in the administrative-command system.

In addition to reorganising industry, the central authorities attempted to 'perfect' the existing system of economic control through the proliferation of material balances and planning indicators such as net production and net profit. According to Gerhard Schürer, head of the State Planning Commission, an army of 25,000 full-time planning personnel at central, regional and district level was responsible for the operation of the planning levers (*Wirtschaftswoche*, 30, 20.7.90, p. 15).

As part of their grand strategy Mittag and his colleagues sought to promote economic growth through a revamped economic modernisation programme, in which microelectronics was to play the central role. The intensive production commenced in 1977–8 after earlier developments in the 1960s had been allowed to founder. Microelectronics virtually acquired the status of a magic formula and was identified by Honecker at the Eleventh SED Party Congress in 1986 as one of the 'key technologies' which were decisive for the growth of labour productivity. Various organisational measures were introduced to solve the perennial problem of the slow diffusion of the country's research effort. For example, the research activities of the Academy of Sciences of the GDR, the country's major research centre, were linked more closely to the needs of industry. In 1986, 47 per cent of the Academy's research capacity was tied to agreements with combines, an increase of 12 per cent in one year, and higher education's research commitment rose from 42 to 52 per cent.

By the mid-1980s, the GDR had made a partial recovery from its earlier economic troubles. It was once more creditworthy, the net hard currency debt was falling, produced national income growth in 1984 and 1985 was slightly above the target figure of 5.1 per cent and some savings had been made in the consumption of energy and raw materials. Yet these were essentially 'one-off achievements', the result of what John Garland called 'de-extensification' rather than of 'comprehensive intensification' (Garland 1987: 7). In other words, the SED had demonstrated considerable skill in manipulating the administrative-command system but it was reluctant, perhaps psychologically unable, to grasp the nettle of fundamental reform. Such a challenge now beckoned with the advent to power of Mikhail Gorbachev.

Withstanding Gorbachev, 1985–1989

The SED leaders' discomfort with the early stages of glasnost and perestroika developed into open antipathy and then outright hostility when it became apparent in the autumn of 1986, but particularly after the Communist Party of the Soviet Union (CPSU) plena in January and June 1987, that Gorbachev was embarking upon a basic overhaul of the Soviet Union's economic and political structures. Despite many vital conceptual uncertainties and confusion, there was an undeniable movement towards a dualism in the ownership system, a shift of decision-making from the central planning authorities towards the production unit and the utilisation of selected market elements. Moreover, Moscow's belief, which had been crystallising since early 1987, that each socialist country must find a solution to its own problems released ever more radical reform impulses in eastern Europe, above all in Poland and Hungary. Widespread market reform and a partial de-nationalisation and privatisation of industry emerged as the platform of many reformers. Greater leeway also meant that the east European communist regimes would not be able to call upon the Soviet Union for life support and would thus become more dependent on their own resources for purposes of regime legitimation and survival.

The SED gerontocracy was alarmed at what it regarded as a

radical, ill-conceived and highly risky departure from the fundamentals of the traditional socialist economic system and it anxiously sought to prevent the spread of the reform virus to the GDR. The spectre of capitalism appeared to be haunting 'real existing' socialists. Dire warnings were issued against Hungarian and Polish plans to introduce market elements 'imported' from capitalism. Price rises and rent increases introduced in these two countries were denounced as incompatible with the GDR's own social system. Direct attacks were made on Soviet attempts to implement changes in the cornerstone of the traditional socialist system, the social ownership of the means of production (Nick and Radtke 1989: 229–31). Harry Tisch, SED politburo member and Chairman of the Free German Trade Union Association (FDGB), inveighed against the deployment of 'capitalist' elements such as job insecurity and competition in order to raise the efficiency of a socialist economy. No socialist country, he maintained, had demonstrated that borrowing from the 'arsenal' of capitalism would benefit the GDR (*Tribüne*, 22.5.89, p. 4).

The alleged success of the GDR economy was a vital part of the SED's Canute-like effort to hold back the tide of reform. At a meeting with Party District Secretaries in February 1987, Honecker asserted that the GDR was now reaping rewards in the form of higher labour productivity and greater social security from the decision taken in 1971 to gear the economy towards intensification. Each country, he concluded, had to take heed of its own specific conditions and its own level of development (*Dokumentation* 1987: 440–1). The imposition of a uniform socialist model, it was averred by SED spokespersons, was incompatible with the diversity of social, ethnic and economic developments in the socialist world and would be harmful to the greater efficiency of the more advanced GDR economy.

But at the same time as the SED was propagating the virtues of its own version of the traditional socialist system, influential figures within the Soviet political and academic elite were becoming increasingly sceptical of SED claims (Weißenburger 1990: 85–6) and were initiating a debate on the existence and nature of the general crisis of the administrative-command system of socialism. Oleg Bogomolev, the Director of the Institute for the Economy of World Socialism, contended that this crisis had its roots in the original sin of imposing the flawed Stalinist model on eastern Europe.

Vyacheslav Dashichev, one of Bogomolev's colleagues, was in no doubt that the GDR, too, was caught up in the general crisis of communism. The GDR's relatively high standard of living, he argued, was sustained to a considerable extent by numerous West German transfer payments and by imports of relatively cheap raw materials and energy from the Soviet Union. He attributed the GDR's poor economic performance to the obsolescent administrative-command system, whereas, in his view, West German prosperity derived from its federal political system, its market economy and its full incorporation into the international division of labour. As a way out of the impasse, he advocated a gradual drawing together of the two German states, culminating in a confederation or unification on the basis of guarantees for the security of all European countries (*Der Spiegel*, 5.2.90, pp. 148 and 152).

In retrospect, the retention of the administrative-command economic mechanism, the many technocratic adjustments notwithstanding, was a fateful decision, for the advent of Gorbachev could possibly have legitimised a reform process which, if initiated in time, might have arrested the symptoms of socio-economic decay which became increasingly malignant in the twilight years of the Honecker era, especially after the General Secretary's visit to Bonn in September 1987. However, Honecker, obdurate to the bitter end, clung to outmoded principles: 'We never turned our economy into one great experiment and made our actions ever more precise while involving ever broader sections of our economy' (*Foreign Affairs Bulletin*, 27, 2.10.89, p. 211). When Gorbachev, during his short but momentous visit to East Berlin in October 1989, warned his host that whoever comes too late will be punished by life itself, it was in fact already too late for Honecker and his associates.

The GDR Economy in Crisis, 1989–1990

As SED rule crumbled in the autumn of 1989 and the curtain lifted on the true state of the GDR economy it became painfully clear that that economy had been living not only on borrowed time but also on borrowed money. The facts could at last be separated from SED rhetoric. The future had been mortgaged by the SED leaders to keep the population quiescent and to preserve the 'Stalin mausoleum'. The country faced a series of acute short-term problems – a declining national income, a heavy foreign debt and a budgetary deficit – as well as the more deep-rooted problems associated with the structural defects in the traditional economic mechanism. The situation demanded a radical reassessment of the whole economic system and not just a reassembling of the myriad of balances, indicators and normatives. What were the main symptoms of the economic crisis?

(1) The major, albeit crude, indicator of the health of the economy, produced national income, had been in decline since the mid-1970s. The fall was particularly pronounced in the later 1980s. For example, whereas the average annual growth of produced national income was about 4.5 per cent between 1981 and 1985, it dropped to about 3.1 per cent from 1986 to 1989 ('Zur Lage der Volkswirtschaft der DDR' 1990: 3).

(2) The subvention of the 'Main Task' was proving increasingly counterproductive. The state subsidies for rents, public transport and basic foodstuffs had rocketed from 16.9 bn marks in 1980 to 49.8 bn marks in 1988. Wastage was encouraged by the ready availability of low-priced energy for domestic users and cheap foodstuffs, bread, for example, often being squandered as fodder. A kilogram of rye bread cost as little as 0.52 mark (barely 15 pence sterling at official exchange rates). The heavy state subsidies diverted resources from urgently needed investment in industry and infrastructure. Investment in the producing sector as a proportion of national income utilised dropped from 16 per cent in 1970 to 8.1 per cent in 1985, although it did stage a partial recovery thereafter (Cornelsen 1990: 77).

The housing programme, the core of the SED's whole social policy, it was now revealed, had been financed by credits amounting to 55 bn marks. Despite the many improvements in the housing stock, the emphasis on the construction of new units had left many old buildings in a dilapidated condition, and East Berlin's privileged position in the programme had created a serious gap in the quality of the housing stock between the capital and the rest of the country, a difference which was bitterly resented by the provinces.

(3) A particularly serious consequence of under-investment was the failure to replace much obsolescent plant and equipment. In 1989, 27 per cent of industrial plant was less than five years old but 52 per cent was between five and twenty years and 21 per cent aged over twenty years ('Zur Lage der Volkswirtschaft der DDR' 1990: 3). At the beginning of the 1980s, the value of machinery and plant in the producing sector which was virtually a total write-off amounted to about 58 bn marks; by the end of the decade, this had grown to 133 bn marks. The ageing machinery and plant required frequent servicing and maintenance: 280,000 workers were engaged in repair work and it had been impossible since the start of

the 1980s to reduce the proportion of manual labour in centrally managed industry (Stinglwagner 1990a: 240).

(4) The economic modernisation strategy by means of the application and development of the key technologies had proved to be a palpable failure, despite the diversion of considerable resources into this area. About 14 bn marks, it was estimated, had been invested by the beginning of 1989 in microelectronics. And in order to circumvent restrictions introduced by CoCom (the Co-ordinating Committee for Multilateral Export Controls, a Paris-based organisation created in 1949 to co-ordinate its members' national controls over the export of strategic materials and technology to communist countries) on the export of high technologies to the state socialist countries, sophisticated instruments had been purchased on the black market at three times their normal value (*Der Spiegel*, 16.4.90, p. 129).

A distorted investment programme meant that other sectors, for example transport and communications, were under-resourced, but even in the more favoured areas the new technologies proved to be a false investment in many enterprises as they were not integrated into the production process. Robots and other equipment frequently lay idle because of the lack of a compatible production structure and the requisite technical expertise among the workforce. In consequence, the GDR was unable to close the technological gap with the advanced capitalist states. For example, one of the most prestigious developments, the 1-megabit chip, which was first displayed in autumn 1988, had not commenced serial production in 1990. Yet NEC of Japan, one of the world's largest chip manufacturers, was already producing four million of the 1-megabit chips by the end of 1988. This kind of delay in marketing a product had serious repercussions for the competitiveness and profitability of the GDR's products. A case of too few silicon chips in Jena and too many smokestacks in Bitterfeld.

(5) Labour productivity lagged far behind that of West Germany and as an indicator of the inability of the administrative-command economic mechanism to respond to the challenges of the scientific-technical revolution, the gap was increasing in the final decade of the Honecker era. The German Institute for Economic Research calculated that in 1968 average labour productivity was about 68 per cent of West Germany's, and measured according to working time a further 21 per cent lower in 1983 (Gutmann 1990: 17). Considerable variation existed between and within sectors and branches. The situation in the clothing industry was particularly

problematic: a West German annual turnover of DM 146,000 per employee contrasted with the low GDR figure of DM 20,000. In the machine tools industry, which was heavily engaged in the export trade, labour productivity was half that of the Federal Republic (Stinglwagner 1990b: 13).

(6) The low motivation of the workforce was a constant problem, particularly as workers lacked an adequate system of material and non-material incentives. A reform of the wage system had commenced in 1976 with the aim of relating bonuses to real performance and of penalising failure to attain norms. Given the continuation of slack plans, the reform failed to make the desired impact. The mediocre could still feel secure, the ambitious and talented lacked stimulus. Employees still regarded bonuses as their right and too many workers, or so it was popularly believed, were able to earn an adequate wage without undue effort. The former Minister of Wages and Labour, Hannelore Mensch, revealed that the failure of the new wage system to stimulate performance was reflected in the fact that since 1975, and in particular in 1976, 1987 and 1988, the ratio of average wages had not been correlated with the growth of labour productivity (*Arbeit und Arbeitsrecht*, 1, 1990: 3).

One frequent complaint concerned the narrowness of income differentials. Engineers and master foremen in highly responsible positions were aggrieved that all too frequently they earned no more than skilled production workers. In their turn, some workers were tempted to give up skilled jobs as they were able to earn the same pay for less effort in jobs such as window cleaning. This was a dilemma for the SED as, on the other hand, many East Germans set great store by the egalitarian features of wage policy. A comparison of West and East German wage and salary structures highlights the nature of this 'levelling downwards' process. Although personnel with a degree employed in research and technology enjoyed salaries 27 per cent above the GDR average, their West German counterparts' earnings were 65 per cent higher than the national average (Gornig and Schwarze 1990: 1621).

(7) Foreign trade, too, was giving the utmost cause for concern. In addition to the usual problems – in particular the limited opportunities to utilise the advantages of the international division of labour – new ones had emerged. The SED's crisis management strategy in the early 1980s had been heavily dependent on the processing of mineral oil and the sale of mineral oil products to the west. The fall in the value of these products, following the drop in world oil prices in the later 1980s, occurred at a time when the

country's sales to western customers were being undermined by competition from the newly industrialising countries such as Singapore, Taiwan and Hong Kong.

The weakening competitiveness of GDR exports can be illustrated in various ways. For example, foreign trade turnover between 1986 and 1988 increased more slowly than the growth of produced national income, despite a general expansion of world trade ('Zur Lage der Volkswirtschaft der DDR' 1990: 3). Ever more marks had to be pumped into the economy in order to earn hard currency abroad: whereas in 1980 2.40 marks realised DM 1.00 in trade with the west, by the end of 1988 4.40 marks had to be invested. The Polygraph combine, whose trade with western customers represented over half its foreign trade turnover, expended 2.9 marks in order to acquire 1.00 Valuta Mark (the special foreign exchange accounting unit). The Mikroelektronik and Robotron combines fared even worse: 1.00 Valuta Mark per 7.2 marks (Haendcke-Hoppe 1990: 652). One result of this sharp deterioration in the GDR's terms of trade was a dramatic shift in its trade structure. Western industrial countries' share of GDR exports increased from 24.1 per cent in 1980 to 48.5 per cent in 1989, whilst that of the Comecon countries fell from 65.4 per cent to 43.2 per cent. The import profile exhibited a similar pattern over the same period, Comecon's percentage share of GDR imports falling from 60.2 to 39.4 and that of the industrial west's increasing from 30.4 to 53.1 (*Statistisches Taschenbuch* 1990: 110).

The plight of the GDR was acknowledged in a memorandum drafted in September 1989 by five economic experts, including the Chairman of the State Planning Commission, Gerhard Schürer, and the GDR's main hard currency adviser, Alexander Schalck-Golodkowski, known as Big Alex. The document's contents were intended for the top leaders, not for public debate. The GDR's annual credit-raising operations, it was estimated, totalled DM 8 bn to VM 10 bn, a considerable sum for a small country like the GDR but necessary for covering its import requirements from the capitalist world. Debt servicing was expected to rise from DM 5.6 bn in 1989 to VM 7.0 bn in 1990. In consequence, the GDR was heavily dependent on West German, Japanese and other foreign creditors. Schürer and his colleagues were extremely concerned about the consequences of International Monetary Fund involvement in a debt rescheduling process if debts continued to soar. In order to redress the situation, they proposed a reduction in consumption in favour of investment and a renewed export drive whilst simultaneously reducing imports. The seriousness of the GDR's indebtness, they concluded, put at risk not only the country's economic development but also its political stability (*die tageszeitung*, 19.3.90, p. 4).

(8) Finally, the SED claim that environmental problems could only be solved under socialism was revealed as pure fabrication. Outdated production methods, the wasteful consumption of energy and raw materials, the ruthless application of agro-chemicals, and the promotion of the lignite and carbo-chemical industries, partly for reasons of economic autarchy, all contributed to a pollution nightmare which, when it was revealed, did irreparable damage to the GDR's reputation as a leading industrial power. Over 50 per cent of forests had suffered some damage and the water supply was badly polluted. It was reckoned that life expectancy would improve by five years if the emissions of sulphur dioxide (5.2 mn tonnes per annum), ashes and dust were reduced by half in the most heavily polluted areas. The situation bordered on the catastrophic in certain parts of the GDR, notably the industrial regions of Leipzig and Halle, the upper valley of the Elbe in the Görlitz area, the districts around the Schwedt petro-chemical combine, the Erfurt–Arnstadt area and the eastern Erzgebirge. The environmental degradation and the social malaise in the conurbations of the south were undoubtedly a significant factor in the generation of the popular unrest which exploded on the streets of Leipzig, Dresden, Halle and Erfurt.

The opening of the Berlin Wall confirmed popular perceptions in the GDR of the yawning gap in the quality of life with the west and fostered widespread disillusionment with the GDR system. Emigration in 1989 and earlier had undoubtedly been stimulated by the desire on the part of East Germans to attain a higher standard of living, although, as was frequently observed at the time, the 1989 emigrants, mainly young and skilled workers, were reasonably well-off in basic material terms. Investigations into the motives for emigration showed that political factors narrowly outweighed economic ones. Later, however, as the shackles of the Stasi and SED-PDS were removed, an improvement in economic well-being became overwhelmingly the most significant motive behind emigration to the west. Final proof of the failure of real existing socialism, according to Gerhard Schürer, was the fact that not even the unemployed in the west wished to live in the GDR (*Wirtschaftswoche*, 30, 20.7.90, p, 15).

Towards Monetary Union

The rapid collapse of the old order and the transparent failure of the administrative-command economic mechanism to cope with the demands of the scientific-technical revolution triggered off an animated public debate on the nature of a radical economic reform. The debate embraced not only the representatives of the old order – the SED and the management teams in the combines – but also the newly emerging political groups such as New Forum, Democracy Now, the United Left, Democratic Renewal and the SDP, as they emerged from the chrysalis of civil society. In the autumn of 1989, these new groups were committed to a separate GDR with an economic system which combined both market and socialist elements. For a few weeks, it appeared that the GDR might become the testing ground for the development of a socialist market economy. Even the SED, in its reformed guise as the SED-PDS, sought, towards the end of 1989, to propagate the concept of a third way between what Gregor Gysi called administrative-centralistic socialism and the rule of transnational monopolies. This hybrid was to blend the advantages of the market economy with those of public ownership (Becher 1990: 688).

Responsibility for the day-to-day problems of running the economy as well as producing a reform programme fell to the SED-dominated government of Hans Modrow. Although Modrow and his Economics Minister, Christa Luft, adhered at first to the notion of a third way, they were forced to abandon it in January 1990. With great reluctance, they began to move towards a market economy: subsidies were to be eliminated in a three-stage programme; restrictions were to be lifted on private ownership, with traditional public ownership being confined to key areas such as energy, heavy industry and transport; the combines were to be released from the shackles of the state planning system and the all-pervasive bureaucracy; and the GDR mark was to be made fully convertible within five years.

The rapidly deteriorating political, economic and social situation had forced the Modrow government into abandoning the third way. The continuation of the mass exodus to the west – about 2,000 per day in late January and early February – was depriving the GDR of a disproportionate number of young, highly skilled workers and causing disruption to the production process and in the health sector. The economic statistics provided cold comfort to the beleaguered Prime Minister. The 1989 economic report which appeared in January showed that national income was 4 bn marks less than planned, and that during December industry had suffered losses of 80 million marks per day. Christa Luft added to the gloom by revealing a balance of payments deficit of $2.46 bn in 1989 and a gross hard currency debt of $20.6 bn (Colitt 1990). As January came to a close, strikes and slow-downs were disrupting production, demands for wage and benefit increases of up to 40 bn marks were jeopardising the survival of firms and the true extent of the environmental nightmare was becoming public knowledge. In order to restore stability, Modrow negotiated with the opposition groups a government of national stability and on his visit to Bonn on 13 and 14 February he appealed, in vain, for an aid package of DM 10 to 15 bn. The initiative was clearly with Bonn, where the modalities of German monetary union were being framed.

Early in the new year, the conventional wisdom in Bonn and Frankfurt was for a gradual adaptation of the GDR's economic and financial structures to the rules of the market. The West German Economics Minister, Helmut Haussman, envisaged a three-stage process towards completion of full monetary union in 1992. Basic economic reform, to be realised in the first stage, was to encompass the introduction of private ownership of the means of production, the gradual easing of wage and price controls and the devising of a realistic exchange rate for the GDR mark. Leading Bundesbank representatives such as the President, Karl Otto Pöhl, and the Deputy President, Helmut Schlesinger, believed that the enormous difficulties inherent in the transition from a planned to a market economy made rapid monetary union an unrealistic aim; monetary union, in their view, should be the culmination of the restructuring of the GDR economy.

Much to Pöhl's embarrassment the evolutionary path was abandoned at a Cabinet meeting on 7 February, when Chancellor Kohl, with one eye on stemming the mass influx of East Germans and the other on the kudos to be earned as the architect of unification, offered East Berlin immediate talks on monetary union. The embattled GDR premier accepted the offer on 13 February, during his visit to Bonn, and a joint commission responsible for drafting the legislative framework for rapid economic and monetary union started work one week later. The countdown had begun for the socialist economic system.

The advocates of rapid monetary union, while conscious of the many transitional problems, envisaged that a shock therapy was required to force the GDR government to address without procrastination vital issues such as freedom of trade and privatisation. The old political cadres and economic managers, it was argued, would be obliged to surrender their control over the enterprises, West German companies would be encouraged to participate in the restructuring of the GDR economy and the introduction of the D-Mark would prevent the development of a flourishing black market and give East Germans the incentive to remain at home. On the other hand, without underestimating the need for urgent action, critics of rapid monetary union warned that a sudden confrontation with the pressures of competition on the world markets would lead to the precipitous collapse of the many uncompetitive GDR enterprises and consequently a high level of unemployment and a corresponding burden on the social security network (Götz-Coenenberg 1990: 53–70 and 76; von Dohnanyi 1990).

While the proponents of a gradual union possessed, at least in theory, a valid economic case, the majority of East Germans wanted to take the fast lane with the Chancellor. In a survey conducted shortly before the *Volkskammer* elections in March 1990, 91.1 per cent of respondents were in favour and only 7.6 per cent were opposed to rapid monetary union (Gibowski 1990: 19). During the election campaign, Chancellor Kohl sought to allay East German fears of the negative repercussions of German economic, monetary and social union by backing a one-to-one conversion rate for small savers. After the Alliance for Germany's electoral triumph, the new GDR government of Lothar de Maizière wasted little time in pledging itself to rapid union, thus enabling GDR citizens, in de Maizière's words, to go on their summer holidays with D-Marks in their pockets. In late April, the two governments started negotiations on economic, monetary and social union. A treaty was signed on 18 May to come into operation on 1 July.

While the negotiations on GEMU were proceeding, analysts attempted to predict the speed with which the benefits of the West German social market economy would come into operation in the GDR and thus narrow the disparity between the two countries in labour productivity, living standards and output. According to one model, given a GDR labour productivity 40 per cent below that of the Federal Republic, it would take the GDR fifteen, twenty or thirty years to catch up with West Germany if GDR labour productivity grew on average at 8.5 per cent, 6.75 per cent or 5.25 per cent respectively while that of the Federal Republic increased by 2 per cent per annum. These high rates of increase in the GDR would depend upon removing impediments to growth such as overmanning and low motivation and upon the GDR attracting a high level of outside investment (Götz-Coenenberg 1990: 38–40). Predictions of the impact of GEMU on employment varied wildly. Some forecast unemployment accelerating rapidly to 3.8 million in 1992 and 1993; by contrast, others anticipated a growth in demand for labour as early as 1991 and a labour shortage of about 3 per cent by the end of the century.

One particularly animated debate centred around whether the conversion rate should be one GDR mark for one or two D-Marks. Anxious to dampen inflationary tendencies and to reduce the liquidity problems of firms having to pay interest in D-Marks on the high level of existing collective debt of 260 bn marks gross, the Bundesbank proposed two GDR marks to one D-Mark, except for small savings. The West German Finance Minister, Theo Waigel, also favoured this kind of solution. The response in the GDR was immediate: tens of thousands of demonstrators took to the streets in East Berlin, Leipzig and Halle in protest against what Helga Mausch, chairperson of the Confederation of Free German Trade Unions (FDGB – Freier Deutscher Gewerkschaftsbund), described as a threat to reduce East German wages to below those of Taiwan (*Der Spiegel*, 9.4.90, p. 25).

A conversion rate of two-to-one would indeed have decimated wages in the GDR. In 1988, average monthly pay was 1,100 GDR marks gross and 925 GDR marks net, compared to DM 3,300 gross and DM 2,200 net in the Federal Republic. The advocates of parity argued that a halving of wages would depress motivation and stimulate emigration, especially when price increases started to bite after the removal of consumer price subsidies. It was, of course, recognised that the wage bill would not be the sole determinant of a firm's survival and competitiveness; the quality of products and the productivity of the workforce would have an important bearing, too. There was, however, a certain degree of artificiality in the whole debate in that it would ultimately be impossible to maintain such wide disparities in wages and salaries in an open economy.

The savings accounts of East Germans was yet another highly sensitive issue. Between 1980 and 1989 total savings had risen from 99,730 mn to 159,671 mn GDR marks. Most of the savings were small, 70 per cent being below 5,000 marks. Whereas popular feeling was strongly in favour of parity for all accounts, the main argument advanced against such a proposal was that parity might stimulate an extra purchasing power with inflationary effects.

The final agreement on GEMU, which went into effect on

1 July, represented a compromise between the many diverse interests (Informationsdienst 1990). Wages, salaries, rents and pensions were to be converted at one-to-one. The basis for the conversion of wages and salaries was the level of payments as of 1 May 1990. Pensions were to be raised to 70 per cent of West German levels. Financial assets and liabilities were to be converted at two-to-one. As for savings, a conversion rate of one-to-one was allowed for up to 4,000 GDR marks per capita for GDR citizens aged 15 to 59 and up to 2,000 marks for young people under 15 years of age. Citizens aged 60 and over were allowed this rate for accounts of up to 6,000 marks.

No less important than the monetary aspects of union was the GDR government's agreement to adopt the principles and practices of a social market economy: private ownership of the means of production, freedom to choose a profession and to exercise economic activity, the liberalisation of trade and capital movements, the introduction of well-defined property rights and the encouragement of a wide variety of small and medium-sized businesses. The GDR was obliged to undertake the rapid implementation of West German environmental standards and regulations. The Bundesbank was empowered to act as the bank of issue of the common currency area. Finally, GDR agriculture was enjoined to adopt EC standards, including the introduction of market regulations and adjustment to West German producers' prices. However, transitional arrangements were provided for in sensitive areas and agricultural subsidies of DM 5.3 bn and DM 9.1 bn were approved for the second half of 1990 and for 1991 respectively.

The economic and monetary aspects of monetary union were buttressed by a third component – stipulations concerning a social union. The GDR was expected to adopt, though with some modifications, the West German labour, trade union, welfare and tax legislation. Many of the laws, relating, for example, to pensions and unemployment were to be introduced gradually.

The treaty made provision to meet some of the anticipated costs of unification. The West German government agreed to contribute DM 22 bn for the remainder of 1990 and a further DM 35 bn in 1991 to cover the GDR budget deficits. Furthermore, it agreed to payments of DM 750 mn towards the new pension insurance scheme and DM 2 bn towards unemployment insurance during the second half of 1990. A unity fund of DM 115 bn was to be created by the federal and the *Länder* governments to help finance restructuring until the end of 1993. Savings in the federal budget were to release DM 20 bn, while the remainder would be raised by bonds and other means. Finally, provision was made for DM 7 bn for the remainder of 1990 and DM 10 bn in 1991 to help enterprises facing closure during the transitional phase.

While it was impossible to predict with any precision the overall cost of restructuring the GDR economy, the infrastructure and the social security system, Bonn, partly for reasons of political calculation, especially with December's all-German election in mind, leaned towards the lowest calculation. Various estimates, however, were produced which provided a rough guide to the magnitude of the transformation. According to the deputy head of the Institute for Economy and Society in Bonn, F. J. Heidemann, the investments, whether private or public, required for restoring the infrastructure alone were in the region of DM 1,000 bn, including DM 200–250 bn on the motorways and railways, DM 10–15 bn on the telephone, radio and television network and about DM 200 bn on the housing stock (Götz–Coenenberg 1990: 21–2).

Responsibility for the privatisation and restructuring of the GDR's 8,000 formerly state-owned firms was assumed by the *Treuhandanstalt* or Trusteeship which had been in existence since the beginning of March. The Trusteeship was endowed with real power only after the passing of a Law on Privatisation and People's Own Assets on 17 June. Officials of the agency could have harboured few illusions about the nature of their task for, at the end of July, Reiner Maria Golke of the Trusteeship estimated that hardly one of the GDR's firms was competitive and 30 per cent were not fit for restructuring (Beyer 1990b: 1333). The Trusteeship found itself on the horns of a dilemma: whereas its preference was to sell off the firms and then let the new owners reinvigorate them, the claims of former owners and the economic unattractiveness of so many firms meant that potential investors and purchasers were reluctant to step in unless there were attractive inducements or some restructuring had already taken place; however, the latter course entailed the extension of subsidies to flagging firms. Just one indication of the complexity of the operation was the fact that by the end of November almost half of the land and property of East Germany, according to the Trusteeship, had been claimed by former owners, mainly West Germans (Marsh 1990b). Under these circumstances there could be no prospect of the Trusteeship achieving a favourable balance sheet: while about DM 1.5 bn was anticipated by the end of 1990 from sales, between DM 12 bn and DM 15 were required for liquidation, restructuring and environmental improvement schemes, (*Der Spiegel*, 29.10.90, p. 146; Marsh 1990a).

The Downward Spiral: The East German Economy between Plan and Market

The problems of the Trusteeship were symptomatic of the vertiginous downward spiral of the East German economy. Throughout 1990 gross national income, production and exports were all falling rapidly, while unemployment, closures, social unrest and some retail prices were on the increase. With the economy in sharp decline emigration remained heavy throughout 1990. The most pessimistic forecasts of the short-term impact of the shock therapy seem to have been confirmed.

East German gross national product fell by 3.4, 6.1 and 30.8 per cent during the first three quarterly periods of 1990 compared to performance during the equivalent periods in the preceding year (Müller-Krumholz 1990: 652–3). Overall, gross national product was expected by leading economists to decline by 16 per cent during 1990 and by about 8 to 10 per cent in 1991 ('Die Lage der Weltwirtschaft . . .' 1990: 633).

The decline in gross national product was a reflection of a dramatic fall in demand for East German products and a sharp rise in imports, especially from West Germany. Even western retailers were taken aback by the East German mania for western goods. Looking ahead, it was expected that purchases from western countries, above all from West Germany, would be one-third higher in 1991 than in 1990; and about half of consumer goods were expected to come from outside East Germany ('Die Lage der Weltwirtschaft . . .' 1990: 615). Industrial production, according to the GDR Statistical Office, fell by 7 per cent during the first half of 1990 compared to the equivalent period in 1989 (Beyer 1990a: 1178). The decline continued thereafter: in August production losses in percentage terms amounted to 15 in refrigerators, steel 34, lignite 37, shoes 59, cement 68, integrated circuits 72, meat 76 and coffee, tea and sweets 77 (*Süddeutsche Zeitung*, 12.11.90, p. 21). As production contracted, even top companies were having to implement radical adjustments. Carl Zeiss Jena, burden by debts and social security payments in the region of DM 2.4 bn but with an anticipated turnover of DM 850 mn, announced plans to reduce its workforce in Jena from its present level of 27,500 to a level of about 10,000 during 1991 (*Süddeutsche Zeitung*, 19.12.90, p. 27).

The situation in agriculture was equally gloomy. East Germany's 3,844 over-large agricultural enterprises encountered serious difficulties in disposing of their products in the face of competition from high quality western goods. Between April and June 1990, output fell by 41.1 per cent and then in the next quarter by 30.1 per cent compared to the corresponding periods in 1989 (Müller-Krumholz 1990: 653). Debts were soaring and about 50 per cent of work-place were held to be at risk. The depression in agriculture triggered off public protests and strikes. On 15 August, about 250,000 angry farmers protested on the streets of the GDR, including 50,000 on the Alexanderplatz in East Berlin.

East Germany's foreign trade, including trade with West Germany, was in serious trouble. In the third quarter of 1990, supplies to western customers fell by one-third and a deficit of about DM 19 bn was recorded in commodities and services, primarily because of the shift in demand from home to foreign products. Trade with the Soviet Union increased by about 19 per cent during this period, mainly because of the artificially high conversion rate of DM 2.34 for the transferable rouble (Lahmann 1990: 701). Trade with Comecon countries, above all with the Soviet Union, had long been crucial to the East German economy as about 850,000 work-places were directly and a further 600,000 were indirectly dependent on trade with former socialist partners. However, the future of trade with the rapidly disintegrating Soviet bloc looked bleak: an appreciable decline was expected in 1991 due to a shift in East German consumption patterns, the recording of transactions in D-Marks, the general restructuring problems in Comecon, the Soviet Union's shortage of hard currency and high level of indebtedness and its intention to reduce oil exports (*Süddeutsche Zeitung*, 31.10/1.11.90, p. 33). All this was most disturbing for former GDR firms. Whereas many had hoped to use their traditional trading links with Soviet partners as a buffer during the transition to the market economy, they were having to contemplate the near certainty of a dramatic collapse of exports to the Soviet Union. This was the prospect faced by one leading company, Umformtechnik Erfurt, 70 per cent of whose total exports had traditionally been destined for Soviet customers (Piper 1990).

The economic situation within what used to be the GDR was not helped by wage and salary increases awarded to East German workers naturally anxious to reduce the gap with their West German counterparts. Before GEMU, from January to April 1990, there had been a number of wage increases, for example the 10 per cent raise in gross wages in industry and construction. After 1 July, wages continued to rise – by about 30 per cent in the most important sectors such as electrotechnics, chemicals, the railways and metalworking – but without commensurate productivity agreements and with little differentiation of the wage structure (Gornig and Schwarze 1990: 1620–1). While the wage increases have been an extra burden on sorely pressed firms, they neither removed the stigma of second-class citizenship nor stemmed East Germany's demographic haemorrhage, over 100,000 having left for the West since GEMU and early November 1989. Some 10,000 qualified workers, it was disclosed by the Economics Minister of Saxony, were leaving Saxony each month for work in the West. About one thousand East Germans per day were expected to leave for the West in 1991 (Marsh 1990c; *Süddeutsche Zeitung*, 20.12.90, p. 2).

Unemployment increased sharply during 1990: 15,000 in February, 38,000 in March, 65,000 in April, 100,000 in June, 272,000 in July, 361,000 in August, 537,000 in October and 589,000 in November. It was still rising in the new year, reaching 757,000 in January 1991. Yet these figures understated the true extent of the social dislocation. A more accurate picture required the inclusion of employees on short-time work. The latter was intended to cushion the psychological shock of unemployment among a population unaccustomed to structural unemployment, and to provide workers with an opportunity for retraining. By the end of July 1990, there were 650,000 short-time workers and 1,856,000 in January 1991. Bearing in mind the fact that about 52 per cent of short-time work involved no work activity, the equivalent of 970,000 workers should be added to the unemployment figures. This meant an unemployment rate in the region of 21 per cent. The majority of short-term workers received 90 per cent of their wages, most of whose cost was covered by contributions from the federal government. Bonn's commitment was supposed to come to an end in June 1991, along with the agreement on protection against unlawful dismissal. An explosion of the unemployment figures was then anticipated; the President of the Metalworkers' Union, Franz Steinkühler, predicted a rise to 2.5 mn (Scheremet 1991; *Süddeutsche Zeitung*, 31.12.90/1.1.91, p. 6).

Faced by a rapidly mounting unification bill, the Finance Minister conceded that his ministry's original estimate in the summer of 1990 was wide of the mark. Part of the government's optimism had lain in its expectation of a rapid expansion of the service sector and in its belief in the widespread willingness of private industry and business to invest in the restructuring of East Germany. Some of these hopes were realised. During the first ten months of 1990, 226,000 new businesses were registered in the GDR, over half of them in the retail sector and in the hotel and catering trade (Walter 1991). Siemens invested about DM 1 bn in twenty projects in East Germany in the fields of telecommunications, power generation and automation (Goodhart 1990), and Opel a similar amount in a project to build a new car plant in Eisenach. However, western private investment, which was expected to reach over DM 15 bn in 1991 ('Die Lage der Weltwirtschaft . . .' 1990: 616) proceeded much more slowly than anticipated because of uncertainties over property rights, the heavy debts of enterprises, the underdeveloped infrastructure, overmanning and recent wage trends. Tax and financial incentives such as the idea of a low-tax zone in East Germany, as proposed by the Free Democrats in December 1990, were argued for in order to attract more West German firms and to relieve the public purse.

Total transfer payments from West to East Germany in 1991, it was anticipated, would reach DM 100 bn, that is DM 6,000 per head of population, and would constitute a large proportion of the public sector deficit of at least DM 140 bn which the Finance Ministry was forecasting for 1991. This figure was already DM 40 bn higher than estimated in June 1990 (Marsh 1990c). The DM 100 bn did not include the DM 30 bn to DM 40 bn per annum which the Trusteeship required to pay off the legacy of the old corporate debts and to cover new ones. It had originally been hoped that part of the unity bill would be offset by increased tax and other receipts from East Germany. However, by early 1991, the Finance Ministry was expecting tax receipts of DM 40 bn instead of the DM 53 bn originally projected for that year. While as a share of gross national product (about 5 per cent) the public borrowing requirement of DM 140 bn was not the highest ever raised in one year on the capital markets, the Bundesbank was concerned lest the rising public sector indebtedness worked against controlled credit and money supply growth (*Monthly Report* . . . 1990: 10). The Finance Ministry desperately searched for ways to relieve the burden, for example by reducing subsidies for West Berlin and the former inner-German border regions and by making cuts in defence spending. The West German regional governments were also called upon to bear a greater share of the costs. Chancellor Kohl's election pledge of no direct tax increases to pay for unity thus came under increasing pressure. For example, one leading CDU politician in the east, Kurt Biedenkopf, the newly installed Minister President of Saxony, foresaw no alternative to raising taxes to defray the economic and social costs of unification which he put at DM 100–110 bn per annum over the next five years (*Süddeutsche Zeitung*, 2.11.90, p. 33). With the costs of unification running out of control, the government was forced into a major policy U-turn. At the end of February 1991, it announced heavy across-the-board tax increases to come into effect on 1 July.

After forty years of socialism, the immediate future appeared extremely gloomy as the citizens of what had been the GDR undertook the difficult and uncharted transition to a market economy. High rates of unemployment and emigration, at least in the early 1990s, served as a painful reminder of the inequalities between the two parts of Germany. Heavy public investment will be needed to rebuild the damaged infrastructure and provide jobs before, perhaps towards the end of the decade, private as well as public investment will, hopefully, be able to reinvigorate the economy of the former GDR. Given the magnitude of the reconstruction and the potential for social unrest and political instability, this is a formidable domestic task which faces the new all-German government at the same time as it has to redefine its international role.

Acknowledgement

I am grateful to the Nuffield Foundation, the British Academy, and the School of Humanities and Social Sciences, Wolverhampton Polytechnic, for the financial assistance which enabled me to undertake the research for this paper.

References

Becher, Jürgen, 'Das Ringen um die Wirtschaftsreform in der DDR', *Deutschland Archiv*, 5, 1990, pp. 687–96
Beyer, Achim, 'Wirtschaft. Wirtschaftliche Daten', *Deutschland Archiv*, 8, 1990a, p. 1178

——, 'Wirtschaft. Probleme der Treuhandanstalt', *Deutschland Archiv*, 9, 1990b, pp. 1333–4

Colitt, Leslie, 'E Germany lifts Veil from "Secret Economic Details"', *Financial Times*, 4.1.90, p. 2

Cornelsen, Doris, 'The GDR Economy in the Eighties: Economic Strategy and Structural Adjustments', *Studies in Comparative Communism*, 1, 1987, pp. 39–53

——, 'Die Wirtschaft der DDR in der Honecker-Ära', *Vierteljahreshefte zur Wirtschaftsforschung*, 1, 1990, pp. 70–9

von Dohnanyi, Klaus, 'Das deutsche Wagnis. Die Risiken der deutsch-deutschen Vereinigung', *Der Spiegel*, 24.9.90, pp. 162–3, 166, 168, 170, 172, 174, 177, 180, 182

'Dokumentation. Erich Honecker vor 1. SED-Kreissekretären', *Deutschland Archiv*, 4, 1987, pp. 436–44

Garland, John, 'The GDR's Strategy for "Intensification"', *Studies in Comparative Communism*, 1, 1987, pp. 3–7

Gibowski, Wolfgang G., 'Demokratischer (Neu-)Beginn in der DDR. Dokumentation und Analyse der Wahl von 18. März 1990', *Zeitschrift für Parlamentsfragen*, 1, 1990, pp. 5–22

Goodhart, David, 'Siemens Sees a Profit in East Germany within Two Years', *Financial Times*, 14.12.90, p. 24

Gornig, Martin, and Schwarze, Johannes, 'Hohe pauschale Lohnsteigerungen in der DDR gefährden die Wettbewerbstätigkeit', *Deutschland Archiv*, 10, 1990, pp. 1619–24

Götz-Coenenberg, Roland, *Währungsintegration in Deutschland: Alternativen und Konsequenzen*, Bundesinstitut für ostwissenschaftliche und internationale Studien: Cologne, 1990 (Berichte des Bundesinstituts für ostwissenschaftliche und internationale Studien, 20)

Gutmann, Gernot, 'Produktivität und Wirtschaftsordnung. Die Wirtschaft der DDR im Wandel', *Aus Politik und Zeitgeschichte*, 33, 10.8.90, pp. 17–26

Haendcke-Hoppe, Maria, 'Außenhandel. Umbewertung der Außenhandelsstatistik', *Deutschland Archiv*, 5, 1990, pp. 651–2

Informationsdienst der Bundesregierung (ed.), *Der Vertrag über die Schaffung einer Währungs-, Wirtschafts- und Sozialunion zwischen der Bundesrepublik Deutschland und der Deutschen Demokratischen Republik. Erklärungen und Dokumente*, Bundesdruckerei Zweigbetrieb: Bonn, 1990

'Die Lage der Weltwirtschaft und der deutschen Wirtschaft im Herbst 1990', *DIW Wochenbericht*, 43/44, 25.10.90, pp. 605–35

Lahmann, Herbert, 'Zur Entwicklung des Außenhandels der Bundesrepublik Deutschland im dritten Quartal 1990', *DIW Wochenbericht*, 50, 13.12.90, pp. 696–701

Marsh, David, 'Treuhand Chief Gives Bleak View of Sell-off in the East', *Financial Times*, 1.11.90a, p. 3

——, 'Claims against Half E German Property', *Financial Times*, 22.11.90b, p. 21

——, 'The Costs of Unity Keep Rising', *Financial Times*, 13.11.90c, p. 22

Michel, Jeffrey, 'Economic Exchanges Specific to the Two German States', *Studies in Comparative Communism*, 1, 1987, pp. 73–83

Monthly Report of the Deutsche Bundesbank, 9, September 1990

Müller-Krumholz, Karin, 'Die wirtschaftliche Entwicklung in Deutschland im dritten Quartal 1990', *DIW Wochenbericht*, 46, 15.11.90, pp. 645–54

Nick, Harry, and Radtke, Gerd-Rainer, 'Gesellschaftliche Entwicklung und sozialistisches Eigentum', *Einheit*, 3, 1989, pp. 225–32

Piper, Nikolaus, '"Der Russe schließt nicht ab"', *Die Zeit*, 21.12.90, pp. 23–4

Scheremet, Wolfgang, 'Arbeitsmarkt im Sog des wirtschaftlichen Gefälles zwischen Ost- und Westdeutschland', *DIW Wochenbericht*, 7, 14.9.91, pp. 57–62

Statistisches Amt der DDR (ed.), *Statistisches Taschenbuch der Deutschen Demokratischen Republik '90*, Haufe: Berlin, 1990

Statistische Zentralverwaltung für Statistik (ed.), *Statistisches Jahrbuch der Deutschen Demokratischen Republik 1977*, Staatsverlag der Deutschen Demokratischen Republik: Berlin, 1977

Stinglwagner, Wolfgang, 'Schwere Zeiten für die DDR-Wirtschaft', *Deutschland Archiv*, 2, 1990a, pp. 237–41

——, 'Nur langfristige Umstrukturierungen helfen', *Das Parlament*, 14.9.90b, p. 13

Walter, Norbert, 'Country in a State of flux', *Financial Times*, 3.1.91, p. 12

Weißenburger, Ulrich, 'Die wirtschaftswissenschaftliche DDR-Forschung in der Sowjetunion', *Vierteljahreshefte zur Wirtschaftsforschung*, 1, 1990, pp. 80–7

'Zur Lage der Volkswirtschaft der DDR', *Neues Deutschland*, 11.1.90, p. 3

PART II

Aspects of Political Culture

-5-

Changes in Political Culture and the Transformation of the GDR, 1989–1990

Henry Krisch

Assessing the relationship between political culture and the policies of the GDR leadership during the 'high noon' of Honecker's 'welfare authoritarianism' (cf. Henrich 1989), I stated my belief that it made sense to begin with the assumption that the regime's policies were designed, *inter alia*, to 'increase the congruence between the political structure and the values of the dominant political culture' (Krisch 1988b: 151). During this period of relative political stability (roughly between 1976 and 1987), the regime seemed indeed to have propagated effectively a mixture of revolutionary, traditional and alternative elements that granted the system of *Realsozialismus* sufficient support to minimise the regime's need to allow structural modification of its political and social order.

In the years after 1971, the Honecker leadership had shown itself quite flexible in selecting and modifying a variety of such elements so as to increase its support by broadening the basis of its appeal while leaving unchanged the basic power relations of the society (cf. Krisch 1988a). Thus, in addition to the original base of revolutionary attitudes, it sought to add traditional values based on a broader acceptance of German history and cultural traditions (Thomas Müntzer *and* Martin Luther, so to speak), as well as stressing the technocratic and meritocratic elements in the communist tradition. Moreover, while it clearly opposed the political and cultural implications of alternative or youth cultures, it nevertheless strove to incorporate at least some elements from this tradition into the dominant culture mix. For example, throughout the latter years of the old order, it was official policy to attempt incorporation of elements of popular culture (especially in music and entertainment more generally). Moreover, despite episodes of repression, the authorities never quite suppressed unofficial societal initiatives on such topics as the environment or nuclear armaments, nor did they interfere seriously with the Evangelical Church that provided these movements with logistical support and a psychological anchor.

The political culture of any society, however, is by its nature a constantly changing set of attitudes. No political culture pattern ever represents a universal set of attitudes; the proportion of the politically aware population that responds to political life in a particular way is always a shifting one. Political stability, then, depends on a proper balance being maintained between overt policies designed to attract support and social changes that produce divergent attitudes among significant sectors of the population.

Throughout the industrialised world in recent years, in both communist and non-communist nations, attitudinal change has been a constant, if not increasing, fact of political life (Gibbons 1989: 23–4). The most central tenets of the Leninist political system have been called into question, including the central role of the ruling party, the basic features of the command economy, and the basic orientation of the people to the existing political system and to its historical and ideological legitimation. This change in attitudes has been demonstrated in a number of ways in the Soviet Union and in the states of eastern Europe; these include surveys of public opinion, results of elections and public demonstrations. The basic thrust of such changes is to call into question the fundamental relationship of Soviet and also GDR politics: that between a vanguard political leadership centred in the Party, and a mobilised mass population.

In the GDR, this momentous shift in political attitudes affected most of the bases of system legitimacy. The central policy feature of the Honecker era, the 'unity of social and economic policy', had led to expectations of continued economic growth and expanded material benefits to the population. But the relative slow-down of economic growth, which led to the GDR economy's poor performance in matters of consumer goods and services, served to erode a major system-maintaining attitude among the population.

A clear sign of this change of perspective was the attitude of many of those fleeing the GDR in the summer and autumn of 1989. Although they came in many cases from materially privileged strata of the GDR population, their palpable sense of diminishing opportunities in the face of rising expectations showed how little was left of the attitude, diligently sponsored by the Honecker leadership, that 'hard work will pay off' for GDR citizens. The

GDR's liberalised travel policies in late 1987 and 1988, by providing increased basis for West–East comparison of living standards, may have been politically counterproductive. The constant strain of an inadequate supply of modern manufactures was ill-suited to the regime's desired self-image of the GDR as a highly developed industrial state. For the mass of the population, the highly touted achievements of the key technologies (*Schlüsseltechnologien*) which the government favoured could not compensate for the more pervasive shortages (cf. Bohley *et al.* 1989: 156–8).

Another major element of the dominant political culture was the evocation of a separate GDR identity. Whether in the form of a separate GDR 'state consciousness', a goal fostered especially after 1971 by a deliberate policy of *Abgrenzung* (or demarcation), or in the effort of the early 1980s to anchor the GDR in a broader German historical tradition (approval for Luther, Frederick the Great, etc.), the GDR was to be perceived as the desirable political home for its population. In the crucial months of autumn and winter 1989, the attitudes of the GDR population were divided between those whose political reference point was West Germany, as indicated either by fleeing westward or by voting behaviour in the March 1990 general elections, and the smaller group whose literal (cf. the slogan 'We are staying here!' – 'Wir bleiben hier!') and electoral behaviour indicated that a reformed GDR remained their political focus.

The most important shift in political culture revealed by the upheaval in the GDR concerns political participation. Here we observe a change of attitudes which includes at least three important aspects. First, there was a change in the relationship of the individual to organisational authority; second, there was a demand that the participatory and representational potential of such existing structures as the People's Chamber (*Volkskammer*) and the political parties be realised; finally, there was the creation of new institutions or the conversion of existing ones into channels of participation. It was the failure of the regime to respond, promptly and adequately, to demands arising from such changing attitudes that destroyed its authority in the eyes of the population, as evidenced by mass behaviour on the streets and squares of the GDR during critical days in October and November 1989.

The changes in political culture outlined above may have come to fruition in 1989, but their overt manifestation in determining behaviour must have been preceded by a lengthy period of incubation. Unfortunately, until scholars have ready access to survey or interview data from before the *Wende* (as the period of change at the time of the 1989 revolution is usually called in Germany), we must rely on the same sort of indirect evidence hitherto used to determine GDR political culture. Thus the remainder of this chapter will rely on both statements made and behaviour displayed during the period September 1989 to March 1990 (and, in some cases, beyond) in order to determine the scope and nature of political culture change.

What direct evidence we do have of changing attitudes, however, tends to corroborate these indirect findings and thus justify our acceptance of them. For example, there is a longitudinal series of attitude surveys of GDR university students undertaken by a Leipzig research centre (Abteilung Studentenforschung, Zentralinstitut für Jugendforschung). This study suggests that regime socialisation policies achieved some measure of success in disseminating supportive political attitudes among this critical constituency (Heublein and Brämer 1990). In 1979 more than half of the sample identified (to be precise, expressed *Verbundenheit*) with the SED as a ruling party; a decade later, only 28 per cent did so, while only one in five identified with the SED's economic policy, and a vanishing five per cent with its information policy (an astounding loss of public credibility!). This poor view of the SED may lie behind a distaste for supporting leadership by politicians; an astonishing 72 per cent named 'non-partisan experts' as best able to resolve the country's problems. Positive attitudes towards the GDR as such, however, were more persistent than positive views of the SED. As late as spring 1990, for example, just over half the sample favoured a confederation of two German states for the near future. Moreover, by margins ranging from 86 to 94 per cent, students approved of specific items of social policy, such as secure opportunities for education and training, and a liberal abortion policy. Such items are the very same sort of accomplishments the regime liked to herald, suggesting that the growth of negative attitudes was not due to particular policy disagreements.

That a possibly significant minority of the GDR population was moving towards a pattern of negative attitudes towards the exercise of power in the GDR was clear from developments in the country in the decade preceding the *Wende*, and especially in the last few years of that decade. (There is an enormous literature, in both English and German, on the rise of alternative political activity in the GDR. See, somewhat at random, Woods 1986; Glaeßner 1990; Süß 1989.) Increasingly, GDR citizens, many of whom had lived their adult lives in the GDR after Honecker's accession to power, gave up – to use Albert Hirschman's (1970) terms – 'loyalty' and chose 'exit' (this is true of those whose negative stance was influenced mostly by the failures of GDR socio-economic policies) or 'voice', these latter being the increasing numbers of GDR citizens who became active in the Church-sheltered environmental, peace and feminist movements. The very number and variety of political pressure groups that sprang up in the summer and autumn of 1989 point to the prior existence of informal circles of like-minded people. (A sampling of the literature on these new organisations would include: Rein 1989; Schüddekopf 1990; *Dokumentation* 1990; Hamilton 1990.) In general, these issue-oriented movements attempted to act in parallel to official policy, retaining a potentially supportive function. One of the first harbingers of a challenge to the regime's political authority came with the demonstrations of January 1988 in conjunction with the Luxemburg–Liebknecht memorial observances.

Although political culture patterns are not changed by single or even a few events, these can serve a catalytic function. In the two years prior to the downfall of the Honecker leadership, there were several such events. What distinguishes them is that each touched on those attitudes whose transformation was to undermine the legitimacy of the GDR order. One was a series of rebuffs to the movement of perestroika and its possible relevance to the GDR: the bans on Soviet publications, the critique of artistic products of glasnost; and the general, self-satisfied conviction that the GDR did not need to re-paper its sociopolitical walls. It was apparent that people in the GDR had internalised the conviction that 'fraternal permission' would be needed for the GDR to avoid political disasters like those in Budapest or Prague in 1956 or 1968. Now that the Soviet Union supported reform, it seemed a cruel joke that the GDR leaders would not follow the Soviet lead.

While the Soviet Union slipped out of favour with the leadership in Berlin, China suddenly stood in its place. The SED leaders, and Krenz in particular, became notorious for their support of hard-line Chinese policies (especially in connection with the student demonstrations in Tiananmen Square). Press coverage of the People's Republic's national holiday on 1 October was unusually lavish. The broad hint was not lost on the people of the GDR.

Another such event was the controversy over the results of communal elections in May 1989, which helped to discredit

Honecker's October successor, Egon Krenz, as the man who had been in charge of organising the elections. To the authorities, it must have been an infuriating aspect of these protests that they seem to have been conducted along entirely legal, not to say legalistic, lines. (See the instructions from the head of the Ministry of State Security, Mielke, to Stasi administrative units, in Mitter and Wolle 1990: 42–5.) To bring an important political ritual into disrepute for no pressing political reason was a political error of great magnitude, and indicates the extent to which the regime, despite lengthy and detailed Stasi reports, had drifted out of touch with mass attitudes.

A similar misjudgement was the regime's reaction to the flood of refugees swarming through Hungary and via West German embassies into what Honecker had once called 'hostile foreign territory'. The public display of a combination of stubbornness and opportunism (denouncing those fleeing, blaming western media, etc., but then arranging transport to the west, routing the trains for protocol's sake through the GDR, but then beating those who tried to join the exodus!) strengthened the conviction, in both the public and the Party, that the ageing SED leadership had lost the capacity to govern. In the mental balance between a 'subject' orientation that accepts direction from above, and an evaluative, participant outlook, the latter perspective was powerfully reinforced by the performance of the leadership itself. In a report to Mielke of early September 1989, it is reported that, with increasing frequency, workers were asserting that the leadership was too old to cope adequately with the GDR's problems (Mitter and Wolle 1990).

As the crisis deepened on the level of political action, the signs of a rapidly changing pattern of political culture manifested themselves. We may sum up these changes under the headings of organisation, process and goals. In each case, the attitudes towards political life that the regime had sought to propagate were abandoned and replaced by others. All three aspects had a common theme: the demand for a shift from vanguard politics and mobilised pseudo-participation to a broad-based, democratic system within a framework of laws.

Such a shift indicates two important things about the sources of change of political culture in the GDR. One is that this change was common to similar movements in the USSR and eastern Europe. Political change in the GDR, both in the realm of political culture and in political life generally, was moved by forces common to European communist polities, indicating a general, systemic crisis for regimes of this type. Secondly, while subjective political errors of often ageing leaders may well have contributed to the problems that arose in 1989, the source of the difficulties lay in the incongruence between social development and political forms. It is ironic that a leadership committed to an ideology of social and historical change would blindly exempt its own system of rule from such processes.

These system-weakening viewpoints had two sources. One was the daily political practice of West Germany, as mediated by an increasingly intensive network of intra-German contacts, but especially of course via West German television broadcasting to the GDR. This influence made itself felt more strongly as time went on, and more strongly among the mass of the population as opposed to the artistic and scholarly elite. The other was derived from socialist ideology itself (aspects of which were contrasted with GDR practice), and was especially influential with the intellectuals as a social group, and with reform-minded members of the SED itself.

The organisational aspect of this shift of attitudes is related to a perception of what are the proper channels for civic action. Such issues are common in regimes of various types, as shown by western debates as to the propriety of street demonstrations. It is a particularly pressing question for communist regimes because of the ideologically legitimated monopolisation of access to political action by the ruling party or its designated instruments.

Through the decade of the 1980s, political action outside party-approved channels grew under the sponsorship of (some elements of) the Evangelical Church. Discussion groups, peace services, environmental libraries, mass demonstrations: the scale of political action through the Church was broad and clearly went beyond narrowly pastoral concerns. None the less, a church environment is necessarily a restrictive one, although in the summer of 1989 the authorities were moving towards a confrontation with the churches precisely over the latitude they permitted social activists. What the *Wende* brought was a proliferation of organised activism that bespoke a greatly changed attitude towards the sources and nature of political organisation.

Most of the organisations were outgrowths of the earlier movements and were led by activists from that period. Many of the new leaders were, in fact, clergymen themselves. Such groups as Democracy Now (Demokratie Jetzt), Initiative for Peace and Human Rights (Initiative für Frieden und Menschenrechte) and, above all, New Forum (Neues Forum) demonstrated the extent to which activists in the GDR were willing to seek new organisational outlets for self-directed and legitimated action (see, among other sources, *Analysen, Dokumentationen* 1990). These organisations were not, at first, designed to be political parties, and indeed some never took that further step. It is clear that they were founded in the expectation that the GDR as a state, and perhaps most of its political institutions, would remain in existence for the foreseeable future. What would change would be the *mode of participation*. Still later, in the early months of 1990, these organisations played a positive role in holding the system together pending elections, by participating in an *ad hoc* consultative forum, the Round Table (*Runde Tisch*). The parallelism between this institution and its Polish, Czech and other Soviet bloc counterparts is another striking example of the parallel political development in these countries.

In addition, however, some new political parties were founded. Given the West German example and the environmental awareness linked to church groups, it is not surprising that Green parties were established. More important was the re-establishment of a Social Democratic Party. Given the history of the SPD's semi-forced absorption into the SED, an SPD revival meant harking back to a pre-Stalinist practice and, given the prominence of the SPD in Bonn's *Ostpolitik* and the shared perception of the SED and SPD regarding the need to encourage discussion of areas of conflict which had previously been taboo (*Streitkultur*), it meant an infusion of West German attitudes.

Later, in anticipation of the *Volkskammer* elections of 18 March 1990, there were internal changes in the former 'Block' parties, these being especially important in the CDU, which emerged with the largest vote in those elections. Moreover, inasmuch as the names of twenty-four parties appeared on the March ballot, it is clear that a great many had been formed during the immediately preceding months.

One further organisational change is noteworthy: the movement to reform drastically the then still ruling party, the SED. Much of the struggle to transform the SED into an internally democratic, intra-systemic party, re-naming it in the process as the PDS, involved changing the behaviour and attitudes of party members. The fund transfer scandals of November 1990 showed how difficult this can be. Nevertheless, the line of SED membership was hardly one that divided reformers from their enemies. This is clear, for example, from an account of a rank-and-file SED rally outside the then Central Committee building ('Unerträgliche Selbstgerechtigkeit', *Der Spiegel*, 46, 1989, p. 40. Cf. Brie 1989). The development of so-called 'platforms' within the Party, and their legitimation by the new leadership, was another sign of a widespread desire for more participatory channels (Staritz 1990: 15). As the reconstituted PDS, it has remained an important electoral force and, despite its heritage, provides an avenue of self-directed political activity for some elements in parts of Germany.

In the realm of process, the most striking themes in the 1989 upheaval were the calls for participation and discussion. The widespread sense of civic disenfranchisement showed the nature of the gulf between officially sponsored attitudes, and those that had grown up in the population. A measure of this is the sudden outburst of political statements from normally non-political sources such as actors and musicians. A resolution of 18 September 1989, issued by 'rock musicians, balladeers, and entertainers', may serve as one example, it being instructive to note that the substantive demands of this manifesto concerned issues of political participation, rather than policy in the realm of popular culture ('Resolution der Rockmusiker, Liedermacher und Unterhaltungskünstler: Wenn wir nichts unternehmen, arbeitet die Zeit gegen uns', in Rein 1989: 150). The manifesto of New Forum provided a classic statement of this theme: 'Communication between state and society in our country is poor. Evidence of this is widespread dissatisfaction, including even withdrawal into the private sphere or mass emigration' (Rein 1989: 13).

Behaviour followed demands: the last months of 1989 in the GDR were characterised by a constant stream of meetings and discussions. Prominent were those meetings arranged in Dresden and Leipzig by non-partisan figures (such as Gewandhaus conductor Kurt Masur) and the mass meeting called for Berlin's Alexanderplatz on 4 November by the artists, actors and writers of the city. A parallel set of public forums were those held by party leaders trying to establish 'dialogue' with the population, as in the case of Berlin's SED leader, Schabowski (cf. Neues Forum Leipzig 1990: 273–8).

As far as goals were concerned, the most interesting aspect of this change in values and attitudes was the almost conspicuous agreement on policy questions between regime and opposition. In the New Forum manifesto quoted above, it is clear how careful its authors were to call for 'economic initiatives but no cut-throat [*Ellenbogen*] society'. Most groups, perhaps out of tactical considerations in the early stages, called for some form of reformed socialism. If there was one additional theme, it was the call for greater environmental awareness.

This seeming focus on citizenship values, on the political process, may be misleading because of the prominent role played by intellectuals, often of 'socialist sympathies', in the dissident movement. While thousands marched in the streets or stood in squares, only a relatively small number participated actively in the organisations we have been describing. A Leipzig scholar has estimated that only 10,000 to 15,000 persons had some links to the oppositional groups (Pollack 1990: 1217). The increased activity of students is evidenced by figures showing that the average GDR student took part in four demonstrations in the last four months of 1989, with every fifth student being involved in more than five. On the other hand, in many a town in the GDR without concentrations of students or artists, large and determined demonstrations did take place (Heublein and Brämer 1990; Connelly 1990: 71–89).

The difference in constituencies may account in part for the noticeable change in public sentiment that seems to have taken place at the turn of the decade. Aggressive anti-socialism, German nationalism, and increased anti-foreigner (or, as has been suggested, 'anti-official anti-fascist') sentiments came to the fore. This transition has sometimes been summed up as the shift from 'We are the people' to 'We are one people'. This seems overly simplified, since national themes had certainly been a part of the set of political attitudes the old regime had favoured. Without the controlling hand of the SED, however, this dangerous game with German national sentiment spelled a turning away from attitudes that could produce attachment to (or indeed a need for) a separate GDR.

As the political focus in the GDR shifted to the election campaign of March 1990, yet other attitudes came to the fore. Broad-based, often spontaneous political activism gave way to the more organised campaigns of political parties. Many of these, in turn, were supported and advised (not to put it more strongly!) by West German organisations. Indeed, in the GDR, the turbulent political events of the first half of 1990 may be summed up quite neatly from a political culture perspective by saying that the dominant political culture values were (or seemed to be) those of the Federal Republic. It would not be surprising if, in the process of 'growing together', German political culture took on many, perhaps even most of the attributes of West German political culture.

The symbolic moment for such a shift may have been the rejection in April 1990, by the *Volkskammer*, of a draft constitution for the GDR. It had been drawn up by many of the same scholars who had argued for a reformed socialism and indeed a reformed PDS as a viable future for the GDR. Of course, such a shift is not by its nature either undemocratic or undesirable. It does mean, however, that the new all-German political culture may have relatively little of the GDR's heritage in it.

Nevertheless, some GDR influences may well persist into a new social setting. The increase in Germany's population by a quarter through unification has brought a strong admixture of feminist, small-group activist and environmentalist attitudes. The political impact of German religious life will surely be changed by the influence of the former 'Church in Socialism'. Participation may also mean greater social responsibility for ordinary people, directed against the political gigantism of both former German states. (I take this to be the message of many recent writings of Erich Loest, as for example his essay 'Das Jahr der Täter' (Loest 1990).

What changes may the process and excitement of recent time have brought to Germans' political attitudes? The importance of this question lies in its implications for future democratic stability in Germany. As Ralf Dahrendorf has argued, a broad-based political class committed to participation would produce those political culture attitudes that would uphold democratic institutions: 'without political culture no reliable institutions' (Dahrendorf 1990). Have the experiences of the past year or so strengthened democratic elements of political culture in erstwhile East Germans? Will they strengthen similar tendencies in Germany as a whole? Or has the rapid unification that followed upon the commitment to a single currency allowed Germans in the former GDR to transfer a dependent sociopolitical relationship, with its attendant non-participatory behaviour, to a new authority?

Clearly, it will take time, and a great deal of field research, to answer such questions. Certain preliminary observations may be in order already. From the perspective of many thoughtful East(ern) Germans, the triumph of democracy in the GDR came too quickly and, thanks to Bonn's help (or, if one likes, interference), too easily. 'Democratisation' in 1989 was uncomfortably similar to 'anti-fascism' in 1945; the beginning struggles were blighted by the regime's collapse – into the arms of the Federal Republic, so to speak. Why, asks Hans-Joachim Maaz in an essay, was there never an armed attack on the Berlin Wall from the eastern side? He worries that the speed of unification deprived GDR citizens of a chance to develop an 'identity as expressive adults' (Maaz 1990: 216–18).

On the other hand, there are signs that anti-authoritarian social elements will survive unification, especially in social spheres important in the special development of the GDR, such as women's affairs (Matte 1990). Konrad Weiß, a leader of Democracy Now, has described the dependent and ultimately undemocratic behaviour patterns that characterised his own life in the GDR. When he failed to protest against the expatriation of the songwriter and singer Wolf Biermann in 1976, he availed himself of all the then current rationalisations, but 'inwardly I knew that I had been cowardly' (Weiß 1989: 296). That it could take him so long to accept civic responsibility seems to him to indicate a lack of democratic political culture. Yet from the perspective of the President of the Federal Republic, Richard von Weizsäcker, the Germans in the GDR were lucky because, unlike their materially better-off western brethren, they attained their freedom through effort, instead of receiving it as a gift (*Der Fischer Weltalmanach* 1990: 350–1).

References

Analysen, Dokumentationen und Chronik zur Entwicklung in der DDR vom September bis Dezember 1989, Gesamtdeutsches Institut: Bonn, 1990

Bohley, Bärbel, *et al.*, *40 Jahre DDR . . . und die Bürger melden sich zu Wort*, Büchergilde Gutenberg/Hanser: Frankfurt a.M., 1989

Brie, Michael, 'Vom Versagen des administrativen Sozialismus', in Hubertus Knabe (ed.), *Aufbruch in eine andere DDR*, Rowohlt: Reinbek, 1989, pp. 181–91

Connelly, John, 'Moments of Revolution: Plauen (Vogtland), 7 October 1989', *German Politics and Society*, 20, Summer 1990, pp. 71–89

Dahrendorf, Ralf, 'Die Quadratur des Zirkels. Wie entsteht politische Kultur?', *Frankfurter Allgemeine Zeitung*, 3.9.90

Dokumentation zur Entwicklung der neuen Parteien und Bürgerrechtsbewegungen in der DDR (November 1989–Februar 1990), Gesamtdeutsches Institut: Bonn, 1990

Der Fischer Weltalmanach. Sonderband DDR, Fischer: Frankfurt a.M., 1990

Gibbons, John R., 'Contemporary Political Culture. An Introduction', in John R. Gibbons (ed.), *Contemporary Political Culture. Politics in a Postmodern Age*, Sage: London, 1989

Glaeßner, Gert-Joachim, 'Vom "realen Sozialismus" zur Selbstbestimmung. Ursachen und Konsequenzen der Systemkrise in der DDR', *Aus Politik und Zeitgeschichte*, 5.1.90, B1–2/90, pp. 3–20

Hamilton, Daniel, *After the Revolution: The New Political Landscape in East Germany*, American Institute for Contemporary German Studies: Washington DC, 1990 (German Issues 7)

Henrich, Rolf, *Der vormundschaftliche Staat*, Rowohlt: Reinbek, 1989

Heublein, Ulrich, and Brämer, Rainer, 'Studenten im Abseits der Vereinigung', *Deutschland Archiv*, 9, 1990, pp. 1397–410

Hirschman, Albert O., *Exit, Voice and Loyalty. Responses to Decline in Firms, Organizations and States*, Harvard University Press: Cambridge, Mass. and London, 1970

Krisch, Henry, *Politics and Culture in the German Democratic Republic*, University of Michigan: Ann Arbor, 1988a

——, 'Der Wandel der politischen Kultur und politische Stabilität in der DDR', in Gert-Joachim Glaeßner (ed.), *Die DDR in der Ära Honecker*, Westdeutscher Verlag: Opladen, 1988b, pp. 151–64

Loest, Erich, 'Das Jahr der Täter', *Frankfurter Allgemeine Zeitung*, 13.10.90

Maaz, Hans-Joachim, 'Stalinismus als Lebensform', *Der Spiegel*, 9, 1990, pp. 216–18

Matte, Christina, 'Scheidungen in Weiß', *Neues Deutschland*, 27/28.10.90

Mitter, Armin, and Wolle, Stefan (eds), *Ich liebe euch doch alle! Befehle und Lageberichte des MfS Januar–November 1989*, BasisDruck: Berlin, 1990

Neues Forum Leipzig, *Jetzt oder nie – Demokratie. Leipziger Herbst '89*, Bertelsmann: Munich, 1990

Pollack, Detlef, 'Zur Rolle der alternativen Gruppen im Umbruchprozeß der DDR', *Deutschland Archiv*, 8, 1990, pp. 1216–22

Rein, Gerhard (ed.), *Die Opposition in der DDR*, Wichern: Berlin, 1989

Schüddekopf, Charles (ed.), *'Wir sind das Volk'*, Rowohlt: Reinbek, 1990

Staritz, Dietrich, 'Ursachen und Konsequenzen einer deutschen Revolution', in *Der Fischer Weltalmanach. Sonderband DDR*, Fischer: Frankfurt a.M., 1990, pp. 14–43

Süß, Walter, 'Perestroika oder Ausreise', *Deutschland Archiv*, 3, 1989, pp. 286–301

Weiß, Konrad, 'Vierzig Jahre in Vierteldeutschland', in Hubertus Knabe (ed.), *Aufbruch in eine andere DDR*, Rowohlt: Reinbek, 1989, pp. 294–9

Woods, Roger, *Opposition in the GDR under Honecker 1971–85*, Macmillan: London, 1986

–6–

The Failure of GDR Cultural Policy under Honecker

Ian Wallace

KEIE: We made a paradise on earth for them.
MORDRET: And wanted to make them enter that
paradise by use of force.
Christoph Hein, *The Knights of the Round Table*

Throughout the short history of the GDR its ideological spokesmen consistently stressed what they saw as the indivisible unity of politics, economics and culture in the Party's efforts to push forward the socialist revolution. Since the dramatic demise of the country at the end of the 1980s the political and economic dimensions have understandably been the subject of extensive analysis. Far less attention, however, has been paid to the failure of cultural policy, even though this was no less spectacular and, it could be argued, was at least as fundamental as the collapse of the SED's political and economic strategies. For the particular task which had been entrusted to cultural policy was that of promoting a socialist consciousness among the population at large, a sense of loyalty to the brave new socialist experiment to which the 'better' Germany had committed itself following the fall of fascism. By voting with their feet at such speed and in such numbers, the GDR's citizens demonstrated in the autumn of 1989 just how far short of success the experiment had fallen. The policy which had been intended to promote social integration and thereby to solidify the Party's power base was seen to have been built on sand.

From today's vantage point it is clearer than ever that, whichever way they turned, the GDR's cultural politicians could not defuse one simple fact of which the ordinary citizen was only too aware: if persuasion proved ineffective, the Party was prepared to use force to push through its policies even in the cultural sphere. Nor was this something it sought to conceal. On the contrary, believing themselves to be the guardians of truths entrusted to them by the science of Marxism-Leninism, Party stalwarts felt justified in ensuring people's 'happiness' even against their own will. Hermann Kant, for many years a leading exponent of cultural policy in the literary field, now admits that this was always ˉa fundamental mistake:

> We looked for a different path than the west – not in order to detract maliciously from people's happiness but because we saw that happiness quite differently. I am afraid we approached social changes as if we were introducing smallpox vaccination: this is something we have to do, it is good for you, and because not everyone appreciates this, there will have to be a law to force your happiness on you: end of discussion. We probably only understood how inappropriate this approach to social changes was once nobody wanted to listen any more. (Fink 1990: 68f.)

As Kant's statement makes explicit, the orthodox concept of culture which prevailed in the GDR had an assertive, pro-active dimension which clearly provided the seed-bed for such a fundamentally mistaken policy. According to the *Kulturpolitisches Wörterbuch* (Berger *et al.* 1978), which faithfully reflects the Party's view on such matters, culture cannot be understood simply as what is often called in the west 'high culture' (although the idea, much favoured in the early post-war years, that ordinary people of limited formal education could also come or be brought to an appreciation of high culture was never lost sight of). Nor, on the other hand, does it encompass every aspect of human life – that is, everything that man does and thinks and makes of the world in which he lives. This is rejected as a value-free concept of culture characteristic of some 'bourgeois thinkers'. By contrast, the Marxist-Leninist view of culture embraces two basic, complementary propositions. First, the development of human society depends on certain objective laws which underlie the processes of history. These processes are directed towards a definite goal, expressed in a succession of historical phases which progress from primitive society to slavery, then feudalism, capitalism, socialism, and finally communism. Secondly, however, the progress of history is significantly influenced by what human beings themselves achieve in appropriating and reshaping nature and in developing and changing their own social conditions. What they achieve here – in producing certain historical conditions and in developing the human personality – may be defined as culture. At the heart of this concept of culture is an emphasis on the progress and development of society which it promotes, i.e. it is dynamic in nature, it pushes forward the socialist revolution, it is 'progressive'. The converse is obviously also taken to be true. Culture which is not progressive in nature does nothing to promote socialism and, at worst, actually seeks to undermine it. In fact, this is not culture at all in the Marxist-Leninist sense and must be actively opposed by all available means.

Such ideological considerations apart, the term 'culture' remains, in the context of the GDR no less than elsewhere, notoriously difficult to pin down, resembling a concertina which can be stretched or squeezed according to requirement. What is clear, however, is that, in practice, the word is normally used in a much narrower sense than that favoured by the *Kulturpolitisches Wörterbuch*, this in spite of the fact that determined attempts were made from the 1970s on to assert the predominance of the broader concept (cf. Haase *et al.* 1988: 367f. and 480). It is normally taken to refer to literature and the arts in general – not unlike in the United Kingdom, in fact, which perhaps for that reason prefers to have a Minister for the Arts rather than a Minister of Culture. Unlike the United Kingdom, however, the GDR always accorded to culture in this narrower sense an enormous political significance, perceiving in it a Jekyll-and-Hyde quality which could make it seem at one moment the apologist of the SED's brand of socialism and at another the principal agent of its subversion from within. It can, of course, be argued that this is to attach an exaggerated importance to the likely impact of literature on the political and social consciousness of the country at large. A measure of scepticism is certainly justified in the face of claims that writers had a direct line to ordinary citizens and were able to articulate or even shape their hopes and convictions, this in spite of the fact that the statutes of the Writers' Union (as revised in 1973) confidently referred to writers as 'active co-shapers' of socialist society: 'The members of the Writers' Union of the GDR take an active part in shaping the socialist present. Their art helps to form the thoughts, feelings and actions of the people constructing and completing socialism' (Statut 1974: 291).

However great or small the actual impact of GDR literature on its readers may have been, it should not be overlooked that it did enjoy a special status in the GDR, if only by default. Press, television and radio were no more than the stultifyingly unimaginative mouthpieces of Party ideology, so that the arts in general and literature in particular provided the only significant public outlet for any form of alternative thinking. The Party was fully aware of this, of course, and to that extent was right to see in its relationship with the country's writers 'the central concern' of its cultural policy after the Eighth and Ninth Party Congresses (Walther *et al.* 1991: 100) and the most critical test of its ability to nurture a particular form of socialist consciousness. This relationship will therefore be the focus of our attention in turning now to a consideration of Honecker's cultural policy.

No Taboos?

When, in 1971, Erich Honecker replaced the authoritarian Stalinist Walter Ulbricht as First Secretary (later Secretary-General) of the SED and therefore as leader of the country, his accession gave rise to the widespread hope that the Party might renounce the familiar, strong-arm approach to cultural policy, deeming it inappropriate to an era of détente in which the GDR seemed set fair to shed its image as an international pariah and to take its place in the international community of states. In spite of Honecker's leading part in the crude attacks on Wolf Biermann, Stefan Heym, Werner Bräunig, leading film-makers and others at the now infamous Eleventh Plenum of the SED's Central Committee in December 1965, his apparent willingness to introduce a more liberal cultural policy (without, of course, calling into question the leading role of the Party in this as in all other spheres) was widely accepted at face value. In a long speech which the new leader delivered in December 1971 two short sentences attracted particular attention and, despite their wooden German, became the fruitful source of much speculative exegesis: 'If the starting point is the firm position of socialism, there can, in my opinion, be no taboos in the field of art and literature. This applies to questions both of content presentation and of style – in short: to the questions of what is called artistic excellence' (Rüß 1976: 287). What was the significance of the expression 'in my opinion'? Should it be read as proof of the new leader's modesty? Or of his willingness to engage in genuine dialogue? Did it indicate that not everyone in the leadership shared his view? Or should one see in it a conscious allusion to the strictly experimental nature of what was being said, with the unspoken hint that the experiment could be terminated just as suddenly as it had been initiated?

How seriously one should ever have taken Honecker's (qualified) promise that there would henceforth be no taboos in literature and the arts generally remains a matter for debate, but it is clear that the new policy was widely welcomed among writers, not infrequently with something approaching euphoria. The years between 1971 and 1976 can be regarded as the honeymoon period in Honecker's cultural policy, years of hope in which it seemed possible that an atmosphere of trust between the Party and the different branches of the arts might gradually be built up. Congresses organised by the various arts organisations during this period were notable for the relatively open nature of their debates. Books which had previously been suppressed, such as Stefan Heym's *Die Schmähschrift*, *Lassalle* and *Der König-David-Bericht*, were now able to appear. Volker Braun's play *Die Kipper* was at last performed and, after some hesitation, his controversial story *Unvollendete Geschichte* appeared in the journal *Sinn und Form*. The poet Adolf Endler sent the feathers flying with an unusually and refreshingly unrestrained attack on orthodox literary scholars in the GDR, whom he likened to a wizened governess directing abuse at the flowering garden of GDR lyric poetry, while Ulrich Plenzdorf's *Die neuen Leiden des jungen W.*, written in the late 1960s with little belief in the likelihood of early publication, enjoyed enormous public success both in the theatre and as a prose text.

Nevertheless, a more careful analysis of Honecker's 'no taboos' speech might have encouraged greater scepticism. Certainly the significance of one passage was all but overlooked. This made it clear what Honecker meant by a 'socialist position' and 'artistic excellence': 'To attain artistic excellence demands first of all clarity about the role of art in the intellectual conflicts of the present – from the position of socialism and of the relentless ideological class struggle with imperialism' (Rüß 1976: 288). Dealing sensitively with the arts did not mean making concessions to views which were 'foreign to our ideology'. In other words, the Party was certainly interested in encouraging a more trusting relationship with writers and other practitioners of the arts but only on condition that the latter showed a sense of responsibility by never questioning the Party's ideology. Given that the essence of the new cultural policy seemed to many to be the much greater freedom from tight Party control which it held in prospect, this invitation to self-censorship was bound to lead to conflict sooner or later.

Virtually from its inception there had been clear signs that the new policy might prove less attractive in practice than official pronouncements suggested, but it was not until the autumn of 1976 that the extravagant hopes invested by many in Honecker's alleged liberal intentions were finally and irrevocably dashed. A second, infinitely darker phase in post-Ulbricht cultural policy began on 29 October when Reiner Kunze, who had been a thorn in the side of the Party ever since his protest against the role of the GDR in the invasion of Czechoslovakia in 1968, was thrown out of the Writers' Union following publication in the west of his volume of short prose texts *Die wunderbaren Jahre*. An even more serious blow to Honecker's liberal reputation followed less than three weeks later, on 16 November, when perhaps the GDR's most famous dissident and a particular *bête noire* of the SED for at least twelve years, Wolf Biermann, was deprived of his citizenship of the GDR after giving in Cologne his first concert during an officially approved tour of the Federal Republic. Like many commentators, Biermann quickly came to the conclusion that, after denying him permission to perform publicly in the GDR for eleven years, the leadership of the Party had been deceitful in granting him permission to undertake a tour in the west, since its intention from the outset (as the writer Jurek Becker had warned) had been to lock the door behind him (Seyppel 1982: 139). The next day, eleven well-known writers and the sculptor Fritz Cremer took the unprecedented step of addressing a respectful letter of carefully modulated protest to Erich Honecker in which, wisely noting that Marx was on their side with his view that the proletarian revolution must be constantly open to self-criticism, they urged the GDR's leaders to view with tolerance Biermann's provocations:

> We do not identify with Biermann's every word and every act and distance ourselves from attempts to misuse the events surrounding Biermann to attack the GDR. Biermann himself has never, in Cologne or elsewhere, left any doubt which of the two German states, for all his criticism, he supports. We protest against his expatriation and request that the action which has been taken be reconsidered. (Lübbe 1984: 310f.)

Even though this letter was published only in the western press, it gained the public support of over 150 other intellectuals in the days that immediately followed. There were many like Klaus Schlesinger who experienced an overwhelming sense of release and excitement as the protest spread (Schlesinger 1990: 162–4). On the other hand, given the almost excessive restraint of the letter's wording, Karl-Heinz Jakobs may not have been alone in feeling initially that there was something not so much revolutionary as ridiculous in his signing it (Jakobs 1983: 177). The open letter was followed by yet another, this time written by Bernd Jentzsch and addressed to Erich Honecker personally. Jentzsch had been living in Switzerland since 20 October, working on an anthology of Swiss literature for publication in the GDR. He could therefore perhaps afford to be less circumspect than the drafters of the first letter: 'The damage which the GDR has done to itself through these measures is immense. But it is my hope that further damage to the GDR can be averted if these hastily made decisions are reconsidered and reversed' (Lübbe 1984: 338). In particular, he stated openly that the treatment of Kunze and Biermann had not come out of the blue but had been preceded earlier in the year by unmistakable evidence of an increasingly hard line in cultural policy. He chronicled the previously little-known but all-too-familiar catalogue of oppression – the long cross-examination of writers by the security police (Stasi); house-searches; confiscation of manuscripts, notes, diaries, letters and books; the banning of public performances, of books, and of films.

There were, of course, those who from the outset had viewed Honecker's apparent promises with caution. Writers such as Volker Braun (Braun 1979: 103) and Erich Loest (Loest 1990: 60) were not swept off their feet but insisted that the proof of the pudding must be in the eating – a wise precaution given both the history of cultural repression in the GDR and the statement by at least one leading functionary in Berlin, even as he initiated an assembly of writers into the details of the new policy, that 'we can strike again at any time' (cf. Jäger 1990: 1834). As the published extracts from his diaries reveal, Erwin Strittmatter was another who was sceptical, first asking somewhat disbelievingly whether certain politicians had really come to appreciate the pointlessness of dogma in matters of art (Strittmatter 1990: 34 – entry for 26 Sept. 1973), but in time absolutely certain that the promise of no taboos was no more than 'a rhetorical trick to win over those in the arts in a party-political sense' (Strittmatter 1990: 97 – entry for 25 July 1975), an allegation he substantiates by pointing to Honecker's alarmed and threatening response when Braun had the hero of his play *Die Kipper* refer to the GDR as the most boring country on earth.

In a campaign clearly orchestrated by the SED, *Neues Deutschland* published in the days that followed a series of declarations in which workers and party hacks as well as widely respected intellectuals such as Anna Seghers, Konrad Wolf, Peter Hacks, Ludwig Renn, Paul Dessau, Willi Sitte and Hermann Kant distanced themselves from Biermann with varying degrees of emphasis (and, in Hacks's case, with particularly venomous contempt). Fritz Cremer and Ekkehard Schall found reason to withdraw their support for the original letter of protest, while another signatory, Volker Braun, objected only to its alleged misuse by western commentators in what he described as a fruitless attempt to try and drive a wedge between Party and writers.

As if in recognition of the widespread confusion and dismay caused by the drastic switch in its cultural policy, the SED developed for cosmetic purposes a different and, as it doubtless seemed, more sophisticated approach to particularly troublesome intellectuals such as Stefan Heym and Robert Havemann. Although the latter's house-arrest – imposed in November 1976 for what was alleged to be persistent defamation of the GDR in the western media – was surprisingly rescinded in May 1979, this proved to be only a tactical prelude to his being accused a few days later, with Heym, of currency irregularities. Although both had published books in the west without first seeking the written approval of the Copyright Office (which, as Heym pointed out, was no more than 'the extended arm of the censor' (Heym 1990: 168)), it had been decided to prosecute them not for disregarding the requirement to go through the normal licencing procedure which applied to any form of publication but instead to charge them with fraud – that is, with having pocketed in full the hard currency royalties earned by publications in the west. The accusation smacked of privilege and self-enrichment, and it was doubtless calculated that firm action against such alleged misdemeanours was more likely to meet with the approval of the ordinary citizen than a somewhat arcane dispute about the proper procedure for publishing texts in the west. Havemann was subsequently fined 10,000 marks and Heym 9,000 marks. A determined attempt was made in newspaper reports to suggest that they were no better than petty criminals, the back page of *Neues Deutschland* carrying on 23 May a brief report on Heym's fine, carefully placed between two items entitled 'Burglars were apprehended' and '17 traffic louts lose driving licence'.

Both refused to be cowed, however. In a defiant interview with a West German television reporter (who, for his pains, was immediately required to leave the GDR) Heym proclaimed that, for all the fuss about currency violations, what was really at stake was freedom of speech. In a latter of solidarity with Heym, eight colleagues (Jurek Becker, Klaus Poche, Klaus Schlesinger, Erich Loest, Kurt Bartsch, Adolf Endler, Dieter Schubert, Martin Stade) protested against what they saw as more and more frequent attempts to defame critical writers, to reduce them to silence, or, as in the case of Heym, to prosecute them through the law. Such linking of the criminal law with censorship, they asserted, was obviously intended to prevent the publication of critical literature: 'We are against the arbitrary use of laws: problems in our cultural policy cannot be solved through criminal proceedings' (Walther *et al.* 1991: 65). In the inevitable escalation of hostilities which followed, they too were publicly denounced by Party loyalists, while Dieter Noll broadened the attack with crude abuse of his fellow writers Stefan Heym, Joachim Seyppel and Rolf Schneider. The culmination of this campaign was the fateful meeting of the Berlin branch of the Writers' Union at which five of the letter's signatories (the exceptions being Becker and Stade, who had already left the Union in 1977 and 1978 respectively, and Loest, who left in 1980 after it had proved impossible to find a majority in the Leipzig branch prepared to vote for his removal) as well as Heym himself, Karl-Heinz Jakobs, Schneider and Seyppel were deprived of their membership, explicitly because of what the President, Hermann Kant, and the First Secretary of the Writers' Union, Gerhard Henniger, regarded as their defamation of the Party's cultural policy (Walther *et al.* 1991: 78 and 105). Among the approximately sixty dissenting votes were those of Christa Wolf, Ulrich Plenzdorf, Günter de Bruyn and Stephan Hermlin.

A number of authors, including Wolf, Elke Erb, Franz Fühmann, de Bruyn, Plenzdorf, Günter Kunert, Kito Lorenc, Wulf Kirsten, Rainer Kirsch, Heinz Czechowski and Hein, wrote letters of protest to the Union's leadership, requesting that it not confirm the decision to expel their nine colleagues (Walther *et al.* 1991: 17). It is clear, too, that the treatment of the nine writers caused some ripples in the population at large, since similar letters were sent from all corners of the country, while *Sonntag*, the weekly newspaper published by the League for Culture, dared to suggest that numerous GDR citizens, not least students and other members of the younger generation, were discussing and questioning the decree. Although all the letters of protest were ignored (those sent to the Writers' Union were found ten years later in an unmarked envelope) and the expulsions were duly confirmed on 14 June 1979, the Party evidently felt obliged to react to such evidence of unease. At a meeting attended by the member of the politburo with overall responsibility for culture Kurt Hager, the Minister of Culture H.-J. Hoffmann, the President of the Academy of Arts Konrad Wolf, and representatives of the League for Culture and other important arts organisations, Honecker made a token attempt to breathe new life into his policy of 'no taboos' but then in effect undermined this by adding that freedom in the cultural field must be protected against those who would misuse it.

It therefore surprised no-one when, on 28 June 1979, the *Volkskammer* duly rubber-stamped changes to the Criminal Code which were clearly aimed at punishing such 'misuse' by those who dared to publish their criticisms in the west without first consulting the Copyright Office. Thus, an extension to paragraph 219 of the Code made it illegal to disseminate or to cause to be disseminated abroad any kind of information (including publications, manuscripts or 'other materials') such as might 'damage the interests of the German Democratic Republic'. Similarly, in order to avoid in future the kind of joint action undertaken by writers and artists both in the Biermann affair and in defence of Stefan Heym, significant modifications to paragraph 218 were made, the maximum prison sentence for taking part in an illegal organisation being raised from two to five years and the term 'organisation' itself being complemented by the much vaguer 'any other group of persons'.

Within weeks, however, it became clear that the legal stick which the Party had begun to wield as the main instrument of its cultural policy had not led it to forget entirely the uses of an occasional carrot. Hinstorff, a publishing house in Rostock which included some of the GDR's best critical writers on its list, announced the forthcoming (re-)publication of works by Schlesinger, Schneider and Becker. At the same time Poche, Kunert and Seyppel accepted the offer of long-term visas allowing them to take up residence in the west. In November Heym was given permission to read from his works in Amsterdam and to visit the Netherlands, while Loest was allowed to give a reading in West Berlin. Schneider received a visa which enabled him to travel back and forward to Mainz, where he was to act as adviser to the General Manager of the civic theatre from October 1979 until February 1980. He interpreted his presence in Mainz as a positive sign for the future: 'There have been assurances on both sides that we want to make an honest attempt to get along . . . I am in good heart and see the fact of my being here as a sign of our wish to move away from conflict to an atmosphere of trust, of mutual understanding, even of mutual respect. That has always been the stated intention. It will be a matter of realising it again and again in practice' (quoted in *Deutschland Archiv*, 12, 1979, p. 1234).

Further positive signs came with unmistakable frequency. The warm congratulations showered on Hermlin on his sixty-fifth birthday were followed on 1 May 1980 by the award to him of the Fatherland's Order of Merit in Gold. The premiere of Müller's play *Der Bau* at last took place, after a wait of fifteen years. The Deputy Minister of Culture, Klaus Höpcke, announced the forthcoming publication of Lukacs' *Ästhetik* and held out hope that Ernst Bloch's works too might soon appear. Heym's novel *Goldsborough* was re-issued, and the author was allowed to travel to the opening of an exhibition on 'Propaganda leaflets in the Second World War' in West Berlin, although only a year earlier he had not been allowed to attend the same exhibition in Mainz.

These and other measures were clearly an indication that the Party wished some form of reconciliation with its troublesome writers. However, the laws which it had so recently modified remained an effective threat which was not easily overlooked. Jurek Becker surely spoke for many when he confessed that they effectively made it impossible for him to continue working in the GDR:

> There are a couple of new laws in the GDR which I cannot respect unless I wanted to change my profession. This means that almost everything I have in mind as a work project for the immediate future constitutes some sort of criminal offence. The fact that many people say reassuringly that the laws will not be as strictly applied as was feared is no consolation to me. They can be pulled out at any time, and to write in a state of fear is unacceptable. (*Der Spiegel*, 10, 1980, p. 452)

The stream of those leaving the GDR – notably Klaus Schlesinger, Bettina Wegner, Jürgen Fuchs, Karl-Heinz Jakobs, Klaus Poche, Joachim Seyppel, Erich Loest, Günter Kunert – continued unabated. Fuchs has produced a list of seventy-seven names, and there is no doubt that not even this tells the full story (taz [1989]: 160). All left in line with the new policy towards dissident intellectuals, which was simply to grant them a visa of one sort or another, rather than to expel them and to revoke their citizenship. In theory at least, this left open the possibility that some would return, particularly since it was suspected that the western press would quickly lose interest in them once they had left the GDR and had therefore ceased to be a fruitful source of newsworthy material.

By insisting on negotiating a separate visa for each individual who left and by applying in the process criteria known only to itself, the Party sought to give the impression of a controlled and carefully considered approach to its new policy. In fact, however, as Erwin Strittmatter confides to his diary as early as 16 November 1979, three years to the day after Biermann's expulsion, the Party's cultural policy (*Kulturpolitik*) in the late 1970s and indeed beyond was no more than cultural bungling (*Kulturpfuscherei*) (Strittmatter 1990: 200). For it seems clear in retrospect that the Party's attempts in 1979/80 to secure peace on the cultural front were no less an expression of the bankruptcy of cultural policy than the treatment of Kunze and Biermann had been in 1976.

The crisis in the second half of the 1970s had at least two consequences which proved that the clock could not be put back to the repressive days of the late 1960s. First, leading critical intellectuals did not simply accept the Party's decision to dispose of Biermann but spoke out, cautiously but without hesitation, against what they saw as a serious mistake. The fact that the main protesters were soon put in their place, suffering a variety of (relatively mild) punishments for their temerity, was not the end of the story, for this incident inflicted a wound on relations between the Party and some of the country's most important writers and others in the arts which was to remain unhealed throughout the remainder of the GDR's existence. Secondly, it led the SED to introduce a new element into its cultural policy which was to have far-reaching consequences – namely, the decision to export, under varying degrees of duress, the most disaffected members of the cultural elite to the Federal Republic in the hope that this would bring an end to the disruption caused by the Biermann affair and its aftermath. The fact that obvious efforts were made to introduce a certain amount of sophistication into this process by varying the conditions under which particular individuals could leave (and perhaps return) did nothing to reduce the sense that the country's cultural life was being seriously damaged. Nor did it do anything to discourage those who felt trapped within the GDR's borders from drawing the obvious conclusion that it was after all possible to find ways of leaving their country for the west – by persuading the government it was more of a problem to keep you than to let you go. It could be convincingly argued that the origins of the later, widespread popular demand to be allowed to leave the GDR can be traced back to this phase of cultural policy. Heinrich Mohr implies as much: 'With uncustomary generosity visas for one or more years' stay in the west were granted on request to notables or semi-notables, often but not always with the right to travel back and forth at will. Exit visas were usually approved. "Oh to be a writer" sighed the man in the street' (Mohr 1988: 611).

One particularly bitter irony of the exodus was that, despite the regime's policy of *Abgrenzung* (or demarcation) – that is, its wish at every turn to insist on the GDR's complete sovereignty and to stress its distinctive and separate identity, it became all but impossible to define with any degree of precision exactly what was meant by a specifically GDR literature. Did this require residence in the GDR? Were those who had left on short- or long-term visas still GDR writers? In other words, in the very sphere which was intended to nurture a socialist consciousness in the reader and a sense of identity with the GDR a strong feeling of doubt about what 'GDR' could be taken to mean had been introduced. Similarly, intellectuals who found the GDR's media closed to them, as well as ordinary citizens who wished to be more fully informed about current conflicts, turned increasingly to West German television and radio, thus building up and reinforcing a widespread dependence on a German–German system of communication which completely undermined the Party's attempts to cut off contact with the class enemy. Here too, what Kurt Hager had hoped would be no more than a storm to clear the air – more aptly described by Christoph Hein as the beginning of a Stalinist backlash intended to rid the GDR of its most troublesome dissidents (Hein 1989) – had proved a disastrous miscalculation.

The following years confirmed the impression of a cultural policy which was devoid of any coherent long-term strategy and simply stumbled more or less helplessly from one short-sighted decision to another. For no obvious reason some critical works continued to be banned while others which might equally have been expected to incur official disapproval, such as Strittmatter's *Selbstermunterungen* (1981), Hein's *Der fremde Freund* (1982), or even works by Becker, Kunert and Seyppel, were published. 'Is there still such a thing as a "cultural policy" or just a zigzag?' asked the latter (Seyppel 1982: 220). Nothing was apparently done to stem the steady flow of intellectuals to the west, despite the increasingly obvious damage this was inflicting on the country's cultural fabric. The Party seemed equally paralysed in the face of the younger generation of *Hineingeborene* (those born and brought up within the GDR, with no direct experience of life in the west or in pre-war Germany) who openly declared their independence of an official policy which was irrelevant to their lives and set about establishing an autonomous culture from their base in the Prenzlauer Berg district of Berlin. There could be no clearer confirmation of the crisis in cultural policy than the Party's unwillingness or inability to act in the face of this declaration of its own redundancy.

The Path to Change

If, in the early 1980s, there seemed no substantial reason to suppose that the slide into crisis, however severe and protracted, represented an immediate threat to the Party's control over the cultural sphere, the effects after 1985 of the introduction of Gorbachev's policy of 'new thinking' perceptibly shifted the balance of power away from the SED's policy-makers. Kurt Hager's attempt to play down the importance of events in the Soviet Union by comparing them to a change of wallpaper – a change which, he asserted, the GDR had made long before the Soviet Union and therefore did not now need to imitate – could not prevent an increasingly open challenge to the Party's control mechanisms. Thus, at the Tenth Writers' Congress, held in November 1987 in Berlin, Christoph Hein and Günter de Bruyn led a bold and determined attack on the practice of censorship in the GDR. Despite some desperate rearguard action, the Party was quickly forced to make a notable concession, decreeing that decisions about publication or non-publication of individual works of literature should in future be made not by the Ministry of Culture or, more particularly, its Department for Publishing and the Book Trade (headed by Klaus Höpcke), but by the publishers themselves. Although this change may have been essentially cosmetic in nature, since it did nothing to loosen the Party's grip on the levers of cultural policy, it remains important as one particularly clear indication among many that writers and intellectuals played a major role in preparing the way for the revolution which swept across the GDR in the autumn of 1989.

Yet that role became a matter of controversy. On the one hand, the courage shown by writers such as Wolf, Heym and Hein was undeniable. That this gained for them the trust of large numbers of ordinary people appears at the very least highly likely. The West German journalist Marlies Menge, who was part of the crowd of 5,000 at a demonstration in East Berlin organised by writers and other intellectuals on a Saturday in November, states categorically: 'They are all credible because they were the first to identify with the concerns of the population and to deal in their books, plays and songs with problems which had officially been swept under the carpet' (Menge 1989). Looking beyond the events of the day, it can be argued that it was precisely the work of leading writers which prepared the ground for radical change. This conviction is clearly shared by Christa Wolf, who combines her praise for the arts with a reproachful dig in the ribs for representatives of other, less deserving branches of intellectual endeavour: 'How nice it would be if journalists, sociologists, historians, psychologists, social scientists and philosophers would now likewise do their public duty' (*Wochenpost*, 43, 1989: cf. Wolf 1991: 27). It came as no surprise to learn in November 1989 that Democracy Now, one of the more important political groupings spawned by the changes, should have proposed Christa Wolf for the office of State President. In the west, too, important voices were raised in praise of the GDR's writers and others from the cultural sphere. *Der Spiegel* celebrated them as the initiators of change in the country (*Der Spiegel*, 49, 1989, p. 230) while, in November 1989, Willy Brandt accorded their names a place of particular importance in the history of the revolution.

On the other hand, exceptional and well-known figures such as Wolf, Heym and Hein could not defend writers in general from the accusation that for too long they had kept quiet in order to protect their alleged privileges and that they only began to speak out once the direction of events had become clear. This feeling could only be strengthened when even a figure like Hermann Kant, widely regarded as an SED mouthpiece who, as President of the Writers' Union through most of the Honecker era, had played a leading part in the implementation of the Party's disastrous cultural policy during and after the Biermann affair, was suddenly to be heard attacking the complacency of the leadership and the lack of openness in GDR society. This was, of course, by no means the only sighting at this time of the 'wryneck' (*Wendehals*) – the term widely used to describe those who were only too anxious to forget their part in stabilising the old system and to make a display of their new democratic credentials. (Interestingly enough, the term is known to have been used in a similar sense as early as 1943/4 by Friedrich Meinecke when discussing in his memoirs an earlier German revolution, that of 1918. Cf. letter to the editor by Reimer Hansen in *Der Tagesspiegel*, 28.10.90.)

The more critical attitude towards writers and other intellectuals appears to have become predominant once the first, 'gentle' phase of the revolution, culminating in the impressive mass demonstration on the Alexanderplatz on 4 November, was over. It is possible to see here the same shift in mood which also expressed itself in the transformation of the slogan 'We are the people' into 'We are one people' – the change, that is, from a concern with democracy and non-Stalinist forms of socialism to a demand for unification with West Germany (and, in its more extremist forms, even a return to the borders of 1937). In this new context the writers were no longer seen as the spokespersons for a better future *within* the GDR but as obstacles to a better future *after* the GDR. In mid-January 1990 Wolfram Schütte spoke for many observers when he described the writers and intellectuals for whom 4 November had been a unique and unforgettable experience of solidarity with the people as 'now speechless, orphaned, and even the target of hostility' (Schütte 1990).

First signs of this development were in evidence as early as 26 November 1989 when the appeal 'For our Country' was issued by leading intellectuals including Wolf, Heym and Braun. The appeal saw the GDR as facing a stark choice between two possible futures: either the country could insist on its own independence and distinctiveness, building up a society based on the ideals of solidarity, peace, social justice, individual freedom, freedom of movement, and the protection of the environment, or, succumbing to strong economic pressures and accepting the humiliating conditions which representatives of the Federal Republic would wish to attach to any aid programme, it could abandon its own values and sell out lock, stock and barrel to West Germany.

There were those in the GDR who made no secret of their opposition to the manifesto, however. The response of a group of intellectuals in Dresden, for example, was to issue an alternative declaration entitled *Enough of Experiments*. In the view of Günter de Bruyn, a writer of impressively liberal pedigree, the manifesto made the fundamental error of dressing up in new clothes 'the old slogans of demarcation and the image of "the enemy"' instead of simply stating that German unity should not be allowed to take precedence over and therefore endanger European unity (de Bruyn 1990: 28). For him, the manifesto represented a continuation of the vain, unrealistic attempt over two decades to make the German question a no-go area. Rolf Schneider was even more blunt, characterising it as 'one of the most foolish things I have ever come across' (Schneider 1990: 204). Its very title reminded him more of the hit-parade than of a manifesto. Its view of West Germany ('a Federal Republic bristling with capitalist egoism') was a half-truth.

As for selling off the GDR, all the best bits had already gone and what was left was in such a scandalous state that one should be glad if anyone were even interested in buying it up. To believe that 'true socialism' could now be built in the GDR 'demonstrates the kind of chauvinistic presumptuousness and arrogance for which a German writer cannot be forgiven'. One of the worst consequences of this belief was that the desire for German national unity was ignored and handed over as an issue to the political right.

Some of the loudest voices raised in criticism not only of this particular document but also of the role played by prominent writers in the revolution as a whole – for example, in organising and taking part in the massive demonstration at the Alexanderplatz on 4 November – belonged to writers who had moved west since 1976. Monika Maron bitterly dismissed the document's appeal for a new experiment in socialism in the GDR as a 'repeated laboratory test with unwilling guinea-pigs' (Maron 1990: 70). She was particularly scathing in her attack on Stefan Heym, who only a short time before had been feted in East Berlin as the Nestor, or grand old man, of the revolution. Like Braun and others, Heym saw in the collapse of the GDR a defeat not for socialism but for the corrupt and inefficient political system which had been established in the GDR and falsely given the name of socialism. Far from representing the defeat of socialism, the crisis in the GDR was for him an opportunity, at last, to set up a truly socialist state worthy of the name. When it became dramatically clear, however, that the ordinary people of the GDR were not interested in any further experiments in socialism and preferred to use their newly found freedoms in order to indulge in some of the basic consumer pleasures which for so long they had had to forgo, Heym reacted with sarcasm and scorn, like a grand seigneur appalled at the primitive table manners of the common people. Maron certainly spoke for many when she censured Heym's arrogance and pointed with unconcealed distaste to the fact that, as a privileged intellectual, he himself had long had access to the riches of western consumerism which he now evidently would wish to deny to his less advantaged compatriots.

The same accusation is levelled at intellectuals in general by Günter Kunert in an angry article published in the *Observer*:

We see today the crowds in Leipzig and East Berlin. They are raging at a system that has cheated them all their lives with its feudal structure of hierarchies. We see people whose most heartfelt desire is for an existence without fear or deprivation – a normal existence. And they are answered by writers and intellectuals who, having never known such deprivation, call for a purified, revitalised socialism . . . [These authors] set themselves up, once again, to dictate how life should be and how we should behave within their hypothetical construct, revealing, thus, their contempt for ordinary people. (Kunert 1990)

It is doubtful whether, at this late stage, the signatories' call for a socialist alternative to the Federal Republic could in any case have significantly influenced the course of events, but, paradoxically, whatever chance of success the appeal might originally have had was eliminated by the disastrous decision to invite anyone wishing to support its aims to append their names to it. What the original signatories undoubtedly sought was an expression of popular support and therefore democratic legitimation for their aim of rescuing the GDR from the west's clutches. What they naively overlooked was that this presented the representatives of the old SED apparatus with a heaven-sent opportunity of jumping on the bandwagon, which some duly did. The most damaging recruit, only one day after the appeal appeared, was Egon Krenz, still the leader of the country and still the subject of widespread suspicion. Little wonder Stefan Heym reportedly came to regard this development as catastrophic (*Der Spiegel*, 49, 1989, p. 233).

Judged by the emotions it aroused, however, the controversy surrounding the manifesto gave no more than a foretaste of the bitterness which attended the publication early in 1990 of Christa Wolf's prose text *Was bleibt* and was to dominate the debate until the end of the year. This story, which at its most obvious level treats of the thoughts and experiences during one particular day of a narrator who is under surveillance by the state security police, was seen by her most severe critics as a transparently opportunistic attempt to claim for herself the status of a resistance fighter and thus to rescue and build on the moral authority widely attached to her name. Although West German critics such as Frank Schirrmacher of the *Frankfurter Allgemeine Zeitung* played a leading part in the attempt both to expose this best-known and most respected of all GDR writers as no more than a *Staatsdichterin* (a writer in the service of the state) whose essential function was to cement the power base of the SED and also, through her representative dismantling, to disqualify on moral and political grounds GDR literature as a whole (Schirrmacher 1990), it was the particularly virulent attacks by former GDR writers now in the west – described by Wolf herself as 'a kind of witchhunt with a strong element of revenge' (*Süddeutsche Zeitung*, 13.9.90) – which reveal most about the deep wounds inflicted on the literary community by a disastrous cultural policy. Perversely, it was precisely at the moment of its disappearance that the destructive impact of that policy on relations between writers it had forced into one of two camps became most pronounced, with any hope for a rapid reconciliation and healing of old wounds soon proving illusory. Indeed, hostilities between those who had left the GDR and those who had stayed, with the claim being made on each side that what they had done was the only effective way of promoting change in the GDR (e.g. Königsdorf 1990, and Maron 1990), resembled in their uncompromising intensity the conflict between those who, barely fifty years earlier, had either left or remained in Hitler's Germany.

One of the bitter ironies of the dispute revolving around the figure of Christa Wolf was that the atmosphere of mistrust which it promoted discouraged the very writers who had been least willing to bend to the will of the cultural politicians from initiating public discussion of any mistakes they might have made in the past (Günter de Bruyn was a notable exception). Even more seriously, it distracted attention from those orthodox loyalists to whose literary work the reproaches of the critics might more justifiably have been addressed. In general, these writers tried to lie low and, where possible, to undo at least some of the damage they had inflicted on the literary community. Thus, as early as November 1989, the Stalinist leadership of the Writers' Union, including the discredited Hermann Kant, made a desperate and ham-fisted attempt to turn the clock back, announcing that the writers who in 1979 had been excommunicated for daring to support Stefan Heym had had their membership restored with all its concomitant rights and duties (Walther *et al.* 1991: 131). In what was patently a ploy to forestall any investigation into the injustice done to Heym and his colleagues in 1979, there had evidently been no time in the resulting scramble to take even the elementary step of first contacting the writers in question. Thus Bartsch, Jakobs and Schlesinger learned of their return to grace from their newspaper. Bartsch's case was particularly unfortunate since, only a few days earlier, he had been turned back at the border as an undesirable. Even more embarrassingly, Schneider flatly refused to accept the renewed membership so crudely thrust upon him, on the grounds that the Union's letter had included not a word of apology to the members of his family for the injustice and suffering meted out to them.

The attempt by the Stalinists in the cultural apparatus to salvage something from the wreckage of the policy they had helped to conceive and administer was in vain. Their main representatives – Kurt Hager, Hans-Joachim Hoffmann, Hermann Kant, and others – were one by one dismissed from office or pressured into resigning. The principal victims of the Stalinist backlash of the late 1970s and early 1980s were once again allowed into the GDR. Having been denied entry as late as 4 November despite an invitation from Bärbel Bohley to take part in the mass demonstration at the Alexanderplatz, Wolf Biermann was permitted to give a concert in Leipzig barely a week later. In December Erich Loest was able to return to Leipzig and read from his novel *Völkerschlachtdenkmal*. Soon afterwards he set up in Leipzig a branch of his own publishing house, the Linden Verlag, and began the process of publishing in the GDR all his most recent books, none of which had previously appeared in the GDR. Indeed, a long succession of works which had previously been banned now appeared as a matter of urgency, notably two novels which had particularly provoked the wrathful scorn of the GDR's cultural politicians in the late 1970s: Heym's anti-Stalinist *Collin* (which was also serialised in, of all places, the SED's mouthpiece *Neues Deutschland*) and Schneider's *November*, with its unmistakable echoes of the Biermann affair. Even works which had been banned under Ulbricht were no longer taboo, prime examples being Heym's novel on the workers' uprising in 1953, *5 Tage im Juni*, and Fries's *Der Weg nach Oobliahdooh*. It was not only books which were rehabilitated. Walter Janka, Ernst Bloch and Robert Havemann were just the best-known of a long list of notables to have their public reputations restored. The damage inflicted by the infamous Eleventh Plenum of the Central Committee in 1965 was assiduously undone. Thus the twelve feature films produced by DEFA (Deutsche Film-AG) which had been banned because they were critical of some social and political aspects of the GDR were retrieved from the archives, any compulsory cuts that had been imposed were restored (at a reported cost of between DM 150,000 and 250,000 for each of the first six films rescued: *Neues Deutschland*, 6.2.90, p. 4), and all were made available for showing in GDR cinemas, on West German television and at a variety of film festivals.

Facing the Future

The critical intellectuals who, despite the harsh criticisms subsequently levelled at them, had played a crucial part in preparing the ground for the revolution by challenging the old cultural policy did not succeed, however, in developing a convincing alternative to replace it. With no ready-made blueprint to guide and reassure them, their understandable euphoria at being liberated from the ideological tyranny of the past soon gave way to widespread anxiety that this would in future be replaced by a new, economic tyranny. With the disappearance of the generous state subsidies to which they had grown accustomed, they saw a danger that the state would henceforth abandon what they felt was its proper responsibility towards culture and hand them over to the tender mercies of cut-throat market forces. West German commentators who insisted that such fears were exaggerated and largely based on ignorance of the way in which cultural subsidies in the Federal Republic actually worked could do little to console those who watched with a mixture of anger and apprehension as familiar cultural institutions in the GDR, such as houses of culture or the many libraries set up at the work-place to ensure ease of access, were closed or converted to other uses.

At least three aspects of the cultural intelligentsia's response to such obvious evidence of irresistible change require emphasis. First, they sought to join existing trade unions in the west or to set up similar organisations of their own in order to defend their interests more effectively as the new political and economic order began to take shape. By January 1991 approximately 700 of the 1,056 writers who were members of the Writers' Union when it was disbanded at the end of 1990 had already applied to join the Federal Republic's Union of Writers, a part of the trade union IG Medien. How realistic the hopes invested in such organisations will prove to be in the long run only time can tell, but it seems at best unlikely that they will be able to prevent a substantial reduction in the number of people who, not least because of the GDR's generous, not to say profligate, subsidies in the cultural field, have hitherto been able to earn a living in the arts.

Secondly, they campaigned for an explicit recognition by the state, the regions and local government of their joint responsibility to guarantee a secure future for the arts. The fact that article 35 (section 2) of the Unification Treaty specifies that 'the cultural substance' of the old GDR shall not be damaged is due not least to their efforts. However, it cannot be disguised that the parlous economic state of the five new regions will scarcely allow the survival of all or even many of the 217 theatres, 87 orchestras, 719 museums, 16,883 libraries and 1,709 houses of culture which existed in the GDR on 3 October 1990 (according to Gabriele Muschter, *Staatssekretärin* in the Ministry of Culture at that time: cf. *Der Tagesspiegel*, 20.2.91). Even the future of DEFA, the prestigious film studios in Babelsberg which have built on the tradition established by Universumfilm-AG, is anything but secure.

Thirdly, they asked what specific contributions GDR culture might make to the new cultural mix in a united Germany. Although there were those in the west who denied there was anything worth saving, while the list of suggestions which was drawn up in the east quickly began to look unrealistic, there are at least two elements which deserve mention. The first is the so-called *Kulturfonds*, a system developed in the GDR for support of the arts whereby, for example, a small additional charge which was made for access to cultural events – the so-called *Kulturgroschen* – was used to oil the wheels of culture in a variety of ways (Berger *et al.* 1978: 389–90). Article 35 (section 6) of the Unification Treaty provides for its continued existence on the territory of the former GDR at least until December 1994, and possibly beyond that in some new form in the Federal Republic as a whole. The second, and much more significant, element is quite simply their experience of what it was like to live in the GDR and to observe or have a part in its final demise. Coming to terms with and articulating that experience offers perhaps 'our only chance of defending our self-respect or, where we have lost this, of winning it back' (Thierse 1991). For the writer, this confrontation with the past represents an opportunity to redefine his function now that the old cultural policy has been jettisoned. This has clearly been recognised. At an important meeting of West and East German writers only weeks after the fall of the Berlin Wall Jürgen Fuchs identified the struggle to come to terms with the past as a central concern for any future literature written by (former) GDR citizens because it represented a distinctive contribution which only they could make to a future united Germany (*Frankfurter Rundschau*, 27.2.90).

Christoph Hein, too, accepts the writer's duty to subject the GDR's history to unsparingly honest scrutiny, to dislodge and dismantle the officially promoted view of that history at which so many politicians and even historians were willing to connive. For Hein the reworking of the past has a deeply moral as well as political dimension, enabling individuals to see where they lacked courage and therefore share responsibility for events which should never be allowed to happen again. In a passage reminiscent of the promise 'Never again war!', which provided the moral underpinning for both parts of Germany after 1945, Hein reflects on the lessons to be learned from Gustav Just's account of the harshly inhuman treatment meted out to him and other so-called counterrevolutionaries in the late 1950s:

> For our own sake we should use his witness for our future, so that in future we summon up more courage and strength and backbone and never again permit a deformation of our society, never again permit ourselves to be deformed. (Hein 1989)

All translations into English are by the author.

References

Berger, Manfred, *et al.* (eds), *Kulturpolitisches Wörterbuch*, 2nd edn, Dietz: Berlin, 1978 (see especially the sections on 'Kultur' (pp. 364–70) and 'Kulturpolitik' (pp. 403–5))

Braun, Volker, 'Tabus', in Volker Braun, *Es genügt nicht die einfache Wahrheit, Notate*, 2nd edn, Reclam: Leipzig, 1979, pp. 102–4

de Bruyn, Günter, 'Fromme Wünsche, offene Fragen', in M. Naumann (ed.), *'Die Geschichte ist offen'*, Rowohlt: Reinbek, 1990, pp. 23–9

Fink, Heinrich, 'Gespräch mit Hermann Kant', *neue deutsche literatur*, 12, 1990, pp. 56–71

Haase, Horst, *et al.*, *Die SED und das kulturelle Erbe. Orientierungen, Errungenschaften, Probleme*, 2nd edn, Dietz: Berlin, 1988

Hein, Christoph, 'Gustav Just " . . . und andere"', *Frankfurter Rundschau*, 15.12.89 (also published as '" . . . und andere". Für Gustav Just', in Christoph Hein, *Als Kind habe ich Stalin gesehen. Essais und Reden*, Aufbau: Berlin and Weimar, 1990, pp. 230–9)

Heym, Stefan, *Stalin verläßt den Raum. Politische Publizistik*, Reclam: Leipzig, 1990

Jäger, Manfred, 'Kultur', *Deutschland Archiv*, 12, 1990, pp. 1832–48

Jakobs, Karl-Heinz, *Das endlose Jahr. Begegnungen mit Mäd*, Claassen: Düsseldorf, 1983

Königsdorf, Helga, 'Deutschland, wo der Pfeffer wächst', *Die Zeit*, 20.7.90 (cf. Sigmar Schollak's response in 'Affenliebe', *Die Zeit*, 3.8.90)

Kunert, Günter, 'End of a Romantic Dream', *Observer*, 18.2.90 (also in *Granta*, 30 ('New Europe'), 1990, pp. 161–2)

Loest, Erich, *Der Zorn des Schafes*, Linden: Künzelsau and Leipzig, 1990

Lübbe, Peter (ed.), *Dokumente zur Kunst-, Literatur- und Kulturpolitik der SED 1975–1980*, Seewald: Stuttgart, 1984

Maron, Monika, 'Die Schriftsteller und das Volk', *Der Spiegel*, 7, 1990, pp. 68–70

Menge, Marlies, 'Immer mehr Pfiffe für die vielen Wendehälse', *Die Zeit*, 45, 3.11.89, p. 4

Mohr, Heinrich, 'Das gebeutelte Hätschelkind. Literatur und Literaten in der Ära Honecker', in Gert-Joachim Glaeßner (ed.), *Die DDR in der Ära Honecker. Politik Kultur Gesellschaft*, Westdeutscher Verlag: Opladen, 1988

Rüß, Gisela (ed.), *Dokumente zur Kunst-, Literatur- und Kulturpolitik der SED 1971–1974*, Seewald: Stuttgart, 1976

Schirrmacher, Frank, '"Dem Druck des härteren, strengeren Lebens standhalten"', *Frankfurter Allgemeine Zeitung*, 2.6.90

Schlesinger, Klaus, *Fliegender Wechsel*, Hinstorff: Rostock, 1990 (also Fischer: Frankfurt a.M., 1990)

Schneider, Rolf, 'Die Einheit wird kommen', *Deutschland Archiv*, 2, 1990, pp. 202–7

Schütte, Wolfram, 'Aufbruch ins Unversicherbare', *Frankfurter Rundschau*, 13.1.90

Seyppel, Joachim, *Ich bin ein kaputter Typ*, Limes: Wiesbaden and Munich, 1982

'Statut des Schriftstellerverbandes der DDR', in Schriftstellerverband der DDR (ed.), *VII. Schriftstellerkongreß der Deutschen Demokratischen Republik. Protokoll*, Aufbau: Berlin and Weimar, 1974, pp. 291–300

Strittmatter, Erwin, *Die Lage in den Lüften. Aus Tagebüchern*, Aufbau: Berlin and Weimar, 1990

taz (ed.), *DDR Journal zur Novemberrevolution*, taz: Frankfurt a.M., [1989]

Thierse, Wolfgang, 'Die deutsche Einigung als kultureller Prozeß. Hat die Kultur eine Chance in der ehemaligen DDR?', *Der Tagesspiegel*, 3.3.91

Walther, Joachim, *et al.* (eds), *Protokoll eines Tribunals. Die Ausschlüsse aus dem DDR-Schriftstellerverband 1979*, Rowohlt: Reinbek, 1991

Wolf, Christa, 'Ein Deutscher auf Widerruf', *neue deutsche literatur*, 2, 1991, pp. 24–31

The Peace Movement and the Church in the Honecker Years

John Sandford

'Peace' was from the outset both the avowed overriding goal and the central proclaimed achievement of the GDR. More than anything else, it was repeatedly used to legitimate the state's existence, to justify all areas of its activity, and to exhort its citizens to intensify their efforts in whatever field of work, study, or even recreation they might be engaged – for in so doing they would be making their contribution to the strengthening of socialism, of the GDR, and thus of peace. The very existence of the GDR, it was constantly asserted, was a major factor for stability in Europe, and the best guarantee that – in the words of a much-used slogan – 'war could never again emanate from German soil'. Implicit, and often explicit, in this philosophy was the assumption that as long as the West German state existed in its present form this guarantee could never be absolute: hence the tremendous responsibility placed by history upon the shoulders of the GDR for the maintenance of stability until such time as the Federal Republic too would move forward into socialism and thus join the GDR in the active promotion and protection of peace.

But the state was not alone in its concern with the overriding significance of peace. In the course of the Honecker years, and especially in the 1980s, other voices made themselves heard on this issue – voices that were equally insistent that war should never again emanate from German soil, but voices that articulated a different vision of the means by which this goal might be ensured, and that even questioned the very definition of 'peace' as proclaimed by the state. Initially these alternative approaches to the question of peace were closely associated with the Protestant churches, and their vision was strongly influenced by Christian thinking. As the decade drew to a close, though, the groups and individuals involved began increasingly to assert their independence of the Church, and to broaden the focus of their concerns. By 1989 what had originally been a Church-based peace movement was to provide the nuclei of the opposition that fed into the autumn revolution. While the deposed and discredited Honecker found refuge under the wings of the Church, those who had questioned his insistence on holding on until socialism knocked on the door of the Federal Republic found themselves now sharing official responsibility for the fortunes of the post-revolutionary republic.

There was nothing unique or remarkable about the GDR's insistent presentation of itself as a 'peace state'. In a sense, all modern states seek to project this image, but in the Marxist-Leninist states the identification of the state with peace was further underpinned from the outset by an elaborate philosophical construct. The GDR thus shared with the Soviet Union and its fellow socialist states a picture of themselves as the guarantors of world peace, as the elect few destined by history to guide humankind through the troubled and perilous present into a future that would be free of the causes of war. Such a messianic vision obviously had important legitimatory functions at the more mundane level of everyday politics, both domestic and foreign; for the GDR, these functions were especially important, given the state's difficulties in justifying its separate existence both to its own citizens and to the world at large. The promotion and proclamation of the image of the 'peace state' was not, as in other socialist countries, merely a way of asserting the superiority of the existing political system, but even more an assertion of the historical necessity, compounded by Germany's disastrous recent history, for the existence of a separate state on German soil. The prioritising of peace as the cardinal criterion of all political activity was thus conducted in the GDR with a fervour virtually unparalleled elsewhere in the socialist world.

The Marxist-Leninist view of the nature and causes of war and peace claims to be for the first time in history a 'correct' or 'scientific' analysis, thus further legitimating the dismissal, even to the extent of criminalisation, of alternative arguments on the matter. At the heart of this analysis is the location of the origins of wars in the material organisation of societies. From this it follows not only that certain types of society are inherently given to warmongering, but also that other types of society are inherently peaceful. These latter societies come at the beginning and end of human history, in primitive society and in communism, and their peaceful nature derives from the absence within them of the class antagonisms associated with the private ownership of the means of production.

With the Russian Revolution and the emergence after the Second World War of the socialist community of states the beginnings of that war-free final stage of history are ushered in. War now ceases to be *inevitable*, but the utopian condition where it actually becomes *impossible* can only arrive when the whole world has become communist (cf. Hocke and Scheler 1982; Großmann 1985; Militärakademie 1986; entries under 'Frieden' and 'Krieg' in *Kleines Politisches Wörterbuch* 1967 *et seq.* and Klaus and Buhr 1964 *et seq.*).

For the present it falls to the socialist states to 'manage' capitalism in its volatile final phase of imperialism. The task is an awesome one, given the nature of modern weaponry: it implies in effect responsibility for the fate of the human race during the perilous transition from capitalism through socialism and on to communism. Such a task requires of the socialist states that they too be armed – indeed, that their level of weaponry match that of their capitalist adversaries. As one East German textbook put it:

> As long as imperialism threatens peace, socialism will need the most up-to-date weapons, so that it can reliably guarantee its own protection and prevent the most reactionary forces of imperialism from unleashing a war of atomic destruction that would threaten the very existence of humanity. . . . Peace still needs the military might of socialism in order to ensure the existence of humanity and its social progress. (Authors' Collective 1983: 346)

The paradox of a 'peace state', itself inherently incapable of engendering war, requiring a large army and a sophisticated array of deadly modern weaponry, and bound in subservient alliance to one of the nuclear superpowers, was always an uncomfortable one for the GDR's rulers to sustain. All of them had, after all, experienced at first hand the horrors of militarism and war, often with devastating personal consequences. And there was, moreover, another side to the socialist tradition that in its distaste for all things military shaded over into outright pacifism. Such factors made it difficult for the country's theoreticians of military strategy to accept that what their stance amounted to was that very same contradictory practice of 'deterrence' that determined strategic thinking in the west. Their insistence that their strategy of maintaining the conditions for 'peaceful coexistence' was fundamentally different from what they portrayed as an inherently threatening western posture squared uneasily with an asserted readiness to engage in 'devastating retaliation' (Authors' Collective 1983: 347), with all that that implied by way of eradicating the very humanity that it was socialism's mission to save.

The paradoxical principle of preparing for war in order to protect peace had implications that were certainly not acceptable to many outside the ruling circles in the GDR. The Protestant churches in the GDR had long had their own ideas about matters of war and peace, and in the course of the Honecker years the discussions that took place within and around the churches on these matters were to turn into the nearest thing the GDR experienced to a coherent intellectual opposition.

The GDR, it has often been noted, was the only communist state with a predominantly Protestant tradition. Whereas the Federal Republic was established in a part of Germany where the population was divided roughly evenly between Protestants and Catholics, the GDR came into being in a much more solidly Protestant region. Official GDR censuses ceased to record religious affiliation after 1964, but in that year just over 11 million of the total 17 million East Germans were returned as belonging to one of the Christian churches. By the 1980s the figure – now unofficial, but generally accepted – had fallen to about 8 million, of whom just under 7 million belonged to the eight independent regions of the 'Evangelische Kirche', about 100,000 to various 'Free' Churches (predominantly Methodists and Baptists), and the remaining one million or so to the Catholic Church (cf. Büscher 1982).

Church–state relations in the GDR went through a number of phases, with the vicissitudes of official attitudes being felt particularly strongly by the Protestant churches. Unlike the Catholic Church, which for the most part kept its head down and concentrated on its function as a centre of worship, the Protestants found themselves obliged by their particular theology to play a more engaged and active role in matters of public concern. Accommodation with a state and a ruling party that asserted exclusive power was bound to be fraught, and the problems were compounded by the general hostile nature of Marxist-Leninist views on religion. In the early years of the GDR, state pressure on the churches was at its most overt. Discrimination against Christians, the secularisation of school syllabuses and premises, and the abolition of the traditional state-administered church tax went hand in hand with atheist and anti-clerical propaganda and the introduction in 1954 of the *Jugend-weihe* – the socialist and atheist initiation ceremony for fourteen-year-olds that was quite clearly modelled on the churches' own confirmation rituals.

The success of the *Jugendweihe*, which quickly established itself as a rite of passage undertaken by virtually all youngsters in the GDR, seems to have been one of the factors contributing to a more relaxed attitude on the part of the authorities in their dealings with the Church by the late 1950s. Statements about the Church now became less hostile, and attempts were made, though without much success, to woo those Christians who were willing to accept and even affirm the new socialist order as a secular embodiment of their own ideals. Criticism of East German Protestantism in the 1960s came in the indirect form of propaganda against the 'NATO Church' in West Germany which had in 1957 established a ministry to the Bundeswehr. The point was being fairly unambiguously made that it was time the East German churches broke with the 'Evangelische Kirche in Deutschland' (EKD), the Protestant federation that, as one of the last organisational remnants of a united Germany, provided an umbrella for Protestants in both German states. In the event, the break came in 1969, when the East German Protestant churches left the EKD and set up their own federation: the 'Bund der Evangelischen Kirchen in der DDR'.

The beginning of the Honecker era in 1971 was to coincide with a number of events that can in retrospect be seen as ushering in the final major stage of Church–state relations in the GDR, a stage of reconciliation and even co-operation that was to last almost through to the collapse of the socialist order in 1989. In February 1971 a Central Committee statement made it clear that attempts to co-opt the churches were no longer Party policy, and a month later, as a token of the new approach, the state gave official recognition to the new 'Bund der Evangelischen Kirchen in der DDR', from now on accepting as its partners in dialogue the churches' own delegates rather than, as hitherto, 'representatives' picked by the state itself. At the same time, 1971 was also to see the churches coming to terms with the basic facts of life in the GDR with the adoption at that year's Federal Synod of the notion of the 'Church within socialism'.

The formula 'Kirche im Sozialismus' had first been used in 1968 by the Bishop of Thuringia, Moritz Mitzenheim. Notwithstanding what many regarded as Mitzenheim's overly 'collaborationist' approach to Church–state relations, the phrase was picked up and given new life by the 1971 Synod's formal recognition of the churches' place as being '*in* this specific society, not *alongside* it, not *against* it' (Henkys 1982: 70). The prepositions were carefully chosen: from now on, it was being asserted, organised Protestantism in the GDR would not oppose the socialist system, and neither – like the Catholic Church – would it seek to operate in splendid isolation. Instead, in the words of Manfred Stolpe, former Secretary-General of the Federation of Churches, the churches would 'accept the socialist relations of production and regard the question of power as no longer an issue' (Ehring and Dallwitz 1982: 38).

Not surprisingly, there were many in the Church who initially regarded these attitudes with suspicion, seeing them as little more than an adoption at the level of the Church as a whole of the very attitudes that in the 1960s a minority had accepted in their desire to curry favour with the state. In fact, the conception of a 'Church within socialism' was, if anything, to free East German Protestantism from much of the mutual suspicion and hostility that had characterised relations with the state in the two previous decades. The formula was a gesture to the state that the Church did not regard its role as one of opposition ('not *against* socialism'), but at the same time it was also a reminder to the country's Christians that their religion was not simply a private matter ('not *alongside* socialism'), but also something that implied active concern for, and involvement with, the world around them.

The relationship between Church and state in the Honecker years can be seen as a developing exploration of the practical implications of the idea of the 'Kirche im Sozialismus'. Honecker's own assessment of the Church's place within socialism was encapsulated in the phrase 'an autonomous organisation of social significance within socialist society'. The terms were clearly a gloss on, and an acknowledgement of, the Church's own formula, and they too were carefully chosen. In using the word *eigenständig* for 'autonomous', Honecker was stressing that though the Church's roots were located in society it was none the less not independent (*unabhängig* – a term he avoided) in a state where the Party had overall control. Its significance was, moreover, explicitly 'social' rather than political, and it was, by its own recognition, situated within socialist society.

Honecker's observation was made in the context of his historic meeting with the executive of the Bund der Evangelischen Kirchen on 6 March 1978. This was an event that was to set the seal on the new era of cordiality in Church–state relations, and was to bring further concessions on the part of the authorities, who had three years before made an important gesture by granting permission, after twenty years of pressure, for the building of new churches in new 'socialist' communities. Given prominent publicity in the GDR media, the meeting of 6 March 1978 was regarded as cordial and productive by both sides, and resulted in the resolution of a number of outstanding practical questions and in the granting to the churches of wider access to the state radio and television services (*Neues Deutschland*, 7.3.90).

The new mood in Church–state relations was to be put to its first real test later in 1978 when, for the beginning of the new school year that autumn, the state introduced a new subject on to the syllabus for fourteen- to sixteen-year-olds. Called 'Military Studies' (*Wehrkunde* – the term might also more euphemistically be translated as 'Defence Studies'), it involved both theoretical and practical military and civil defence courses for all pupils in the final two years of compulsory schooling. There was nothing new about the militarisation of young people's lives in the GDR: the ethos and activities of organisations such as the Pioneers and the Free German Youth, to which nearly all children belonged, or the popular Society for Sport and Technology for older teenagers, were strongly imbued with military attitudes, and references to the army abounded in the school syllabus in subjects as disparate as German, Social Studies, Sport, or Mathematics. 'Military Studies' in fact represented in quantitative terms only a small addition to the syllabus, being concentrated in a few weeks of the year, but it was for many a highly visible and unprecedentedly explicit token of a further unwelcome militarisation of GDR society. The government's decision to introduce it was to have the unforeseen effect of helping to place the peace issue at the top of the agenda of Church–state relations in the 1980s, to make peace the central concern of dissident politics in the GDR, and ultimately to shape a whole culture of opposition in the country that was to be tangibly different from that of the other communist states at the moment of their collapse.

The 1980s were, of course, a decade of peace protest throughout Europe, but whereas the western peace movements – and in particular the massive groundswell of discontent in West Germany – were triggered above all by the NATO decision of December 1979 to 'modernise' the alliance's nuclear capabilities by installing Cruise and Pershing II missiles on the continent, the birth of the peace movement in the GDR is more appropriately located in the debate about 'Military Studies' in the preceding year. Certainly peace movement activity in the GDR was later to draw much inspiration from the western peace movements, but it would be wrong to see it either in its origins or in its later development as somehow derivative of what was happening across the border. It was symptomatic of the 'Military Studies' issue that it was not so much concerned with broader matters of strategy, that it was not occasioned by the nuclear threat, and that it did not lead to massive displays of public protest. It was instead a matter that, from an outside perspective, perhaps looked decidedly provincial, but one that in reality involved fundamental questions of ideology and state control. It was also, above all, a matter that reawakened the churches and their membership to questions of war and peace.

The year 1978 was not the first in which the GDR churches found themselves confronting the state over the peace question. In January 1962 conscription was introduced in the GDR, some six years after military service became compulsory in West Germany. But in contrast to West Germany, there were no provisions in the new East German law for conscientious objection. None the less, some three thousand young men refused military service in the first full year of conscription, and their case was taken up by the Protestant churches – as it happened, to some positive effect, for in September 1964 the conscription law was amended to provide for the establishment of units of unarmed 'construction soldiers' (*Bausoldaten*) (cf. Eisenfeld 1978 for the most detailed study of conscientious objection in the GDR up to the late 1970s). Although the possibility of serving as a *Bausoldat* provided an alternative to full military service that was unique in Eastern Europe (and, for that matter, superior to provisions for conscientious objectors in many other countries too), it fell well short of the ideal that many saw embodied across the border in West Germany. *Bausoldaten* did not have to carry arms or take part in manoeuvres, but they were none the less soldiers, obliged to wear uniform, subject to military discipline, and, in the early years at least, often obliged to work on military construction projects. The fact that the 'construction units' actually existed was not publicised, and the option of serving in them was to all intents and purposes a secret, carefully hidden from conscripts; moreover, the few who did know of it and chose to embark on it were well aware that they were almost certainly sacrificing the possibility of a decent career in later life, for their pacifist attitudes were taken as clear evidence of a failure to appreciate the obligation to protect socialism, not to say as a token of rebellion in a system that placed an absolute priority on conformity.

In making provisions for conscientious objection that were far from satisfactory, the state was only helping to lay the groundwork for the independent peace movement that was later to be so centrally involved in its overthrow. The ex-*Bausoldaten*, excluded from the privileges of social integration and advancement, but at the same time sharing a common set of values and experiences, were ready-made dissidents, increasing in number at the rate of some five hundred a year, whilst the very imperfections of the construction-soldier provisions ensured that the system remained an issue, an identifiable cause that welded together both current and ex-*Bausoldaten*.

By the time the 'Military Studies' issue surfaced in 1978 there was already a loose but distinct network of former *Bausoldaten* in the GDR, pressing their demands for a genuine alternative to military service, and even holding regular meetings and seminars to discuss these and more general problems of peace. Their association with the Church had from the outset been close: most of them were Christians, acting out of a religiously inspired pacifism, and several were themselves to become pastors or other church workers. The church itself had angered the authorities in 1965 with its 'Recommendation for the Pastoral Care of Conscripts' which had spoken of *Bausoldaten* and absolute refusers as giving a 'clearer testimony' to the commandment of peace than those who did normal military service (Büscher, Wensierski and Wolschner 1982: 22–3 and 49–61). Although more cautious in its pronouncements for much of the rest of the 1960s and 1970s, the Church continued to fulfil the vital role of a 'space' – both literal and metaphorical – within which unofficial peace movement activity could develop.

The Church's response to the Military Studies issue was again more direct, taking the form of expressions of concern to the state authorities, proposals that peace studies form at least part of the new syllabus, and the formulation and publication in 1980 of a detailed set of guidelines for peace education. It was a direct challenge to the state's philosophy of maintaining peace through armed strength, internal and external vigilance, and the attempted inculcation of black and white 'friend–foe' stereotypes. It was also a clear token of the prominent role that the whole peace debate was going to play in the 1980s.

That debate was to be by no means simply a matter of 'Church–state relations': increasingly as the decade wore on the Church found itself obliged to act not just as a 'space' for the articulation of independent peace opinion, but as a mediator between officialdom and an ever more restive youthful counter-culture that was steadily broadening the focus of its concerns well beyond the initial concentration on peace, whilst at the same time expressing growing impatience with the caution of the established Church hierarchy. An early symptom of the mood of the new decade and the problems it was to bring to the Church came in the form of the affair of the 'Berlin Appeal'.

The 'Berliner Appell' of January 1982 was the first document of independent peace thinking in the GDR to achieve widespread recognition beyond the borders of East Germany – indeed, it was almost certainly read more widely outside the country than within, where it could only circulate clandestinely in a limited number of primitively duplicated copies passed from hand to hand. Both what the Appeal said and the events occasioned by its appearance make it a classic example of the nature of peace-movement dissent in the 1980s (Sandford 1983: 95–6; Woods 1986: 195–7; Büscher *et al.* 1982: 242–4; Ehring and Dallwitz 1982: 227–9).

The Appeal was jointly formulated by the Protestant pastor Rainer Eppelmann (later to become Minister for Disarmament and Defence in the de Maizière government of 1990) and the dissident Marxist philosopher Robert Havemann. The inputs of the two men into the Appeal were distinctively different, with Havemann's hand clearly dominant in the first three of its five sections, where the perspective is global and the focus on international and intra-German politics. The lengthier final two sections have a much more recognisably Christian pacifist flavour to them, with a more domestic focus, and are unmistakably the work of Eppelmann. Between them, the two authors managed, in an engagingly *faux-naif* manner, to touch on a succession of taboos that were bound to cause the displeasure of the authorities, and indeed to cause them considerable alarm at the prospect (in reality never realised) of an incipient alliance of dissident Christians and Marxists.

For a start, the Appeal, with its slogan 'Make Peace Without Weapons', opened on a distinctly pacifist note ('If . . . we want to remain alive – away with the weapons!'), which ran directly counter to official insistence on the need for weapons and military preparedness. Equally subversive was the refusal of the Appeal to observe the obligatory distinction between the 'peaceful' weaponry of the east and the 'aggressive' armaments of the west. But the most sensitive of all the taboos that the Appeal broke lay in its breezy references to the German Question: in calling for 'negotiations between the governments of the two German states about the removal of all nuclear weapons from Germany' it managed in one sentence to bring in the awkward term 'Germany' (compounded in the next sentence by the term 'divided Germany') and to draw attention to the fact that the two German states in any case really had little say in the matter of the nuclear weapons stationed on their soil (if indeed there *were* such weapons in the GDR, for even this was unclear). To cap it all, the Appeal then went on to refer without more ado to the 'occupation troops' that the former Allies maintained in 'Germany'.

In its more domestic final two sections the Berlin Appeal began by calling for a 'great debate about questions of peace', for 'free expression', and the encouragement of 'every spontaneous public manifestation of the desire for peace'. Here again, Socratic irony was being used to draw attention to the very absence of the kind of civil society in the GDR that would permit such activities. The topics then proposed for this 'great debate' were equally awkward, including as they did the replacement of 'Military Studies' by peace studies in the school syllabus, the replacement of the existing *Bausoldat* option for conscientious objectors with a 'community peace service', and the renunciation of military parades, 'so-called' civil defence exercises, the production, sale, and import of war toys, and the links between the waste of valuable resources on weapons of destruction and the poverty of the Third World.

Between them, Havemann and Eppelmann had touched on the whole range of issues that were to occupy the independent peace movement throughout the 1980s, and, in their concluding call for a public discussion on the question 'What will bring about peace; what will bring about war?', they neatly distilled the key theme that informed the whole debate. For the authorities, the causes of war and peace were already explained by the 'classics' of Marxism-Leninism, and the conclusions drawn legitimated not just the military posture, but the whole power structure of 'real existing socialism'. For the peace movement, the question and its implications were far from resolved, though like the state they recognised that it was by no means simply a matter of military strategy and weapons deployment. Increasingly, the peace movement was to turn its attention to the links between external peace and internal peace – questions of justice, tolerance, and above all civil liberties were all recognised as legitimate components of the peace debate.

But it was not just the contents of the 'Berlin Appeal' that made it such a classic manifestation of the peace movement. The reaction of both the authorities and the Church also epitomised the complications of their respective and joint relations with the new culture of dissent. As was to happen on many subsequent occasions in the course of the 1980s, the 'Church within socialism' found itself on the one hand in sympathy with the sentiments of the Berlin Appeal, but at the same time politically embarrassed by its radical tone. Eppelmann, who had in the mid-1960s served eight months in jail for refusing to take the military oath on being conscripted, was already known as an outspoken pastor who had tested to the limit the state's tolerance of the kinds of things that were permissible beneath the wing of the Church. Although the Berlin Appeal was not a 'Church document' as such, it was sufficiently close to Church thinking for the religious hierarchy to feel the need cautiously to endorse it as a programme for discussion, but at the same time it was more than sufficiently subversive for them to have to distance themselves from some of its pronouncements.

Rainer Eppelmann was arrested two weeks after the publication of the Berlin Appeal, but was then released twenty-four hours later. What had happened was what had happened before and was to happen many times again: the Church had interceded behind the scenes with the authorities, and the State Prosecutor had abandoned the judicial inquiry into Eppelmann's activities that had just been initiated. The state in its turn now applied behind-the-scenes pressure on the Church – in particular on Eppelmann's diocesan leadership – with the unambiguous message that the Church should both distance itself from the Appeal and advise its members against distributing it further. The response to this came in the form of a statement from the Berlin-Brandenburg diocese that expressed understanding for the 'disquiet and concern' evinced in the Appeal, but at the same time criticised its failure to bear in mind 'the reality of the political and military constellation', and advised emphatically against the collection of further signatures so as to avoid 'misunderstandings and risks' that would be 'prejudicial to the necessary objective discussion' (Büscher *et al.* 1982: 283–4).

Locating the appropriate parameters of that 'necessary objective discussion' was to preoccupy the Church for the rest of the 1980s. The full potential breadth of the peace debate had already been adumbrated in the Berlin Appeal, and as the decade wore on it became clear that at the grass roots in particular Church members were not content with discussing peace simply at the level of counting weaponry, as was frequently the case with the western peace movements. Undoubtedly the state would have preferred it that way, for it was undeniable that the foreign policy – and in particular the European policy – of the GDR government had much to commend it in the eyes of peace campaigners, and due credit was given to Honecker for his active sponsorship of various disarmament proposals. But the Church and the peace movement in the GDR had always regarded peace as a matter not just of international politics but of the domestic order of society too. This meant that increasingly explicit attention was paid to human rights issues, and this in its turn meant that the Church found it ever more difficult to keep a steady balance between the various demands made on it in its roles of mediator, intercessor and advocate.

The state clearly needed the Church in the later Honecker years, and both sides were fully aware of this. The vulgar Marxist insistence that religion would soon wither away along with other remnants of bourgeois ideology was replaced by an acceptance that the Church was here to stay as an active presence in socialist society. Yet at the same time as the state seemed to be coming to terms with the persistence of religious belief, the Church was increasingly worried by the growing pace of secularisation in the GDR. By the latter part of the 1980s scarcely a third of the population were committed Christians, and the young people who gathered on church premises to discuss and campaign on the ever-broadening agenda of the peace movement were often indifferent to the spiritual dimensions of the Church's work. For the most part both the Church and the state accepted this: most pastors did not attempt to proselytise, and the authorities recognised that the churches fulfilled a variety of necessary functions – potentially subversive groups and individuals were after all easier to monitor if they met on church premises, whilst the churches could be expected to exercise a modicum of restraint on the more impetuous members of their flock.

Towards the end of the 1980s this arrangement came under increasing strain. A marked radicalisation of dissident culture occurred in the GDR, occasioned, amongst other things, by the arrival on the scene in the Soviet Union of Mikhail Gorbachev. Although there was initially despair at the deployment of new missiles in west and east, the eventual lowering of east–west tension lessened the perceived urgency of the peace issue and enabled the focus of concern to shift even more strongly to civil liberties. Critical groupings – most notably the Initiative for Peace and Human Rights – began to cut their ties with the Church, whose protection had, in the views of some, been bought at too high a cost in terms of the compromises it involved. Within the Church, too, dissenting voices became louder, and some Christians went their own way by forming in 1987 the alternative 'Church from

Below' (cf. contributions by Ralf Hirsch and Hans-Jürgen Buntrock in Kroh 1988: 181–233).

In retrospect, 1987 may be seen as the year that ushered in the dissolution of the triangular relationship between Church, state and peace movement in the GDR. Although the late summer had seen the authorities (presumably in anticipation of Honecker's visit to West Germany) permitting the most open display so far of independent peace symbols – including the previously banned 'Swords into Ploughshares' emblem – by participants in the officially organised 'Olof Palme Peace March', the year was to close on a much less harmonious note in the wake of an official raid on the East Berlin 'Environmental Library'. Located in the Zionskirche, the Library had for some time functioned as an information exchange and meeting-place for environmental, civil liberties and peace movement activists. Visitors there were able to read publications – especially western journals – otherwise inaccessible to ordinary GDR citizens, and the Library made no secret of the fact that it housed the duplicating facilities on which the 'samizdat' publication *Environmental News* was produced. The *Umweltblätter*, by GDR standards a decidedly subversive organ, enjoyed the protected status of a publication that was for 'internal church use only'. Its sister journal *Grenzfall*, the mouthpiece of the Initiative for Peace and Human Rights, did not, and it seems that the raid on the Zionskirche was occasioned by the authorities' mistaken belief that they would find there the equipment on which *Grenzfall* was produced.

The raid, which was accompanied by seven arrests and the confiscation of documents and printing equipment, marked a turning-point in Church–state relations that was at the same time the clearest evidence thus far of the terminal crisis that the state was suffering. Not since the Ulbricht years had the authorities acted with such overt and clumsy hostility towards the Church, and the spontaneous wave of protests at churches throughout the country indicated the depth of the indignation they had aroused. The situation was to go quickly from bad to worse with the arrest, on 17 January 1988, of over a hundred people who had staged an unofficial counter-demonstration alongside the annual parade in East Berlin commemorating the deaths of Rosa Luxemburg and Karl Liebknecht, to be followed a week later by further arrests of leading figures from dissident circles.

The majority of the 17 January demonstrators had in fact been trying to draw attention to their demands to be allowed to emigrate, and the authorities duly granted those demands a few days later. Some, however, were members of civil rights groups carrying banners proclaiming Rosa Luxemburg's observation that 'Freedom always means being free to disagree'. Although the authorities found it convenient to lump all the protestors together as wanting to turn their backs on their homeland, this was simply not the case – and had never been so – with the peace movement and civil rights activists, who wanted a better GDR for everyone rather than a new life for themselves in the Federal Republic. The lack of freedom of travel had long been an issue that the Church had pursued with the state, but from early 1988 onwards right through to the end of the old GDR it was to become an ever more central and troublesome concern both for the churches and the dissident groups. Calling on people to stay in the country whilst at the same time campaigning for their right to leave left them in something of a cleft stick, and led to much heart-searching and not a little acrimony over the question of just how far would-be emigrants should enjoy the protection and assistance of the Church. It was a debate that paralleled that of the post-revolutionary winter of 1989–90 over the question of whether the GDR was worth preserving as a separate entity from the Federal Republic.

Throughout 1988 relations between state and Church continued to deteriorate as the authorities persisted with their interference in Church affairs. In March, Church newspapers began to suffer censorship of a kind unknown previously in the Honecker years, and would-be churchgoers were turned back on the street by members of the state security service. Voices within the Church became bolder in their demands for political reform, though they were not always so readily endorsed by the Church hierarchy. Such had already been the case with the paper 'Renunciation of the Practice and Principle of Separation', which had originated in an East Berlin parish in early 1987, and was to become a classic statement on the wider implications of the GDR's closed-border policies. (On this paper and the whole notion of *Abgrenzung* cf. Bickhardt 1988.) Of equal importance were the 'Twenty Theses for a Renewal of Society', presented to the Halle Church Assembly in June 1988 by the Wittenberg pastor Friedrich Schorlemmer, which contained a forthright catalogue of proposals for the democratisation of the GDR, and for justice, disarmament and ecological accountability in the wider world. (Text and Schorlemmer's introduction in *epd Dokumentation*, 39a, 26.9.88, pp. 22–5.)

Both of these documents, and the debates surrounding them,

were to feed into the revolution of 1989, with two of the new political groupings that came into being that autumn – Democracy Now and Democratic Awakening – emerging out of the campaigns to sponsor the 'Renunciation of the Practice and Principle of Separation' and the 'Twenty Theses' respectively. The 'Twenty Theses' had laid particular stress on the need for a democratic electoral system in the GDR, and in the first half of 1989 it was this issue that was to preoccupy critical groups both within and without the churches in the run-up to, and the aftermath of, the local elections that were held throughout the country on 7 May. Several groups called for a boycott of what were in the event to be the last elections held under the old system, and at a number of polling stations the voting that did take place was carefully monitored. The outcome showed that even on their own terms – for GDR elections had never pretended to offer the voters a choice between parties – the authorities were rigging the results, with clear discrepancies between the official figures for votes cast and the number of voters counted by the unofficial tellers. Once again the Church joined in the protest over the blatant falsification of the election results, but by the summer of 1989 a more pressing matter was demanding its attention as the numbers of would-be and actual emigrants reached levels unheard of since the erection of the Berlin Wall. As before, the official Church philosophy was to try to persuade people to stay in the GDR, but such pleas seemed to have little effect as the Hungarians opened their border with Austria and the tide of GDR refugees swelled still further.

It will never be known how many GDR citizens, tempted to defect to the west, changed their minds and stayed at home because the Church said they should, but that the Church did enjoy respect among the population as a whole was to be amply demonstrated as the rout of the old regime took hold in the late summer and autumn. Not only did the churches themselves provide a physical focus for the revolution – most famously in the case of the Leipzig Nikolaikirche as the starting-point for the 'Monday demonstrations' – but as established state power crumbled away the Church took on in the eyes of many ordinary citizens the status of a respected and honest authority that could fill the dangerous vacuum that was threatening to arise. That the reins of power were passed relatively painlessly from the old regime to the country's first democratically elected government was due in no small measure to the statesmanship of the interim communist Prime Minister Hans Modrow, but as Modrow himself was quick to point out, the moderating and mediating role of the churches was an essential component in the peaceful nature of the GDR's revolution.

For a while it almost looked as if one of the least religious countries in Europe was being taken over by Protestant pastors, as in towns and villages all over the GDR the power vacuum left by the departure of SED mayors and other civic officials was filled by local churchpeople. The new political groupings, too, contained a high proportion of former activists from within the Church-based peace and human rights movements; the 'Round Tables', partly initiated by the churches, that played such an important part in the transition to democracy, contained large numbers of Church representatives; and when Lothar de Maizière – himself a head of the Berlin-Brandenburg regional Synod – put together the country's first democratically elected government he invited pastors to fill two of the most senior ministerial posts: Rainer Eppelmann that of Minister of Disarmament and Defence (the title was Eppelmann's own invention) and Markus Meckel that of Foreign Minister. Within the new *Volkskammer* the proportion of Protestant pastors was still considerable: twenty-seven deputies – the great majority of them pastors – came from the Church, with fourteen representing the SPD (including the party's parliamentary chairman Richard Schröder), nine the CDU-led Alliance for Germany, three the Bündnis 90/Grüne (including the vice-president of the *Volkskammer*, Wolfgang Ullmann), and one the liberal Free Democrats.

Yet for all the apparent popularity of the Church in the GDR at the moment of revolution, the following months were to see much soul-searching taking place in Church circles. It was not surprising that a degree of disorientation set in in the 'Church within socialism' once socialism disappeared. The very notion of the 'Church within socialism' had already begun to be questioned in the latter part of the 1980s, but now, in 1990, questions were being asked even more specifically about the degree to which the Church had, in the Honecker years, accommodated with a system that was now revealed as even more rotten than many had ever suspected. The common answer was 'too much'. Certainly, the Church-inspired oppositional groupings of autumn 1989 had assumed, like most of the critical papers emanating from the Church over the years before, that the GDR would remain socialist in one form or another, and thus continue to exist as a separate state that was potentially better than the Federal Republic. It was an assumption of which they were to be speedily disabused once the mood of the people as a whole became measurable.

Through the summer of 1990 it became increasingly clear that 'unification' was in fact going to mean wholesale absorption of the territory and people of the GDR into the West German system. As with all other East German institutions, the *raison d'être* of the Federation of Protestant Churches in the GDR was disappearing. The conclusions drawn by the organised Church developed in a way that paralleled closely what was happening elsewhere in the GDR: an initial assumption that unification with the West would be a lengthy process of give-and-take on both sides was replaced by a growing acceptance of full integration on the West's terms as quickly as possible. But the Church lagged significantly behind many other institutions in embarking on these steps: although representatives of the East and West German churches agreed in January 1990 that they should 'grow together', the East German Federal Synod made it clear the following month that rapid unification was not envisaged, and when the two sides again met at the end of May not only did their timetable for amalgamation run to the end of 1993, but the end product was to be based on a new constitution to be worked out by East and West together. Only at the end of September – within days of the end of the GDR – were these 'third-wayist' visions abandoned as the Leipzig assembly of the Federal Synod unanimously resolved the effective dissolution of a separate GDR church by inviting its eight regions to rejoin the West German Evangelische Kirche in Deutschland which they had left in 1969.

In retrospect, the East German Church's failure to stay in step with the popular mood – where it had, after all, only a few months before been so very much in the vanguard – can be seen as further evidence of the peculiar symbiosis that had developed between it and the socialist state. The Church had broken adrift, for the country's new rulers needed the Church less than the communists had done, and there was a telling irony in the fact that Church circles within the West German Christian Democrats in September 1990 produced a paper denouncing leading East German churchmen for their advocacy of socialism under the Honecker regime. The Church's indulgence towards the socialist proclamations of the state undoubtedly rubbed off on the independent peace movement that was so closely associated with it, and which was to turn into the civil rights movement that most clearly articulated the demands of the revolution. Two of the central causes of that peace movement – the abolition of 'Military Studies' from the school syllabus, and the introduction of a genuine alternative to military service –

were indeed finally realised as a result of the revolution, but those who had most openly carried the banner of dissent through the years of persecution found themselves rewarded with a degree of respect but very few votes from the people as a whole in the March elections to the *Volkskammer* and again in the Bundestag elections of December 1990.

The GDR's revolution differed from those that took place in its eastern neighbours not only in the absence of a clear figurehead – no 'man of the people' like Lech Walesa, no respected intellectual like Vaclav Havel – but also in the nature of the country's opposition. Where Solidarity and Charter 77 were quite openly opposed to the existing system, the whole notion of 'opposition' was handled with great caution in the GDR, and the term itself was usually deliberately avoided. In part this may be seen as a result of the fact that the roots of the dissent of the 1980s lay, in the GDR, in the peace movement, whereas Solidarity and Charter 77 were human rights movements from the outset. Peace protest did not necessarily imply fundamental criticism of the system as a whole: indeed, it could be taken to mean accepting socialism for its utopian promise of a world free of the causes of war. But perhaps the most important legacy borne by the East German dissidents of 1989 came from their association with the Church. It was almost as if this were leading them to proclaim: 'We do not want to be an opposition alongside socialism, nor do we want to be an opposition against socialism: we want to be an opposition *within* socialism.' But, unfortunately, that turned out not to be what the people of the GDR wanted.

All translations are by the author.

References

Authors' Collective, *Dialektischer und historischer Materialismus*, 10th edn, Dietz: Berlin, 1983

Bickhardt, Stephan (ed.), *Recht ströme wie Wasser. Christen in der DDR für Absage an Praxis und Prinzip der Abgrenzung. Ein Arbeitsbuch*, Wichern: Berlin, 1988

Büscher, Wolfgang, 'Unterwegs zur Minderheit. Eine Auswertung konfessionsstatistischer Daten', in Reinhard Henkys (ed.), *Die evangelischen*

Kirchen in der DDR. Beiträge zu einer Bestandsaufnahme, Ch. Kaiser: Munich, 1982, pp. 422–36

Büscher, Wolfgang, Wensierski, Peter, and Wolschner, Klaus (eds), *Friedensbewegung in der DDR. Texte 1978–1982*, Scandica: Hattingen, 1982

Ehring, Klaus, and Dallwitz, Martin, *Schwerter zu Pflugscharen. Friedensbewegung in der DDR*, Rowohlt: Reinbek, 1982

Eisenfeld, Bernd, *Kriegsdienstverweigerung in der DDR – ein Friedensdienst?*, Haag und Herchen: Frankfurt a.M., 1978

Großmann, Horst, *Frieden, Freiheit und Verteidigung*, Dietz: Berlin, 1985

Henkys, Reinhard (ed.), *Die evangelischen Kirchen in der DDR. Beiträge zu einer Bestandsaufnahme*, Ch. Kaiser: Munich, 1982

Hocke, Erich, and Scheler, Wolfgang, *Die Einheit von Sozialismus und Frieden*, 2nd edn, Dietz: Berlin, 1982

Klaus, Georg, and Buhr, Manfred (eds), *Philosophisches Wörterbuch*, VEB Bibliographisches Institut: Leipzig, 1964 *et seq.*

Kleines Politisches Wörterbuch, Dietz: Berlin, 1967 *et seq.*

Kroh, Ferdinand (ed.), *'Freiheit ist immer Freiheit . . .' Die Andersdenkenden in der DDR*, Ullstein: Frankfurt a.M./Berlin, 1988

Militärakademie 'Friedrich Engels' (ed.), *Die Philosophie des Friedens im Kampf gegen die Ideologie des Krieges*, 2nd edn, Dietz: Berlin, 1986

Sandford, John, *The Sword and the Ploughshare: Autonomous Peace Initiatives in East Germany*, Merlin Press: London, 1983

Woods, Roger, *Opposition in the GDR under Honecker 1971–85*, Macmillan: London, 1986

–8–

Revolution in a Classless Society

Sigrid Meuschel

I propose to address two questions here. Firstly, why did a revolution erupt in the GDR when a slow and deliberate process of transformation had already been under way in Hungary and Poland (Garton Ash 1989, 1990)? Secondly, why did this revolution itself rapidly undergo further change and abandon an independent polity in embryo in favour of accession to the Federal Republic? These developments were informed by the social and political structures which had been established in forty years of single-party rule. I wish to consider these structures as part of a 'classless society' in order to emphasise the fact that society in the GDR was more homogenised than differentiated. Whereas social differences did persist and were at times actively supported and indeed accentuated by the Party (SED) in an attempt to offset the potential stagnation of a homogenised social structure, social homogeneity predominated.

The notion of the 'classless society' is not without its irony – particularly when considering the avowed aim of all the ruling communist parties, namely to establish a just and equal society while developing the forces of production – because this aim resulted in a homogenised and inflexible social order. This in turn derived from the Party's monopoly on power and its self-arrogated right to dictate all social change. In order to achieve such control all economic, political and other social resources were centralised while independent institutions and regulatory mechanisms such as the market, the rule of law, public spheres and democracy were suppressed. In addition, the Party itself imposed homogeneity in so far as it deprived the social, economic and cultural subsystems of their autonomy or imposed its own ideology on them (Krüger 1988). This process can be described as the withering away of society (as opposed to the state) and of the organisations subordinate to the SED. Although the hegemony and ideological primacy of the Party formed the basis for social homogeneity, it also enabled the various political, economic and cultural spheres to retain their diversity and identity *within* state-sanctioned social organisations and offered limited scope for the articulation of the interests of these subsystems (Pollack 1990).

Society Homogenised and Revolution Reformed

To ask whether the classless and homogeneous society predominated over a differentiated order in the GDR is to ask an empirical question. In response to this question, I do believe that such was the case. Classlessness may have varied according to the various stages of political and social development in the GDR but it did constitute a continuous trend. These developments also dictated the scope for the reforms which sought to overcome the homogeneity and ossification of society.

From the 1970s society became homogenised into state servants, those either employed by the state or not self-employed; similarly, most members of the *nomenklatura* and the bureaucracy were not immune. Although the division of labour did ensure social inequality such differentiation was neutralised because it was not part of independent social subsystems and beliefs. Moreover, salary differentials were broadly minimal and often professional position would not be measured in social status. The result was a broad 'middle class' comprising qualified workers, medium-level employees and highly qualified specialists (*Sozialreport* 1990).

The description of society as homogeneous cannot deny that there was social differentiation; it does, however, emphasise that its scope for development was severely curtailed. Ensuring party power in Soviet-type societies also depended on levelling in social as against political differentiation (Fehér, Heller and Márkus 1983: 125). Appointments to positions of power were ultimately based on the political-ideological criteria applied to the selection of the party cadres and were strictly regulated (Glaeßner and Rudolph 1978: 32ff.). Political qualifications could, in turn, only be gained by means of formal or informal privilege. GDR society was also permeated by separate interests and conflicts of interest often according to professional or demographic factors. None the less, there was no opportunity for interest groups either to articulate or to organise. The self-regulating media such as law, money and the market which could define the limits of such interests had virtually no role to play and conflict remained in a latent state; individuals could not form identifiable groups capable of political action.

Soviet-type societies were afflicted with a further conflict inherent in their structure: the Party sought to reconcile the varied interests represented in sanctioned organisations with the 'general interest'. However, the regulation and direction of social interest by the Party could not produce the formal organisations which the declared political aims of the system and Party rule required. Without embracing formal rationality socialism was not to discover a modern alternative to bourgeois-capitalist order. In ideological terms, however, the satisfaction of the needs of society presupposed the elimination of the anarchy and crisis in the capitalist mode of production and to abolish the formal rule of law and the legal bureaucracy. This explains why a type of administration and socialism emerged which had very little in common with the ideal type projected by Max Weber (Pakulski 1986; Rigby 1982). Despite the fact that the telos of Party state conceived and pursued economics and politics as a complex which could be planned, intermediary institutions and their experts were still necessary. In consequence, the Party bureaucracy was forced to tolerate co-operation with specialists which could involve the risk of removing from Party control part of the inherent logic of the system. There was an attempt to ensure ideological control by combining experts and ideological bureaucrats, which none the less proved unable to resolve the basic contradiction: it remained latent and could resurface at any time.

Since the classless society could not escape its total dependency any lobbying necessarily depended on the various bargaining positions of the official organisations such as the trade unions (FDGB), pressure groups and enterprises. These organisations exerted at best only informal influence on the allocation of resources. Their function lay in reconciling social interests with the precepts of the state in the cause of social peace. As a result, they fell between particular and 'general' interest. In addition, although they followed the interests dictated by the state it did happen that specialist bureaucrats demanded greater scope for expert knowledge. It should be remembered anyway that the processes of informal bargaining and its results continually constrained the latitude of the Party (Konrád and Szelényi 1981).

The most decisive structural conflict in the GDR did not derive from a conflict between ideologues and technocrats, although the sclerosis of the SED in the early 1980s led them to despair. Instead, new conflicts arose as a result of widespread social injustice, or more specifically as a result of the antagonism between the rulers and the ruled. All Soviet-type social orders produced a confrontation between 'society' and 'state'; a sense of 'them' and 'us' (Tatur 1989). However, the GDR differed from Poland and Hungary in so far as it possessed none of the independent social, political or cultural stuctures which could have canalised the impact of social and political antagonism and which could have formed the foundations of a deliberate transformation of 'real existing socialism'. The overthrow of the socialist order could not release the 'classless society' from its fundamental dilemma: because it was dependent upon direction from the centre and upon the Party state, the 'classless society', having overthrown the *ancien régime*, now needed a period in which to regain an independent form. Accordingly, the transition from the classless to the bourgeois or civil society will be a protracted and precarious process which will in turn necessitate co-ordination 'from above' (Staniszkis 1991). Unlike its neighbours, the GDR did not even possess the new and generally recognised political institutions and elites which could have assumed this role; for this reason the people sought a way out of the revolution by turning instead to the Federal Republic.

Revolution and Political Culture

Although we have suggested reasons for the rapid change in direction of the revolution we have not yet addressed the reason why there was a revolution and not – as in Poland and Hungary – a measured process of transformation. The history of the GDR offers examples of attempts to resolve the problem of the homogeneous society. There were the technocratic desire to remove, albeit partially, responsibility for the economy, the sciences and the 'socialist' rule of law from the Party, the plea for a return to the individual in literature, and the advocacy or practical realisation of individual rights by means of discussion, demonstration and association. However, until their breakthrough in the revolution of 1989 all such initiatives were more restrained than in comparable societies in eastern and central Europe. GDR society was broadly stable and lacked both the collective experience of the practice of resistance and repeated attempts to evade the hegemony of the Party. The failure of the Hungarian revolution, the Prague Spring, and the independent trade union Solidarity in Poland had given the people instructive experience; the long-established human rights and other mass movements had provided the seeds of a civil society. This made it possible to embrace glasnost and perestroika – uncertain though their outcome may be – as an opportunity for a transformation.

There are specific factors which determined the lack of preparation in the GDR and the fact that accumulated discontent assumed the form of open revolt. On the one hand the existence of the Federal Republic greatly facilitated the exodus of discontented sections of the population; on the other, the state-organised arbitration of social interests was more effective than in other socialist countries, most notably by means of social policy. GDR social policy stabilised what was a society of state servants by distributing public resources as long as available. In addition, broad sections of the intelligentsia displayed a great willingness either to co-operate with or to accept the dictates of the state in the quest for an improvement of 'real existing socialism' from within the existing system. Conversely, the peace, ecology and civil rights movements had only recently emerged and led a marginal existence in an unpolitical social climate. Such conditions focus attention not on the structural defects of the system but on the specific nature of German political culture. My thesis is that the ruling party in the GDR had a greater capacity to sustain its legitimacy than elsewhere.

German political culture is often taken to imply a society which is unpolitical (Elias 1989). This approach emphasises the unpolitical cultural tradition in Germany according to which the polity was perceived as a cultural and ethnic community or as a moral institution rather than as a formally and rationally regulated society in which conflict occurred and which opposed capitalist-western civilisation, cosmopolitanism and intellectual reason. It is an approach which is ill-suited to an examination of GDR political culture in the sense that a plausible hypothesis about the continuation and reproduction of inherited patterns is first required.

The guiding objective of SED policy was to create a consensual and harmonious society of material justice which was to be underpinned by the 'political and moral unity of the people' and a broad consensus of interests. This telos departed from the rational Marxist critique of capitalist oppression and exploitation; moreover, the struggle of the German workers' movement was guided not by the need for a social community but by the reality of the conflicts in a class society. However, the project of resolving the problems of society was from the outset beset with what Helmuth Plessner has termed *Weltfrömmigkeit*, or a messianic desire to change the world (Plessner 1974: 41). The workers' movement was able to reconcile itself with the modern age in terms of science and technology but not in terms of political outlook. Politics were a means by which to resolve 'ultimate questions' and finally to relegate democracy itself to the realm of mere prehistory. In addition, political practice was charged with the aim of assisting in the breakthrough of the scientifically verifiable laws of history. Social democracy had begun to acknowledge the fact that society was permanently heterogeneous and necessitated compromise in the Weimar Republic at the latest. By contrast, the Communist Party responded to such 'revisionism' with revolutionary radicalism. Although the KPD/SED did not immediately elevate the establishment of a harmonious, communist future society to the status of central doctrine following the defeat of National Socialism, it did none the less from the outset offer the intelligentsia in particular a way out of the despair at the disastrous consequences of capitalist exploitation and what had been seen as the ease with which 'formal' democracy had been manipulated. The cornerstone of antifascism – the unity of all social, cultural and political forces – represented the quest for a new dawn and a hope so perversely nurtured by the barbarity of National Socialism.

Beyond the intellectual milieu the overpoliticisation of life induced by the Party paradoxically reproduced traditional unpolitical attitudes. The SED may clearly have relaxed the all-pervasive mobilisation of the masses in the course of its forty-five years in power. At the same time, however, the rituals of socialist democracy alienated the people from a political process in which any participation existed anyway in form only. As society became increasingly classless so too the signs of retreat into the private sphere and evasion of social responsibility emerged more clearly. Moreover, even if the homogenised moral community did not in fact wholly identify with the Party or the state and instead distinguished between 'them' (the rulers) and 'us' (the ruled), individuals lost their sense of social heterogeneity and of society as a whole. Social integration functioned through small groups such as the family, friends and the work-collective and isolated everything which happened to fall outside this sphere. Such social homogenisation also led people to seek their sense of identity in morality and in the cultivated world of the educated classes.

Social developments of this kind throughout the socialist system were accompanied in the case of the GDR by factors specifically determined by its particular position and which ensured that there was continuity in inherited political and cultural values. As the ruling force of only one part of a divided Germany the SED possessed no given, inviolable foundation as a nation-state. The 'national policy' of the early post-war period, which was aimed at the whole of Germany, and, albeit much later, the concept of a GDR-German 'national identity' represented attempts by the Party to counteract this unfavourable starting point. Although such strategies marked an acceptance of established cultural topoi they were integrated into socialist thinking: only socialism led by the Party could create the basis for a united Germany just as it was later to see itself as the guarantor of the independent statehood of the GDR. The SED therefore accorded the highest priority to the cultivation of 'socialist attitudes' in society.

The quest for a 'GDR model' which adhered firmly to its immutably socialist, anti-western and anti-bourgeois character was not only the avowed aim of a party which sought to remain in power for as long as possible. In sections of the population there existed deep reservations about the bourgeois-capitalist world. The appeal launched in November 1989 under the title 'For our Country' is not the only illustration of such feeling; the alternative groups which had been organising as a political opposition since summer 1989 differed from their counterparts in neighbouring socialist countries in advocating not a 'return to Europe' but a somewhat vague notion of a 'true' – obviously democratic – socialism.

The Portents of Revolution

A broad coalition for the transformation of 'real existing socialism' had been prevented from emerging by the inertia of the Party elite, the weak position of party reformers (unable either to force a debate on possible change from within the Party or to appeal publicly beyond the Party) and by the loyalty of most sections of the intelligentsia. They were all concerned that Soviet, Hungarian and Polish reform initiatives bore too close a resemblance to bourgeois-western structures and that once transposed to the GDR these would inevitably jeopardise the very independence of its statehood. Moreover, the signs of a civil society were slow in coming when one considers that the peace, ecology and human rights groups were to remain broadly marginal until summer 1989. The late emergence of a civil society in the GDR can be attributed to the fact that these groups had only just begun to consider themselves 'oppositional' and to present themselves publicly as a political alternative (Knabe 1990). More importantly, they also operated as a force within a society which through its cultural tradition was unpolitical and had long remained integrated. These factors may help to explain why the revolution in the GDR was 'so late' and why it 'changed direction so quickly' (Wielgohs and Schulz 1990: 24). However, it was in my view the sociopolitical order in its entirety which helps to explain why there was revolution at all.

The social sciences in the GDR barely constituted a medium of criticism. As a result, anyone who wanted information about society was generally dependent upon either works of literature or the analyses and statements issued by Church groups. Without wishing to discredit these sources of information, one can say that the function of literature or religion in criticising the existing social order differs from scientific examination, especially in a society whose foundations were not so much of a political and rational as of a moral and cultural character. Writers and theologians captured the condition of society in terms of its sociopolitical security, economic backwardness, political conformism and narrow confines. They described the situation as one of alienation from work and life and schizophrenia between public conformism and private discontent. GDR literature functioned as a 'surrogate source of information' (Grunenberg 1989: 232f.) for the readers who wanted to know more about their situation and who also learned that concern was in no way theirs alone. It became clear that human warmth, solidarity and security had long since become a myth and that increasing prosperity, the mechanisation and standardisation of work and life in general and the pressures of time and performance had begun to undermine the private sphere. Nervousness and aggression, fear and the loss of speech, monotony and anonymity, the high divorce rate and the special difficulties of women created a second skin in people (Belwe 1988). Whether intentionally or not, literature came to provide the artistic portrayal of the 'political culture of an unpolitical society': literature portrayed the conformism, retreat into the private self and authoritarianism of the 'niche society' (Gaus 1983). The code of behaviour of this society demanded friendliness, not tolerance, reliability, not capacity for conflict. Literature presented a picture of society which knew no conflict or criticism or public realm. Here was a society characterised by apocalyptic feeling, by despondency and despair and one whose tendency to conceive of social change in terms of developing one's personality was not unknown in German history. Public virtue was replaced by 'conformism to the prescribed forms of political rule', the 'delegation of political action to "authorised people"' and a 'retreat into the private world' (Hanke 1987: 310, 313f.)

While writers may have hoped that contact with art and literature would bring about the democratisation of the individual and society, this hope had a peculiarly German character in balking at direct political and democratic action. None the less, many of those involved in the alternative groups did indeed feel stimulated by the literary critique of society. Ultimately, however, it was a critique which did not assume political form (this point also applies to the analyses and statements of the evangelical churches, with certain reservations). Although these churches became increasingly political they retained on the whole a representative character and operated in a religious environment. The churches cannot be criticised for this, although it did influence the direction and action of the alternative groups.

The analyses and statements of the churches, which served both as internal church discussion and understanding with the Party state, were clearly defined. For example, the notion of the 'megapolis GDR' (Neubert 1986b) gave expression both to centralism and thereby to the dominance of the administration over all spheres of life and to the repercussions this had for industrialisation and urbanisation: isolation in concrete tower blocks, the levelling of social differences, disturbed communication, alcoholism and xenophobia. Theologians felt that the 'classless society' 'made the people ill'. They discovered that people were suffering from a sense of inferiority, resignation and despondency and were evading responsibility under severe pressure to conform. They also detected a tendency to retire into the private sphere ('Synod of the Evangelical Churches in Berlin-Brandenburg, East Berlin (24–28.4.87)', in *epd-Dokumentation*, 25, 1987, pp. 31f.). They attributed conformism and deference to authority to the all-powerful bureaucracy, to abuse of office and the impenetrable workings of the authorities and also to the political powers of the party state ('Oecumenical Assembly for Justice, Peace and the Preservation of Creation, Dresden (26–30.4.89)', in *epd-Dokumentation*, 21, 1989, p. 38). The churches were critical of the readiness of people to accommodate themselves and to adhere to a passive 'spectator mentality' (Schorlemmer 1988: 24). Equally, they criticised the political and social structures in place which bore responsibility for the individual's sense of powerlessness, for the lack of public spheres, the discrepancy between public and private language, lack of legal protection, the disintegration of the family and the problems of the elderly, the handicapped and the ill ('Oecumenical Assembly for Justice, Peace and the Preservation of Creation (8–11.10.88)', in *epd-Dokumentation*, 6, 1989, p. 3). The evangelical churches articulated such severe criticism because in the last years of SED rule they came into close contact with the problems of society. A rising number of people wanted to leave the country and turned to the Church for help, which in turn diagnosed these reasons in order to encourage the state to act (i.e. make concessions). The people who wanted to leave and many of those who stayed in the GDR were dissatisfied with the strict limitations imposed on travel, the lack of voting rights and participation, by the fact that reward for performance was a form of political patronage, by the omnipresent bureaucracy, shortcomings in the economy, the propaganda of success in the media and the bombastic distortion of reality by the rulers of party and state ('National Synod in Dessau (16–20.9.88)', in *epd-Dokumentation*, 43, 1988, p. 49).

Shortly before the revolution there was considerable convergence between the critical positions adopted by the churches and the alternative groups – a cause for little surprise given that the churches as the only independent institutions in 'real existing socialism' in the GDR had, since the early 1980s, voluntarily and wittingly become the protective shield of an alternative movement which organised itself as Church groups. A state security (Stasi) report describes them as having been since their foundation 'almost exclusively incorporated into the framework of the evangelical church' and having made 'full use of its technical and material opportunities' (Mitter and Wolle 1990: 47). The report describes in detail how since the late 1970s the peace movement and since 1982/3 the women's and ecology movements had been similarly organised. The Stasi makes particular mention of citizens and human rights groups such as the Initiative for Peace and Human Rights, formed in 1986. Their particular interest stemmed from the fact that they were formed outside the Church; the report refers to the 'specific coordinating functions' of those groups which sought to organise on a secular basis. They included the peace group New Konkret Committee for Peace (1984), the Working Group for a Church of Solidarity (1986), the Environmental Library (1986), the Church from Below (1988), Ark-Green-ecological network (1988) and the Initiative for Peace and Human Rights.

Despite the important role played by theologians here, such

groups did not necessarily adopt theological positions (although they did have a religious stance). This was not only evident in central issues such as the rejection of the spirit, logic and practice of deterrence and – at a later stage – of demarcation; it could also be seen in their common desire for justice, peace and the protection of creation and in their quest for trust, dialogue and the rational resolution of conflict both in society and between society and the state. These aims, if not actually gained from the synods and oecumenical assemblies, were at least shared by the alternative groups with them; they gave the groups and their social critique a kind of 'religious legitimacy' (Neubert 1990: 705). The affinity with religion was, however, most clearly manifest in the search for transcendence and in the almost ritual practice which invoked such indubitable and intangible symbols and values as peace, justice and nature (Neubert 1985). The meditations, peace and religious services, candle-lit vigils and fasting coupled with the importance of the principle of non-violence created the 'culture of resistance' (Neubert 1990: 706) which informed both the peaceful revolution in the GDR and many of its representatives in the Round Tables and citizens' committees.

The political and democratic identity of the positions adopted by the churches and the citizens' and human rights movements also had (in the latter case) a secular background. If one understands civil society to be a reaction to quasi-absolutist rule and a return to secularisation (that is, an undertaking which seeks to establish a forum for public discourse and to introduce democratic procedure precisely because politics are to discuss ultimate reasons and intangible values) then quite clearly the religious environment and Church protection could no longer be home to the alternative groups. Only in the summer of 1989 was this acknowledged by the alternative groups (a minority excepted).

There were several reasons for this hesitancy. The reproduction of religious value-attitudes deviated from predominant conformism and opposed the system-specific and perverse social model of 'credible schizophrenia' (Grunenberg 1989: 228) – a stable balance between acceptance in public and discontent in private. Such refusal is all the more remarkable when one considers that it was amongst the young – workers and, more particularly, students – in the 1970s that socialist beliefs and value-attitudes were consolidated. This trend changed gradually at first at the end of that decade and then suddenly in the mid-1980s. Students, however, retained loyalty to the system longer than any other group (Friedrich 1990). In general, therefore, the mere act of distancing oneself from the official 'social duties' was regarded as an 'indication of an individual's political attitude' (Henrich 1989: 111). In this the GDR was no different from other socialist societies. What was different was that (articulated) discontent remained dependent either on subcultures or on Church institutions. No other agency – the unions, universities, the Free German Youth movement (FDJ), the organisations for the scientific or artistic intelligentsia and least of all the SED itself – would provide either a counter-forum or support. Furthermore, only in the GDR did legions of dissatisfied people have the opportunity to leave for the Federal Republic. Young people in particular made use of this opportunity: 76.6 per cent of emigrants in 1989 were under the age of 40, and 51.4 per cent were single men between 18 and 30 (*Sozialreport* 1990: 43). They were not the apathetic or insecure but the very people who were prepared to find their way in a different, competitive society. In a survey of GDR settlers in the Federal Republic in summer 1989 72 per cent said they wanted to dictate their own lives while 69 per cent complained that in the GDR their future prospects were either non-existent or gloomy (*Sozialreport* 1990: 44).

By the spring of 1989 there were approximately 150 alternative groups in the GDR; another ten were attempting to unify and co-ordinate the alternative movement on a nationwide basis. Most members were between the ages of twenty-five and forty and there was a disproportionately high number of university graduates compared with workers. A significant minority (12 per cent) had no steady employment, and therefore rejected official norms in this central area. Almost 100,000 participated in all sorts of activities, 2,500 were permanent activists and according to Stasi reports there was a 60-strong 'hard core' (Mitter and Wolle 1990: 47f.). The wave of state repression in the winter of 1987/8 and the conflict between activists and the growing numbers of people applying to leave the GDR served to heighten political engagement. Discontent finally lost its marginal position and became more widespread with the protests against ballot-rigging in the May 1989 communal elections. There was already considerable unease amongst the population at the outright refusal of the SED to acknowledge the need for reform, its attempts to consolidate links with the sister parties in Czechoslovakia and Romania, and its open disavowal of the 'dialogue' and 'competition of ideas' it had previously embraced in a joint paper with the West German SPD. This unease was compounded during the communal elections in May 1989 with their customary rituals when the GDR could be contrasted with the changes elsewhere in eastern Europe: in the Soviet Union secret elections in which there were several candidates were being held for the Congress of People's Deputies, while the Round Tables in Hungary and Poland were negotiating transitional arrangements which would eventually lead to free elections. Comprehensive Stasi reports in the GDR meanwhile indicated discontent both with voting procedure in the communal elections and with the reactions of the authorities to the protests which followed – the open letters, petitions and claims to the courts which were either simply ignored or declared invalid (Mitter and Wolle 1990: 29ff. *et passim*).

Tension mounted further when the SED and the *Volkskammer* displayed understanding for the Tiananmen massacre in Beijing and carried on with preparations for the fortieth anniversary of the GDR undeterred either by the occupation of West German embassies in Budapest and Prague or by the exodus of summer 1989. From early summer the alternative groups had moved beyond the roof of the Church (*Analysen, Dokumentationen und Chronik* 1990; *DDR Journal* 1990 and *DDR Journal 2* 1990; Rein 1989; Schüddekopf 1990). Demonstrations got under way in August and September and countered the chant of 'We want out!' by the people who wanted to leave with their own slogan – 'We'll stay here!'. The mass exodus in turn produced mass demonstrations which precipitated the revolution itself. In October and November the system unexpectedly and quite completely collapsed (Glaeßner 1990).

The opposition was not at all prepared for the prospect of sharing power with SED reformers before taking full power themselves. Its political view was in fact informal in nature and the fall of the regime happened too quickly. This sense of being overtaken by events became all the greater since there had been not only a collapse of the structures of the *ancien régime* but also of the GDR itself. One of the founder members of New Forum, Jens Reich, said: 'The collapse of the GDR was even more unexpected than that of the system' (Jens Reich, *Süddeutsche Zeitung*, 24/25.3.90, p. 12). Firstly, the collapse of the GDR resulted from the fact that the revolutionary momentum which destroyed the political structures of 'real existing socialism' also destroyed the socio-economic basis for the democratic-socialist reforms advocated by those at the forefront of the revolution. Secondly, the fate of the GDR stemmed from the point of departure of the revolution itself: the classless society. The socio-economic structures of a new society were prevented from developing by a homogenised social order; even the embryo of political structures did not emerge in time to create an institutional framework in which society could have debated its future course.

Translated from the German by Colin B. Grant.

References

Analysen, Dokumentationen und Chronik zur Entwicklung in der DDR vom September bis Dezember 1989, Gesamtdeutsches Institut: Bonn, January 1990

Belwe, Katharina, 'Zwischenmenschliche Entfremdung in der DDR', in Gert-Joachim Glaeßner (ed.), *Die DDR in der Ära Honecker*, Westdeutscher Verlag: Opladen, 1988, pp. 499ff.

DDR Journal, *Zur Novemberrevolution, August bis Dezember 1989. Vom Ausreisen bis zum Einreißen der Mauer*, ed. Tageszeitung, Berlin, 1990

DDR Journal 2, *Die Wende der Wende. Januar bis März 1990. Von der Öffnung des Brandenburger Tores zur Öffnung der Wahlurnen*, ed. Tageszeitung, Berlin, 1990

Elias, Norbert, *Studien über die Deutschen*, Suhrkamp: Frankfurt a.M., 1989

Fehér, Ferenc, Heller, Agnes, and Márkus, György, *Dictatorship over Needs*, Blackwell: Oxford, 1983

Friedrich, Walter, 'Mentalitätswandlungen der Jugend in der DDR', *Aus Politik und Zeitgeschichte*, 16–17, 1990, pp. 25ff.

Garton Ash, Timothy, 'Revolution in Hungary and Poland', *New York Review of Books*, 13, 1989, pp. 9ff.

——, 'Eastern Europe: The Year of Truth', *New York Review of Books*, 2, 1990, pp. 17ff.

Gaus, Günter, *Wo Deutschland liegt. Eine Ortsbestimmung*, Hoffmann und Campe: Hamburg, 1983

Glaeßner, Gert-Joachim, 'Vom "realen Sozialismus" zur Selbstbestimmung. Ursachen und Konsequenzen der Systemkrise in der DDR', *Aus Politik und Zeitgeschichte*, 1–2, 1990, pp. 3ff.

Glaeßner, Gert-Joachim, and Rudolph, Irmhild, *Macht durch Wissen. Zum Zusammenhang von Bildungspolitik, Bildungssystem und Kaderqualifizierung in der DDR*, Westdeutscher Verlag: Opladen, 1978

Grunenberg, Antonia, 'Bewußtseinslagen und Leitbilder in der DDR', in Werner Weidenfeld and Hartmut Zimmermann (eds), *Deutschland-Handbuch. Eine doppelte Bilanz 1949–1989*, Hanser: Munich, 1989, pp. 221ff.

Hanke, Irma, *Alltag und Politik. Zur politischen Kultur einer unpolitischen Gesellschaft* Westdeutscher Verlag: Opladen, 1987

Henrich, Rolf, *Der vormundschaftliche Staat. Vom Versagen des real existierenden Sozialismus*, Rowohlt: Reinbek, 1989

Knabe, Hubertus, 'Politische Opposition in der DDR. Ursprünge, Programmatik, Perspektiven', *Aus Politik und Zeitgeschichte*, 1–2, 1990, pp. 21ff.

Konrád, György, and Szelényi, Ivan, *Die Intelligenz auf dem Weg zur Klassenmacht*, Suhrkamp: Frankfurt a.M., 1981

Krüger, Hans-Peter, *Die kapitalistische Gesellschaft als die erste moderne Gesellschaft. Philosophische grundlagen der Erarbeitung einer Konzeption des modernen Sozialismus*, Humboldt Universität zu Berlin, 1988

Mitter, Armin, and Wolle, Stefan (eds), *Ich liebe euch doch alle! Befehle und Lageberichte des MfS Januar–November 1989*, BasisDruck: Berlin, 1990

Neubert, Ehrhard, 'Religion in der DDR-Gesellschaft. Nicht-religiöse Gruppen in der Kirche – ein Ausdruck der Säkularisierung?', *Kirche im Sozialismus*, 3, 1985, pp. 99ff.

——, 'Religion in Soziologie und Theologie. Ein Vermittlungsversuch für den Gebrauch des Religionsbegriffes in der DDR', *Kirche im Sozialismus*, 2, 1986a, pp. 71ff.

——, 'Megapolis DDR und die Religion. Konsequenzen aus der Urbanisierung', *Kirche im Sozialismus*, 4, 1986b, pp. 155ff.

——, 'Eine protestantische Revolution', *Deutschland Archiv*, 5, 1990, pp. 704ff.

Pakulski, Jan, 'Bureaucracy and the Soviet System', *Studies in Comparative Communism*, 1, 1986, pp. 3ff.

Plessner, Helmuth, *Die verspätete Nation*, Suhrkamp: Frankfurth a.M., 1974

Pollack, Detlef, 'Das Ende einer Organisationsgesellschaft. Systemtheoretische Überlegungen zum gesellschaftlichen Umbruch in der DDR', *Zeitschrift für Soziologie*, 4, 1990, pp. 292ff.

Rein, Gerhard (ed.), *Die Opposition in der DDR. Entwürfe für einen anderen Sozialismus*, Wichern: Berlin, 1989

Rigby, Thomas H., 'Introduction: Political Legitimacy, Weber and Communist Mono-organisational Systems', in Thomas H. Rigby and Ferenc Fehér (eds), *Legitimation in Communist States*, Macmillan: London, 1982, pp. 1ff.

Schorlemmer, Friedrich, 'Wir sitzen oft hinter Barrikaden und tuscheln über andere', *epd-Dokumentation*, 39a, 1988, pp. 23f.

Schüddekopf, Charles (ed.), *'Wir sind das Volk!' Flugschriften, Aufrufe und Texte einer deutschen Revolution*, Rowohlt: Reinbek, 1990

Sozialreport 1990, ed. Gunnar Winkler, Institut für Soziologie und Sozialpolitik der Akademie der Wissenschaften der DDR (typescript copy), 1990

Staniszkis, Jadwiga, 'Dilemmata der Demokratie in Osteuropa', in Rainer Deppe, Helmut Dubiel and Ulrich Rödel (eds), *Demokratischer Umbruch in Osteuropa*, Suhrkamp: Frankfurt a.M., 1991, pp. 326–47

Tatur, Melanie, *Solidarnosc als Modernisierungsbewegung*, Campus: Frankfurt a.M. and New York, 1989

Wielgohs, Jan, and Schulz, Marianne, 'Reformbewegung und Volksbewegung. Politische und soziale Aspekte im Umbruch der DDR-Gesellschaft', *Aus Politik und Zeitgeschichte*, 16–17, 1990, pp. 19ff.

PART III

Germany and the Outside World

–9–

Gorbachev, the GDR and Germany

Martin McCauley

'The intrigues which were aimed at destroying our Party are already pretty transparent and they have done a lot of harm . . . It won't be long now before it becomes clear where the roots of these developments lay.'
Erich Honecker, *The European*, 2–4 November 1990

The former SED General Secretary is right. He was stabbed in the back – by the man in the Kremlin. The old nightmare of the SED had resurfaced once again: it could not exist without the support of the Communist Party of the Soviet Union (CPSU) but the CPSU could do without the SED. The Soviets, in the end, did a deal with the West Germans over the heads of the East Germans. The bitter irony of the situation was not lost on Honecker. The Soviet Union and the CPSU he served had passed away with Brezhnev; the new man in Moscow, Mikhail Gorbachev, had turned the communist and indeed the rest of the world upside down. Honecker was like Canute and told the tide of perestroika and glasnost to turn back. Instead it rolled on and finally engulfed him. Honecker and János Kádár, the leader of the Hungarian Socialist Workers' Party, were political twins. Both refused to bow to the new spirit of the communist times and held on so long that when they were shown the door the edifice they had constructed collapsed soon afterwards. In retirement, Erich blithely maintains that he was right all along and everyone else was wrong. At some point during the 1980s he became incapable of assimilating information which conflicted with his *Weltanschauung*, or world-view. The refusal or inability of Moscow and the SED leadership to remove him sentenced the Party and the GDR to extinction.

Martin McCauley

The New Political Thinking about Eastern Europe

A fundamental change of direction was signalled by Gorbachev at a Central Committee plenum of the CPSU in February 1988. He spoke of the right of every people and every country to 'choose freely its social and political system'. It was assumed at the time that Mikhail Sergeevich was only talking about countries outside the 'socialist community'; this has proved erroneous, as the momentous events in eastern Europe during the year of revolution of 1989 have demonstrated. Not only has Moscow stood back and allowed politics to take its course but it has, on occasion, speeded up the process of the disintegration of the 'Stalinist' model by intriguing to remove the incumbent Party leader.

Addressing the European Parliament in Strasbourg in December 1989 Eduard Shevardnadze welcomed the events in eastern Europe as the 'natural collapse of the command-administrative system'. In his view, the process would continue until every 'people could, in complete freedom, choose to build a new society in its own way and using its own methods' (*Pravda*, 20.12.89). This meant that the old ideological imperatives no longer applied, and the socio-economic and political institutions could therefore change radically. This was clearly envisaged by Mikhail Gorbachev at the Malta summit with President George Bush which had taken place earlier the same month. In response to a question about the Soviet position on the changes in eastern Europe he said: 'These changes should be welcomed since they are related to the desire of people to give their societies a democratic, human face and to open up to the outside world' (*Pravda*, 5.12.89).

Shevardnadze, at the 28th CPSU Congress, revealed that as early as 1986 the reform group around Gorbachev had come to the conclusion that the regimes in eastern Europe were no longer viable and hence had become a liability. The proper course of action was to initiate there the same process which was taking place in the CPSU. The decision to allow nature to take its course in the region was not merely a political one – it was inextricably linked to the Soviet Union's defence and security needs. Sometime between 1986 and February 1988 the Gorbachev leadership came to the momentous conclusion that a military presence in the region reduced rather than enhanced Soviet security. Once that mental Everest had been climbed Moscow could let perestroika take root in eastern Europe. With the wisdom of hindsight it is clear that the whole process – the quiet revolution (except in Romania) –

developed a dynamic of its own. It is fair to assume that Gorbachev hoped that little Gorbachevs would spring up everywhere and that a truly democratic socialism would evolve. He must have been shocked to observe the ineptitude with which the Communist Parties attempted to cope with the new situation. They had been lulled into a false sense of security by the knowledge that Moscow would always save them from their own crass mistakes; with this crutch now gone they singularly failed to analyse the evolving situation with any rigour. Even when, as in the East German case, the leadership was provided with brilliantly objective situation reports it acted ineptly. Moscow must have been alarmed by the fact that in Poland, the GDR, Czechoslovakia and Hungary social- ism was simply taken off the agenda. Marxists comforted them- selves with the thought that the pendulum was bound to swing back again in the future.

The Gorbachev leadership could not be too critical of the inability of the east European Communist Parties to analyse in depth the crisis facing them. Since no coherent theory evolved, policies which promised success were out of the question. Whereas enor- mous efforts were undertaken by Moscow to refine the 'new poli- tical thinking' in foreign policy, little attention was paid to eastern Europe. As late as May 1990 Egor Ligachev could berate the reformers for not presenting a coherent situation report of the region, still less a vision of future relations. Part of the reason for the lack of analysis was the furious internal Party debate which was raging about events in eastern Europe. Egor Ligachev, for one, deplored the collapse of the Communist Parties and the Soviet retreat from the region. Conservatives such as V. Zhurkin, director of the Europe Institute of the USSR Academy of Sciences, cited 'developments in eastern Europe as proof of the failure of the policies adopted and of perestroika in general' (Zhurkin 1990). They accused the leadership of throwing away the 'socialist com- munity' and of abandoning the region to capitalism. The Soviet military were acutely discomfited by events and saw the security interests of the USSR being infringed. As one admiral put it, the Soviet Union had lost its allies in the west, had no allies in the east and was back again in the same situation as in 1939.

Eduard Shevardnadze launched vigorous attacks on the con- servatives and accused them of being insensitive to the feelings of other people and of regarding the sovereign states of eastern Europe as mere 'buffer states'. The acrimonious nature of the public utterances testified to the heated internal Party debate which was raging. The reformers sought to undermine the conservatives' position by an unflattering analysis of Soviet thinking and behaviour towards eastern Europe since 1945. One writer argued that the 'Soviet gulag' and 'Stalinist totalitarianism' had been forced on the region against its will (Shishkov 1990). The reformers' position can be summarised as follows (cf. Timmermann 1990: 13–27).

(1) The communist regimes in eastern Europe were paper tigers. In reality, they possessed no substance, only a facade. Their collapse was not due to the machinations of foreign agents but to the ideological dogmatism and economic inefficiency of the ruling Communist Parties. The 'command-administrative system' which they deployed had reached the end of its useful life and was incapable of being rendered more efficient; hence the Soviet Union did nothing to prevent what Shevardnadze in his report to the 28th CPSU Congress called the collapse of these 'totalitarian' regimes with their 'alien command-administrative systems' (*Pravda*, 5.7.90). The transformation in eastern Europe, he said, should be welcomed since it opens the way to a fundamental renovation of society there and corresponds to the process of perestroika in the Soviet Union. There will be instability but this is preferable to the enforced pseudo-stability of the past which led to disaster. A partnership between the Soviet Union and eastern Europe which is based on mutual political, economic and cultural interest is far more beneficial to the USSR than one based on common ideology (Zhurkin 1990). History has demonstrated that a relationship based on ideology quickly leads to hostility and acrimony.

(2) Economically the greatest advantage to the Soviet Union was that it would cease to play the role of an imperial power. It set prices and controlled trade flows. This proved to be economically irrational and led to a waste of resources and deprived each country of the ability and responsibility for running its own economy.

(3) Politically the Soviet Union would be freed from the need to observe 'class solidarity' with its allies and to defend their interests even when these were contrary to its own interests. Differing interpretations of Marxism-Leninism led to states claiming to be the 'true' interpreters of the ideology; labelling others as 'revisionist' led to endless conflict. Experience had revealed that Finland, Austria and post-1956 Yugoslavia were more advantageous partners than the 'fraternal' states of eastern Europe.

(4) The endemic instability of the region, resulting from the imposition of the alien command-administrative system, exacerbated relations with the west and fostered the arms race which was

ruinously expensive for the Soviet Union. Allowing the states of the region to move from totalitarianism towards west European pluralist democracy would enhance the security of the USSR, and a pan-European security pact would become a possibility. Western investment in eastern Europe should be welcomed since a prosperous region is more advantageous than poverty- and crisis-ridden states which are an economic liability to Moscow.

A model for the new type of relationship already existed, that enjoyed by the Soviet Union and Finland. During his visit to Finland in October 1989 Gorbachev emphasised especially the mutually advantageous trade and interdependence of the two states. He gave the term 'Finlandisation' a new and more positive meaning. Finland is a member neither of the Warsaw Pact nor of Comecon but is a parliamentary democracy; however, it may not join any military or economic union which is hostile to the USSR. There are no balance of payments crises since no money passes hands. The goal is to balance trade over a period of time. What an advantageous arrangement for Moscow! Under Gorbachev eastern Europe had become an economic millstone. No wonder he actively sought ways of ridding himself of responsibility for the failures of the region.

Finland is a successful market economy so it became inevitable that eastern Europe would move in the same direction. However, the region was not sloughing off socialism completely. Such socialist concepts as social community, the right to a job and social justice had struck deep roots in people's consciousness. Socialism's day would come again but it would be more humanitarian and responsive to society's needs. However, all this must remain an article of faith.

Relations between Moscow and Bonn

Gorbachev was very cool towards West Germany during his first two years in office. This may have been due to a certain extent to the influence of Andrei Gromyko and his circle. The closeness of the Federal Republic's relationship with the Reagan administration, especially on the modernisation of nuclear weapons, also contributed to the general frostiness. All that began to change in January 1988 when Eduard Shevardnadze became the first Soviet Foreign Minister for five years to visit Bonn. The Intermediate Range Nuclear Forces (INF) treaty, agreed by President Reagan and

Gorbachev in Washington in December 1987, was the necessary backdrop to a new Bonn–Moscow relationship. Shevardnadze made it quite clear that Moscow wanted to improve radically its relations with Bonn. Gorbachev still declined to visit the Federal Republic until Chancellor Helmut Kohl had paid an official visit to Moscow. Kohl's visit in October 1988 marked the beginning of a new relationship between the two states. In the run-up to the visit the Soviet press praised West Germany, but one article was of particular interest; it appeared in *Literaturnaya Gazeta* and examined relations between Russians and Germans. It came to the significant conclusion that one could not speak of several German nationalities since only one German nation existed (Pochivalov 1988; cf. Pochivalov 1989). This disposed of the SED argument about there existing two German nations, one socialist and the other capitalist. Gorbachev agreed to make his first visit to Bonn in June 1989.

Gorbachev's sojourn in the Federal Republic was a stunning success. The Soviet President captivated his audiences everywhere by his appeals to construct a new Europe together. 'Gorby' mania broke out as everyone pressed to shake his hand. His simple, direct language, free of ideological expressions, struck a responsive chord everywhere. Reporting to the USSR Supreme Soviet on his return Gorbachev rated his German visit his greatest foreign policy success so far; the barriers were down and 'hostility and enmity' had vanished. It marked a turning point in the post-war history of Europe. A 'line had been drawn under the post-war period' and this permitted Soviets and Germans to 'take a step towards one another'.

West Germany would be one of the cornerstones of the 'common European house'. But what exactly did this new house look like and how would it be constructed? Gorbachev, addressing the European Parliament in Strasbourg in July 1989, played the architect and presented his design (*Pravda*, 7.7.89). Europe was to reach from the Atlantic to the Urals and the Soviet President had a vision of a 'community of free, democratic peoples'. The United States also belonged to this happy grouping. However, inevitably, a price had to be paid. NATO forces and their equipment were not to be modernised. Everyone had to recognise that states with differing social systems existed and would continue to exist. The new emphasis on the sovereignty of all European states signalled the end of the Brezhnev Doctrine (Migranyan 1989). One of the reasons advanced by Migranyan for the ending of the Brezhnev Doctrine was that the USSR recognised that its relations had to be rethought 'in order to integrate organically and painlessly eastern Europe into the western economic system'. This reveals the Migranyan, like many other Soviet commentators, has a limited grasp of market economics and does not perceive that eastern Europe can be integrated neither organically nor painlessly into the western economic system. He is not aware of the fatal weaknesses of socialist economies.

The term 'Brezhnev Doctrine' had been coined in the aftermath of the Soviet invasion of Czechoslovakia in August 1968 and implied that Moscow had the right to intervene in the socialist community where it judged socialism to be in peril. Its demise was spelled out at a meeting of the Political Consultative Committee of the Warsaw Pact in Bucharest in July 1989. A declaration was published which proposed the development of normal relations between states, irrespective of their sociopolitical systems. This ended the distinction which had been applied to relations between socialist states – socialist internationalism – and that with capitalist states – peaceful coexistence.

If the Brezhnev Doctrine had passed away, a Gorbachev Doctrine had come into being. It did not claim that the CPSU should act as a model for other Communist Parties; rather, every Party had the sovereign right to decide all questions for itself. This was given formal recognition in June 1988 when the Central Committee department concerned with relations with ruling Communist Parties was dissolved and relations with these Parties transferred to the department for international relations (Oldenburg 1989: 21). Formal meetings of Central Committee secretaries for ideology from ruling Communist Parties also ceased. Articles laying the Brezhnev Doctrine to rest made it clear that Moscow would accept closer economic ties between eastern and western Europe. The critical economic situation in the socialist community had made it necessary.

What about the Berlin Wall? Would it become part of the common European house or would it be demolished to make way for it? When Gorbachev was asked about the Wall in Bonn in June 1989 he said that the GDR, as a sovereign state, had decided to erect it given the historical circumstances. This gave the impression that Walter Ulbricht took the decision, but such a momentous decision could only have been taken by Nikita Khrushchev, the Soviet leader. The Wall would come down, according to Gorbachev, when the 'circumstances which had given rise to its erection' ceased to exist. But, after all, this is what Erich Honecker was wont to say. With the wisdom of hindsight it is clear that Gorbachev was subtly suggesting that the Wall was an internal German matter. Eduard Shevardnadze, speaking in Vienna in early 1989, had been more forthcoming. Certain circumstances had given rise to the Wall: it was now time to reflect whether they still existed.

Moscow and the Fall of the SED

Gorbachev's ecstatic reception in the Federal Republic in June 1989 alarmed Honecker and the SED leadership. They could only welcome the dramatic change in Soviet–West German relations which, they claimed, corresponded to the goals of GDR foreign policy. However, there was a certain nervousness about their pronouncements. They reiterated that there were two independent, sovereign German states and that this phenomenon was acknowledged, in eastern and western Europe, as a contribution to European stability. Frau Margot Honecker, the Minister of Education, revealed how alarmed the SED leadership was with the rise of Gorbachev's popularity not only in West but also in East Germany. She had always been noted for her hard-line approach to the ideological confrontation between east and west. Addressing the 9th Pedagogical Congress she referred to those promoting political change in eastern Europe as 'counter-revolutionaries'. This was the first time she had used this term of abuse since 1981. Honecker's consort expressed understanding for young people who were disturbed that 'under the motto of pluralism, counter-revolutionaries were trying to achieve their nefarious goals'. The goal of many, under the banner of restructuring in eastern Europe, was not the strengthening of socialism but a return to capitalism. Then she sounded a clarion call for action: 'We are now in a period of struggle which needs young people who are willing to fight to strengthen socialism . . . if necessary, with a rifle in their hands' (*Neues Deutschland*, 14.6.89).

The internal security position of the GDR was of grave concern to the SED leadership. Honecker, during his meeting with Gorbachev in Moscow in September 1988, had expressed alarm at the possible consequences of perestroika and glasnost for the GDR; the Soviet leader merely replied that reforms in the Soviet Union were not a threat to any socialist state. Gorbachev's desire for arms and troop reductions led to heated debate within the SED politburo. Kurt Hager, for one, feared that unilateral cuts would destabilise the situation in the GDR and eastern Europe. Undeterred,

Gorbachev announced Soviet troop reductions at the United Nations in December 1988 and cutbacks even in the National People's Army (NVA) were envisaged in January 1989.

Gorbachev met Honecker to report on his triumphal visit to West Germany in late June 1989. The SED leader called the trip an 'important contribution to the improvement of the situation in Europe' (*Außenpolitische Korrespondenz*, 27, 7.7.89, p. 210). However, the Soviet leader pointed out that more and more West Germans were 'convinced supporters of peace, friendship and good neighbourly relations with the Soviet Union, the GDR and other socialist states', based on existing realities and the need to find mutual solutions to the problems which faced all nations. This appeared to lay to rest the old Soviet accusations about West German 'revanchism', a term of abuse used by Soviet authors implying that the goals of National Socialism as regards territorial expansion had not been given up. In the direct context of the GDR the implication was that West German policy was aimed at the destruction of the GDR's sovereignty and the incorporation of that part of Germany into the Federal Republic. The Soviet side had ceased to make such claims after the visit of Chancellor Kohl to Moscow in October 1988. In Bonn, in June 1989, Gorbachev spoke of the need for the Soviet Union to revise its views about who its enemies were.

The flight of GDR citizens to the West reached crisis proportions during the summer of 1989. The Hungarian government gave the GDR authorities a deadline to resolve the problem; when no solution was forthcoming Hungary opened its borders with Austria on 11 September 1989 and allowed thousands of GDR citizens to leave. This contravened a GDR–Hungarian agreement of 1969; however, the Hungarians had come to the conclusion that the SED regime was no longer viable. They were also encouraged by Bonn to show magnanimity. Thus began the last act of the tragedy of the GDR. Open frontiers to Austria were soon followed by open frontiers to West Germany for GDR refugees in West German embassies in Prague and Warsaw. The Soviet Union ignored pleas from East Berlin to censure Hungary. The Soviet policy of *laissez-faire* meant the SED had to try to put its own house in order.

The last hope of the conservatives in East Berlin was the visit by Egor Ligachev in mid-September 1989. He had repeatedly expressed alarm at the course of events in eastern Europe and warned against the danger of underestimating the threat from West Germany. He said what Honecker wanted to hear: 'Chauvinistic circles in the Federal Republic are always dreaming of swallowing the GDR. We regard such thoughts as attempts to revise all the results of the Second World War . . . Therefore we say to those who engage in such provocations, bring the sovereignty and independence of the GDR into question, that the GDR is our true friend and our proven ally . . . We have a Treaty of Friendship with the GDR . . . and we shall remain true to this treaty' (*Neues Deutschland*, 15.9.89). However, Ligachev flattered to deceive. In Berlin he met yesterday's men and significantly did not encounter the '*Kronprinz*', Egon Krenz. Presumably the latter absented himself on the advice of the Soviet embassy.

Gorbachev's Visit to East Berlin

Gorbachev chose his visit to Berlin in October 1989 to celebrate the fortieth anniversary of the founding of the GDR in order to bring matters to a head. Honecker's refusal to engage in a dialogue and to seek ways of restructuring the GDR meant that he would have to be removed against his will. When he visited the GDR in 1987, General Vladimir Kryuchkov, later chairman of the KGB, began to explore ways of removing Honecker. Wolfgang Seiffert claims that he tried to recruit General Heinz Kessler, GDR Minister of National Defence, as a member of a group to oust Honecker (*Der Spiegel*, 15.2.89, p. 61). Kryuchkov's closest contact, Colonel General Markus Wolf, however, was no longer head of GDR counter-intelligence. He had been sacked by Honecker in late 1986 for being Moscow's man rather than Honecker's man. Nevertheless Wolf had a first-hand appreciation of the GDR situation. Some time later Erich Mielke, Minister of State Security and a close confidant of Honecker, joined the conspiracy. Honecker explicitly trusted Mielke but he confused personal friendship with loyalty to the Party leader. It appears that Mielke had got wind of the fact that Honecker had not been a model anti-fascist inmate during his imprisonment under the Nazis. It was probably Markus Wolf who had procured the relevant documents from West German archives for the Stasi chief. Mielke played an important role in the politburo session on 18 October by hinting that he would publish certain material if Honecker refused to go (*Deutschland Archiv*, 1, 1991, pp. 5–7). There are striking parallels between the roles played by Kryuchkov, Wolf and Mielke in the removal of Honecker and that played by Vladimir Semichastny, head of the KGB, in the ousting of Nikita Khrushchev in October 1964.

Gorbachev had been the KGB's favoured candidate for the leadership in March 1985, as it favoured reform in the USSR. The task was now to find someone in the same mould. There were realistically only two candidates to choose from: Egon Krenz and Hans Modrow. Krenz was the front-runner since he was seen as Honecker's *Kronprinz* and was a full member of the SED politburo: Modrow was not in the politburo and this in the end was decisive. The removal of Honecker and the election of Krenz could be effected smoothly within the politburo, whereas the promotion of Modrow would have been much more complex. It could only have taken place in two stages, the translation of Modrow to full politburo membership and then his election as SED General Secretary. This would have allowed Honecker and this supporters time to attempt to vitiate the whole manoeuvre. Modrow's elevation might have taken on the appearance of a coup and this would have been disastrous in the era of glasnost. Moscow wanted a quiet revolution.

Krenz was a poor choice. He had risen to the top by being a faithful servant of the leader and had never developed, or was incapable of developing, real leadership qualities. He was a ditherer, always hesitating and turning to others for advice on which option to take. He bears comparison with Konstantin Chernenko, who was the interim leader in the Soviet Union between Yuri Andropov and Mikhail Gorbachev. Chernenko had risen from Siberian *izba* (a peasant wooden cottage) to the Kremlin by carrying Brezhnev's briefcase. Krenz had come up the same route. Gorbachev did not receive flattering assessments of Krenz from Markus Wolf and other GDR sources and his own contacts with Krenz strengthened the conviction that Egon was a transitional figure. The clear favourite was Hans Modrow but the succession would have to be a two-tiered process.

Gorbachev took the decision to stab Honecker in the back during the celebrations marking the fortieth anniversary of the GDR. At a gala in the Palast der Republik on 6 October Honecker spoke of the 'forty years of heroic work, forty years of successful struggle for progress in the GDR'. He devoted no attention to the gathering crisis and clearly had no intimation of how serious the situation was. He also failed to grasp that he could not hold back the tide of perestroika flowing from the Soviet Union. Gorbachev spoke of his hope that the SED would come up with 'political answers to all the questions which were on the agenda and which troubled the population'. The following day, 7 October, the occasion of the anniversary, was crucial. In talks at Schloss Niederschönhausen Honecker again presented a rosy picture and failed to address the pressing problems of the hour. Gorbachev, however, devoted considerable attention to the changes in eastern Europe, and in an interview on Soviet television after his return made it clear that he had pressed for reforms in the GDR. After the military parade, accompanied by stirring Prussian military music, Gorbachev went on a walkabout. His message to onlookers was clear and unambiguous: 'Those who come late will be punished by history.' His views about perestroika were very clear but he went even further: 'If you want democracy, take it and it will be yours.' This was an extraordinary appeal to make in the land of 'real existing socialism' and amounted to stating that all SED claims about democracy in the GDR were false. It also implied that the population should oppose the SED! Gorbachev's words spread like wildfire along the opposition grapevine. If the Soviet leader was in favour of change how could Honecker resist it? A new impetus was given to the struggle for reform.

At the dinner in the evening in the Palast der Republic Gorbachev demonstrated to all with eyes to see that the Honecker era was over. On arrival the Soviet President merely shook hands with the SED Party leader. Honecker waited for Gorbachev to embrace him and kiss him on both cheeks, the traditional greeting between Soviet and GDR leaders; Mikhail Sergeevich merely smiled and then walked up to Willi Stoph, the GDR Prime Minister, and ostentatiously shook hands, embraced and kissed him on both cheeks. During the pre-dinner reception two short meetings took place, Egon Krenz with Valentin Falin, a top Soviet adviser on German affairs, and Günter Schabowski and Gennady Gerasimov. The coded message was the same: 'things will change'. The role Schabowski played in the conspiracy against Honecker emerged in conversations with Jens Reich (New Forum). The latter's penetrating documentary was shown on Channel 4 (London) in November 1990.

The Coup against Honecker

Brutus was played by Günter Schabowski. He maintained close links with the Soviet embassy in East Berlin and with Markus Wolf. He had the delicate task of sounding out politburo members about the desirability and feasibility of removing Honecker.

Choosing whom to approach required flair, since an approach to the wrong person could result in everything being reported to the General Secretary. Presumably Wolf and his friends were responsible for the preliminary soundings. Schabowski entered the drama only when the contact sounded promising.

Seven of the twenty-three members of the SED politburo were privy to the plot. But at the last moment, on 17 October, Krenz lost his nerve. He proposed a compromise solution which was to remove Honecker as Party leader but leave him as head of state. Willi Stoph also favoured this. Schabowski and his contacts saw this for what it was, a disastrous retreat from perestroika. Stoph was to meet Vyacheslav Kochemasov, the Soviet ambassador, the same day; according to Schabowski, Kochemasov was briefed to 'turn Stoph round' and succeeded in convincing the GDR Prime Minister that the compromise was not acceptable.

The 9th SED Plenum which convened on 18 October opened in unconventional fashion. Stoph rose to propose that Honecker be relieved of all his functions. Honecker was taken aback and looked at his supporters, but they stayed silent. Those as surprised as the General Secretary, however, were skilled at sensing in which direction the political wind was blowing. It was clearly coming from the east.

Krenz was elected to all three posts held by Honecker: General Secretary of the SED, chairman of the State Council (President) and chairman of the Defence Council. This sealed his fate and also that of the SED. To the opposition it appeared that the only thing that had changed was the name of the leader. Had reform-minded communists been elected to the presidency and the chairmanship of the Defence Council, hopes that the SED could reform itself would have been kept alive.

Gorbachev's generals may have undermined fatally Honecker's authority. Since the Volkspolizei could not cope with the huge demonstrations in Leipzig Honecker gave the order to provide the military, the NVA, with live ammunition. There are conflicting reports about what happened next. Krenz, as Central Committee secretary for security, and the person responsible for carrying out the order, claims that he countermanded the order. He refused to spill blood and re-enact the massacre of June 1989 on Tiananmen Square. Other sources state that the Commander-in-Chief of the NVA was ordered to withdraw his troops from Leipzig and other GDR cities. The order came from the Commander-in-Chief of the Warsaw Pact, to whom the NVA Commander-in-Chief was ultimately subordinate. Given the lack of steel in Krenz's character it is unlikely that he acted on his own initiative. Gorbachev and his generals are ultimately to thank for the fact that the NVA spilled no German blood.

A cruel cartoon sums up Krenz's standing in the GDR. He is depicted as the wolf in the Little Red Riding Hood story. In bed masquerading as grandmother he is not asked why he has such long ears but: 'Grandma, why have you such big teeth?' The message was quite clear. The man who had travelled to Beijing to congratulate the Chinese leadership on their Tiananmen Square massacre was perceived to be ready to devour any opponent in the GDR. However, fortunately for the GDR Gorbachev had him on a long lead. He was called to the Kremlin on 1 November 1989 to give an account of his stewardship of the SED. He failed the test, being quite incapable of elaborating a coherent response to the crisis in the GDR. However, Gorbachev expressed confidence in the SED and stated that all questions affecting the GDR 'would be decided, and decided only, in the capital of the GDR'. The Kremlin now placed its hopes in Hans Modrow who had maintained regular contacts with Moscow through the Soviet embassy in East Berlin. A week later Modrow was nominated to succeed Willi Stoph as Prime Minister. It would be his task, through the instrument of the government, to attempt to save socialism in the GDR. The SED was clearly perceived to be beyond redemption.

So alarmed was Moscow by the weakness of the SED that at a huge demonstration in East Berlin on 4 November Markus Wolf stepped out of the shadows and attacked the regime for failing to move rapidly towards perestroika. This rare appearance of the spymaster may have been prompted by the fact that not even Günter Schabowski could get a hearing from the crowd. It also heralded the desire of Wolf to influence SED policy openly. At the extraordinary Party Congress in December 1989 – during which the SED was renamed SED-PDS – Wolf was elected a member of the consultative committee of Gregor Gysi, the Party chairman. (He retreated to Moscow before unification when it became clear that he would be arrested if he remained on German soil.)

Gorbachev and the Unification of Germany

The end of the Brezhnev Doctrine signalled a return to the doctrine of various roads to socialism which had been in vogue during the period 1945–7. The onset of the Cold War had killed it but the ending of the Cold War resurrected it. A fierce critique of the Brezhnev Doctrine was launched by Vyacheslav Dashichev, an expert on German affairs and an adviser to Gorbachev, in a memorandum dated 18 April 1989 (*Der Spiegel*, 5.2.90). He called for a radical reappraisal of Soviet policy towards eastern Europe which had been transformed from a 'security zone to a zone of danger and instability'. He warned against military intervention, which could only hasten a catastrophe. The twenty-first anniversary, on 21 August 1989, of the Warsaw Pact invasion of Czechoslovakia provided an opportunity to test the new political thinking. Poland and Hungary condemned the invasion, the GDR attempted to justify it and the Soviet Union declined to pass a judgement. Gorbachev clearly sympathised with the critics of the invasion since he allowed the gradual unravelling of communist rule in the region. The intervention was finally condemned by the Soviet government on 4 December 1989 and the Warsaw Pact states acknowledged that the decision to intervene had been 'wrong'.

The decision to abjure the use of force in resolving political problems confirmed that there were various routes to socialism. Friends and foes of communism acknowledged that the Warsaw Pact had a dual function: political and security. It was now shorn of its political role, that of ensuring that ruling Communist Parties stayed in power. This, however, undermined its security role. If member states were at liberty to choose their own way forward they would quickly bring into question the presence of Soviet troops on their territory. What if states abandoned socialism and reverted to capitalism? The logic of the decision not to use the Warsaw Pact for political ends implied that this had to be accepted. The possibility of the Warsaw Pact coming to an end had also to be faced. The key country in eastern Europe, from Moscow's point of view, was the GDR. There were 350,000 troops and 200,000 dependents there. If the GDR was to be allowed to choose its own form of government this would raise questions about the future of the Soviet garrison there. What if the GDR population expressed a desire for unification with the Federal Republic? By the time the Berlin Wall opened Gorbachev and the Soviet leadership had already taken the decision that eastern Europe was not of vital strategic importance. However, this was based on the assumption that the GDR would survive. Instead of a military presence in the region the Soviets would be satisfied with a commitment that eastern European foreign policy would be well disposed towards the USSR. Instinctively the reaction to a possible unification of Germany was negative. The decision to accept Germany unity involved much heart-searching and a fundamental change in attitude towards Germans. Particularly difficult to assess were the long-term consequences not only for the Soviet Union, but for the rest of Europe.

Federal President Richard von Weizsäcker brought up the question of the German nation during his meeting with Mikhail Gorbachev on 7 July 1987. The Soviet leader made it clear that he was not willing to theorise about this subject. For him the political aspect was important. There were two German states with differing social and value systems – such was reality: 'What the situation will be like in a hundred years will be decided by history' (Kusin 1989; Meißner 1990). Gorbachev dismissed the concept of one German nation and one German state in his book *Perestroika and the New Thinking for Our Country and the World* which also appeared in 1987.

A sea change had occurred by the time Chancellor Helmut Kohl was preparing for his official visit to the Soviet Union in October 1988. Leonid Pochivalov's article on Russians and Germans had been published in *Literaturnaya Gazeta* on 20 July 1988 in which he stated that Germans, irrespective of the division of the country, formed one nation (*BPA-Ostinformationen*, 8.7.87; Meißner 1990: 71). The date of publication of this article is also significant: it appeared on the forty-fourth anniversary of the plot by Graf von Stauffenberg and others to assassinate Adolf Hitler. The symbolism seems to be that the Soviets were now siding with the 'good' Germans. They were now perceived to be the heirs of von Stauffenberg and not of Hitler. This must have been a particularly difficult decision, especially for Russians, to take.

The talks between Gorbachev and Kohl went very well and marked a watershed in post-war Soviet–West German relations. The Soviet leader informed Kohl that the 'most difficult period in their relations' was 'over' (Bonn 1989). This made it possible to elevate relations to a new level. In discussions with West German businessmen Gorbachev spoke of the ice having been 'broken'. The breakthrough seems to have been the protocol on consultation which had been agreed by Eduard Shevardnadze in Bonn on 19 January 1988. It was the first Soviet–West German accord since the Moscow Treaty of 1970 and envisaged regular meetings on a wide range of subjects.

Gorbachev's triumphant visit to the Federal Republic in June

1989 brought the standpoint of the two sides closer together. Particularly significant was the statement that 'all peoples and states had the sovereign right to determine their own future and their relations with one another, on the basis of international law' (Bonn 1989). The chief task facing the two powers was to 'overcome the division of Europe'; this was to be facilitated by the construction of the 'common European house'. A key element in the new relationship was to be very close economic links. Gorbachev claimed that both sides had already begun to write the 'first pages of a new chapter' in relations. And even more significantly: 'We have drawn a line under the post-war period. We think that this will allow each of our countries to take a decisive step closer to one another.' The Soviet leader refrained from any direct comment about the German question. He would have been acquainted with Dashichev's memorandum of 18 April 1989 in which the Soviet specialist argued strongly against the view that the division of Germany was in the interests of the Soviet Union (*Der Spiegel*, 5.2.90; Meißner 1990: 73–4). He took the view that if no solution to the German question was found the confrontation between east the west, which had had such baleful consequences for the Soviet Union, could not be overcome. Dashichev was withering in his criticism of the SED which could only stay in power by using 'force'. Honecker's statement that the 'Berlin Wall would stand another hundred years' was dismissed with unconcealed contempt. What was needed was fundamental reform in the GDR. This would lead to a 'revolutionary rapprochement between the two German states' and this would 'defuse the German question'. This, in turn, could lead to a 'confederation of the two German states . . . or unification' providing the security of all European states was respected.

The opening of the Berlin Wall accelerated events and permitted Chancellor Kohl to seize the initiative. His Ten Point Plan for German unity on 28 November 1989 spelled out the various stages towards unification and was to have a decisive impact on the political process in the GDR. It was welcomed neither in Moscow nor in western capitals. Kohl argued that the architecture of the new Germany had to fit the architecture of the new Europe. It was also necessary to construct new pan-European security structures. This was breathtaking stuff and put Kohl in the driving seat of European change. Gorbachev was caught off guard since he was still thinking within the framework of the Helsinki process. It was soon clear that the traditional east–west divide was out of date.

In Moscow Dashichev represented only one strand of Soviet

thinking. If he was willing to contemplate unity, there was another influential group which favoured the two German states living together in amity: this was the confederation option (Besymenski 1989; Portugalov 1989). Gorbachev sided with the second group initially and then moved over to those accepting unification. When he met François Mitterrand, the French President, in Kiev on 7 December 1989 he stated that the existence of two German states was a stabilising influence and that their unification at the present moment was out of the question; however, by the time Hans Modrow, the GDR Prime Minister, had arrived in Moscow on 30 January 1990 Gorbachev had no objections 'in principle' to a gradual unification of the two German states. The whole process of unification had its own 'dynamism'. No one doubted that the German question was now on the European agenda. Germans in the GDR and the Federal Republic had to solve the problems which faced them in a 'responsible' manner and not on the streets. Further impetus was provided by the visit of Chancellor Kohl to Moscow on 10 February 1990. This took place immediately after a plenum of the Communist Party of the Soviet Union which had seen Gorbachev strengthen his position and sweep aside objections to his German policy. The official communiqué stated that at present there was 'no disagreement between the Soviet Union, the Federal Republic and the GDR that the Germans themselves should decide the question of the unity of the German nation, which type of state they wanted, the timing, the speed and the conditions of unification' (*TASS*, 10.2.90). All this was to proceed within a pan-European framework and to take account of the security needs and interests of Germany's neighbours and other states. The new Germany was not to disturb the European balance of power. Gorbachev was effusive about the new nature of relations between Soviets and Germans. The security aspect was of acute importance and at a conference of NATO and Warsaw Pact states in Ottawa on 14 February 1990 it was agreed to convene meetings between the two German states and the four Powers responsible for Germany (the USA, Great Britain, France and the USSR). These became known as the Two + Four talks.

The new Germany was faced with four strategic options; neutrality, wholly within NATO, wholly within the Warsaw Pact or a member of both alliances. This was one aspect of German affairs which would not be left to the Germans to decide. The Soviet position initially was to rule out the whole of Germany becoming part of NATO. Chancellor Kohl was quite adamant; a unified

Germany had to be a member of NATO. On 6 March 1990, during a visit to Moscow by Hans Modrow, Gorbachev went out of his way twice to underline his opposition to German membership of NATO. However, he left himself a way out: if NATO and the Warsaw Pact were transformed then there would not be any conflict over which alliance Germany joined (*Pravda*, 7.3.90). He also made it clear that the GDR could not join the Federal Republic under Article 23 of the Basic Law, according to which the law would become valid not only in the existing regions of the Federal Republic but also in 'other parts of Germany' once the latter had become part of that country by an act of accession.

Gorbachev's tougher stance on German membership was linked to events in the Soviet Union which saw the Soviet military increase its influence (Wettig 1990: 1075–6). Henceforth the Soviet leader had to take carefully into consideration the military's unhappiness with the crumbling situation in eastern Europe. Eduard Shevardnadze, Soviet Foreign Minister, began to promote the idea of Germany being a member of both alliances. This was taken up by Gorbachev at the Washington summit with President George Bush from 31 May to 3 June 1990. It was made clear to the Soviets that this was quite unacceptable to the west. The Soviet negotiating position was critically weakened by the gathering economic catastrophe. Securing economic aid became a top priority. The breakthrough came on Gorbachev's home ground in Stavropol krai in August 1990 when, in relaxed surroundings, he conceded to Chancellor Helmut Kohl German membership of NATO and the ending of Four Power rights over Germany. Kohl agreed that Soviet troops could stay in Germany (it was later agreed that they would all leave by 31 December 1994), that the Germans would pay the military costs, that the Bundeswehr would not take over the GDR and that the all-German Bundeswehr would be reduced to 370,000 men. It was a personal triumph for Helmut Kohl and marked the end of the post-war era. In personal diplomacy, he and his Foreign Minister, Hans-Dietrich Genscher, had negotiated away the final barriers on the road to German unity. Germany would once again be a sovereign state and master of its own security and foreign policy.

The five *Länder* of East Germany were resurrected and joined the other *Länder* of the Federal Republic according to Article 23 of the Basic Law on 3 October 1990. The first democratic pan-German elections to be held in Germany since 1932 took place on 2 December 1990 and resulted in a victory for Chancellor Kohl's CDU/

CSU and FDP coalition. Ironically, the only East German party which performed well and entered the new Bundestag was the PDS, the party which had destroyed the GDR. For this reason many Germans will always be thankful to it.

The Soviet Union promoted the unification of Germany after 1945. It was only in 1955 that Nikita Khrushchev accepted the reality of two German states. The Federal Republic and the Allies always shied away from German unity, fearing that it would bring communism to the banks of the Rhine. By 1990 communism was no longer a threat or even a viable political or economic system. At the moment when Germany was reuniting the Soviet Union was disintegrating. The GDR had disappeared from the map of Europe and is one of the few states to have voted itself out of existence. Before the end of the twentieth century many people will have forgotten that it ever existed. The same fate may befall the Soviet Union. However, Russia will re-emerge and Germany, most likely, will become its chief trade partner. In the past the GDR relationship with the Soviet Union was, at best, that of a junior partner. In the future Germany will be the senior partner and Russia the junior partner. Such is history.

References

Besymenski, L., 'Man muß Angst um die DDR haben', *Neue Zeit*, 50, 1989

Bonn Auswärtiges Amt (ed.), *Die Begegnungen von Moskau und Bonn*, Bonn, 1989

Kusin, V. V., 'Mikhail Gorbachev's Evolving Attitude to Eastern Europe', Radio Free Europe Research, Background Report 128, 20 July 1989

Meißner, Boris, 'Das neue Denken Gorbatschows und die Wende in der sowjetischen Deutschlandpolitik', in Werner Weidenfeld (ed.), *Die Deutschen und die Architektur des Europäischen Hauses*, Verlag Wissenschaft und Politik: Cologne, 1990, pp. 53–80

Migranyan, A., 'The End of the Brezhnev Doctrine', *Moscow News*, 10.10.89

Oldenburg, Fred, *Sowjetische Deutschland-Politik nach den Treffen von Moskau und Bonn 1988/89*, Berichte des Bundesinstituts für ostwissenschaftliche und internationale Studien: Cologne, 63, 1989

Pochivalov, L., 'Nemtsy i my', *Literaturnaya Gazeta*, 20.7.88

——, *Russland, Gorbatschow und die Deutschen*, Verlag Bonn Aktuell: Stuttgart, 1989

Portugalov, N., 'BRD-DDR. Konföderative Strukturen sind möglich', *Sowjetunion heute*, 12, 1989

Shishkov, E., 'Vostochnaya Evropa; vospominaniya i novye realii', *Kommunist*, 10, 1990, pp. 113–19

Timmermann, Heinz, *Die Sowjetunion und der Umbruch in Osteuropa*, Berichte des Bundesinstituts für ostwissenschaftliche und internationale Studien: Cologne, 51, 1990

Wettig, Gerhard, 'Stadien der sowjetischen Deutschland-Politik', *Deutschland Archiv*, 7, 1990, pp. 1070–8

Zhurkin, V., 'Evropa v menyayushchikhsya koordinatakh', *Izvestiya*, 26.5.90

-10-

The Collapse of the GDR and the Break-up of the 'Socialist Camp'

August Pradetto

The death knell of the twentieth century's most tremendous social and political experiment was sounded in the very place where it had started: in Russia. The end of the CPSU's monopoly of power started the disintegration of the communist system at home and the decline of the Soviet sphere of hegemony abroad. The reasons for the collapse of the GDR and the socialist camp are quite obvious: economic failure, the absence of legitimacy in the political system and the authorities' inability to achieve integration. The abandonment of Soviet claims to power and supremacy in the eastern half of Europe signifies the end of a system in an area where it did not arise naturally but was imposed from without. And it also meant an end to the division of Germany. Vernon Walters, accredited as the new American ambassador to Bonn half a year before the Berlin Wall fell, had already summed things up neatly in spring 1989: 'You can't get rid of the Brezhnev Doctrine and keep the Berlin Wall' (Leicht 1990: 4).

At this time hardly any Germans had dared hope for this. As the first refugees from the GDR fled to the Federal Republic via Hungary and Austria in the summer of 1989, followed by the arrival of special trainloads of refugees from the Federal Republic's embassies in Budapest and Prague, the question of German unification first became an issue in the press and media in Britain, France and America – months before the issue was recognised in Germany as a real possibility and placed on the agenda there. What West Germans had only imagined to be a distant possibility, despite years of proclaiming reunification, and what was unthinkable for East Germans because it had been taboo after years of repression, was quickly recognised abroad as an event of immediate significance for a new order in Europe.

The GDR played a special role in the process of the disintegration of the eastern bloc. Up to the summer of 1989 the German Democratic Republic had been the most important factor counteracting the progressive social and political disintegration of the camp and the alliance. Even in the early summer of 1989 there was already talk of two wings within the Warsaw Pact: a 'reform wing' with Poland and Hungary, and a 'hard wing' including all the other Warsaw Pact countries to the west of the Soviet Union. The GDR's role as the 'watch-tower of socialism' was destroyed by the exodus of people from the GDR. When the fall of the Berlin Wall pulled the rug out from under the GDR it signified the end of the 'hard wing' in the Warsaw Pact and the end of the organisation itself in all but name.

Looking at the internal aspects, the collapse of the GDR began when its people took refuge in the Federal Republic's embassy in Budapest in July 1989, followed a few weeks later by the opening of the barriers on the Hungarian–Austrian border during a 'European Picnic' organised by the Paneuropa Movement, after which more refugees took to their heels across the 'Green Border'. As a few holes began to appear in what was then for GDR citizens still the Iron Curtain, tens of thousands of them saw their chance. Travel restrictions imposed on its people by the GDR government had only a minor effect. Too many of them were already in Hungary on holiday, too many had already sought refuge in the Federal Republic's embassies, first in Budapest, then in Prague and finally in Warsaw. When the Hungarian government allowed them to leave on 11 September, the 'march to German unity' had begun, as Peter Vajda remarked in the Budapest journal *Népszabadság* (Vajda 1990).

This march gave the final centrifugal push to the 'camp' which was already in a state of flux. The immediate reactions to the wave of refugees were similar amongst all of the GDR's allies. But their respective actions concealed differing motives. The Hungarian government was trying to stick to its new political line, which it had pushed through against the conservatives in the Hungarian Socialist Workers' Party, and apply its new ideological direction to the question of human rights. Gyula Horn, the Hungarian Foreign Minister, gave a cool demonstration of Hungary's sovereignty in domestic and foreign policy in the face of frantic threats of intervention from the SED. In negotiations with top SED politicians he first explained that his government was being guided by humanitarian considerations, and secondly that 'our country must not allow itself to be turned into a refugee camp' (*Magyar Hirlap*, 11.9.89). Consequently relations between the governments of Hungary and East Germany reached an all-time low.

The Polish leadership was not affected to the same extent as the Hungarian government, but faced similar problems. A few hundred people from the GDR had also sought refuge in the Federal Republic's Warsaw embassy during the summer months. And Poland showed no signs either of wanting to prevent the refugees leaving for the Federal Republic or of wanting to turn them back to the GDR. The problem was considered to be an affair solely for the Federal Republic and GDR. The GDR leadership could hardly expect anything else. At this time a new government was being formed in Warsaw which showed even less sympathy for the communists in East Berlin. And the government members of the Polish United Workers' Party (PZPR) were doing their utmost to avoid worsening their own chances of survival.

The only communist neighbour still intact at this time was Czechoslovakia. Had it made sense, its leadership certainly would have stood behind the GDR's hard policies and not allowed the refugees to leave the Federal Republic's Prague embassy. After all, from their point of view, the GDR was the only 'brotherland' of any significance left since communism had collapsed in Poland and Hungary, and the Soviet leadership was clearly no longer willing to guarantee order in the 'socialist camp'. If the GDR fell, it would only be a question of time before the communist leadership in Prague was toppled. The Czechoslovakian Communist Party elite had little option but to declare the problem to be a German–German affair since the Soviet leadership offered no assistance, and because the GDR leadership had seen no other way than to negotiate with the governments of Poland, Hungary and also the Federal Republic about the arrangements for the departure of those seeking to escape. Against this background the East German exodus had also become a problem in Czechoslovakian domestic politics. As the trains rolled from Prague to West Germany full of GDR refugees in October 1989, the Communist Party leadership in Prague informed the SED: 'if you are going to let your people go, then please not via Prague with all the threats of political infection this could cause' (Leicht 1990: 5).

However, the attempt by a 'rejuvenated' SED leadership under Krenz to channel the exodus directly into the west by means of new visa regulations opened the flood gates. The night these new travel arrangements were announced, 9 November, became the historic date on which the Berlin Wall fell. It was all over a short time later. The offer made by Hans Modrow, elected as the new Minister President of the GDR on 13 November, to form a 'contractual community' between Bonn and East Berlin was the prologue to capitulation. Within a few weeks what was considered to be the Warsaw Pact's most politically stable state had become a legacy which would be easily swallowed up and which scarcely had to make any more independent economic and political decisions. Within a few months this Comecon country, previously referred to as the tenth strongest industrial power in the world, had become an economic ruin. Trade and co-operation with its previous 'brother nations' suffered irreparable losses. Economic disintegration thus rapidly followed the political break-up of the 'bloc'.

The previous system of exchange between the GDR and its partners in eastern Europe formally came to an end when currency union was introduced on 1 July 1990. Gorbachev's agreement to the GDR's integration into NATO at the same time amounted to semi-official acceptance of the fact that the Warsaw Pact Organisation was finished. Thus, a new era of security policy had begun for the countries of eastern Europe.

Precisely what the consequences will be for the former 'socialist camp' as a result of its disintegration is discussed below with particular reference to the GDR and its unification with the Federal Republic. The first section concentrates on the state of economic relations in the former 'community of socialist states'. The second analyses the security aspects following the break-up of the 'bloc'. The third section deals with the issue of new power relationships in the region. At the present time it is obviously quite difficult to draw firm conclusions based on accurate data, reliable statistics and political facts. The situation is too new, too much in a state of flux and simply too chaotic for clear facts to emerge. All that can be attempted here is to present a few of the current problems and some of those trends (perhaps even contradictory) which seem significant.

The Economic Collapse of the GDR and Eastern Europe

Developing the domestic economy and strengthening foreign trade are key factors when it comes to finding out how to combat the profound economic crisis in which the eastern European states have found themselves, how to tackle the effects of crumbling central-ised economic structures and their transformation to a market economy, how to put a stop to declining living standards at all levels and rapidly increasing unemployment, and how to achieve the construction of a new economic system which works. Thus, the economy is a crucial factor in the further social and political development of these countries. Nationalism and anti-semitism are flaring up everywhere, not least because of these current economic difficulties. In such circumstances there are increasing tendencies towards authoritarian solutions and more opportunities for politi-cal 'Pied Pipers'. The chances of survival and development for the new democracies which have emerged are ultimately dependent upon progress in the economic sphere.

One consequence of the GDR's collapse, which quickly became apparent, was (and is) the partial loss of deliveries of East German goods to various countries. Foreign trade between the GDR and the other European Comecon countries developed continually in the 1980s even if growth rates were slowing. Such levels were not reached again in 1990. In the first half of the year GDR exports to Comecon countries (excluding the USSR) had fallen by 3.7 per cent, and imports by as much as 16.4 per cent. In trade with the Soviet Union there was a fall of 3.7 per cent on the export side and 18.7 per cent on the import side ('Innerdeutscher Handel' 1990). It was expected that the GDR's industries would scarcely be able to meet 70 per cent of their export commitments in the second half of the year ('RGW-Export' 1990: 15). At the same time the GDR cancelled huge numbers of import orders from these countries. This brought with it severe balance of payment problems for them, which were aggravated by reduced incomes (from transit traffic and tourism) associated with the changes within Comecon.

Even before these current, dramatic changes in trading condi-tions the Comecon countries had considerable balance of payment problems (see Kulke-Fielder 1990: 18). The situation was no better after the changes in 1990. Those countries which had previously developed a large part of their foreign trade within Comecon were now faced with the problem that, in addition to their difficulties in trade with the west, the 'socialist market' had collapsed (cf. Bos-chek 1990: 11). Andrej Barcak, Prague's foreign trade minister, laid the responsibility for the speed of the collapse of bilateral relations between the Comecon countries chiefly on the process of German unification. The GDR, he claimed, had taken part in hardly any multinational projects in eastern Europe since the start of 1990. Amongst East German firms, moreover, there was an increasing drop in 'delivery morale'. On top of that, he said, contracts for Czechoslovakian computers, foods and cosmetics had been cancelled in large numbers. He even claimed that there had been a severe drop in GDR tourism in Czechoslovakia (Boschek 1990: 11). Armaments, which had been ordered from Czechoslovakia before the 'change', could also be included amongst these major cancellations.

After the opening of the Berlin Wall on 9 November 1989 the progressive decay of the economy in the former GDR began. A number of existing contracts and agreements were then terminated by various economic and commercial bodies in East Berlin, not least because Modrow's government felt driven to make more goods available for the domestic market to ensure supplies in a period of declining production and for the sake of what was left of political stability.

With economic and currency union with the Federal Republic in mind, the process of decline in the GDR along with the break-up of existing trading structures speeded up after the elections to the *Volkskammer* and the new government was formed in March 1990. Termination of contracts was the result of efforts to off-load commitments to those so-called 'soft currency countries' and to shift to new western partners and markets. However, this proved to be shortsighted and premature in many cases. To a certain extent exports could not be delivered on time because component firms fell into difficulties or ceased to exist.

Even before economic and currency union between the two German states, GDR companies were delaying drawing up contracts with other Comecon countries ('CSFR beklagt . . .' 1990: 14). The uncertainty surrounding them made them cautious. The same applied to firms in other former 'real socialist' states. On the one hand, many firms and institutions are still interested in further co-operation and expansion of trade. This has been made necessary by the need to secure jobs and make full use of capacity. On the other hand, there is a great deal of reluctance and caution, because of uncertainty about their own financial situation and about future economic measures and any tax and other burdens which might occur. Equally, there is uncertainty about how to adapt to the new market conditions which have changed and are still changing in these countries. People are also unsure about whether they are up to the new competition which has started. Nobody knows who is going to pay for the necessary reconstruction. It is unclear what the results of changing production and sales to a market economy will be, what opportunities are offered by the western market and what changing consumer behaviour will mean for production in both the domestic and foreign economies of the former socialist countries. Moreover, managements used to the structures of a centralised economy are traditionally less willing to take risks.

Since economic and currency union, businesses in the former GDR have been exposed, in principle, to international competition. This has required them to adjust to the delivery terms and forms of payment which exist in the world market. This too has led the GDR's Comecon partners to adopt a more selective and more restrictive attitude to imports, which is hardly surprising given the existing economic difficulties in the countries concerned. A general reappraisal of existing contracts with other countries was started after the GDR's economic destiny was more or less taken over by the government in Bonn with the introduction of the Deutschmark as the only valid form of payment. This, along with the bankruptcy of GDR firms which began after 1 July, speeded up the fall in exports to other countries.

True, honouring existing contractual obligations was a principle which was included in the German–German Treaty on Economic, Currency and Social Union. With other Comecon countries in mind, the GDR and the Federal Republic declared their intention not to allow the process of unification to disrupt long-established relations. However, this did not amount to giving any external economic guarantees. The principle of honouring existing obligations was to be made more concrete by means of economic and political decisions, negotiations and agreements and was more or less to be put into practice (cf. 'Finanzielle Hilfen' 1990: 4).

First, a few facts which obviously provide only a limited picture of the longer-term development and quality of foreign trade because the restructuring process is only in its initial phase. A whole series of contracts came to an end only on 31 December 1990 and the final shift to hard currency exchange only started on 1 January 1991. At the start of September 1990 representatives at the Czech embassy in Berlin anticipated that the volume of trade under contract in 1990 would fall by a fifth. Existing cancellations or those announced in advance were estimated as being worth over 200 million roubles for the GDR and 100 million roubles for Czechoslovakia.

To halt the balance of payments and trade sliding too heavily into the red, Czechoslovakia's State Bank had created new currency arrangements which were to act as a stimulus for Czech exporters and yet also reduce imports from the GDR ('CSFR beklagt . . .' 1990: 14). The foreign trade ministry in Prague talked of losses of up to 60 per cent in trade between the two countries (Boschek 1990: 11). Imre Vörös, the Hungarian trade attaché in East Berlin, estimated there would be a 30 per cent fall in trade between the two countries despite a boom in exports and imports in some areas ('Beteiligungen' 1990).

There is a clear link between the reductions in exports from the former GDR, because of the aforementioned changes, and the collapse of the domestic economy, and similar developments in other Comecon countries. The latter are now in a very limited position to meet their obligations to the GDR since the changes in 1989. Trade is being strangled by, amongst other things, economic losses, the shift to trading in world market conditions and in 'hard' currency, supply difficulties in the production and energy sectors, and drastic increases in state budget deficits. Exports are getting more expensive. All of what were previously 'soft currency' countries are now in only a limited position to raise the necessary means for those imports paid for in western currency. Moreover, the Polish government's efforts to stem inflation by following a strict money supply policy have reduced demand at home. On top of this, in Poland in 1990 production and domestic turnover dropped enormously, indeed by up to 30 per cent in contrast to 1989 ('Handel DDR–Polen' 1990: 22). The drastic reduction in imports caused by this even led to a surplus in foreign trade with the GDR ('Die Wirtschaftskrise' 1990).

Export restrictions caused by other factors also led to losses in foreign trade. Hungary had drastically reduced its exports to countries tied to the rouble since the start of 1990 in order to reduce its current account balance. In short, Budapest was no longer prepared to continue deliveries to either the Soviet Union or the GDR, whilst its partners were mounting up debts because they had no goods to offer or deliver and were therefore taking advantage of larger and larger interest-free credits, particularly the Soviet Union ('Der Steinzeit-Handel' 1990: 4).

Changes in consumer behaviour have also played a major role in all those countries shifting to a market economy and opening up to the west. Such changes and, in some cases, decreases in levels of consumption have been caused in the first place by rapid price increases and a drop in surplus purchasing power, unemployment and, to some extent, poverty. Secondly, goods produced in eastern

Europe have only a limited turnover, because there is little demand. Both factors have a negative effect on many companies producing and exporting consumer goods and have put them under competitive pressure, accelerated the closure of firms, and reduced trade between the countries concerned.

This has led to a precarious situation for the former GDR's trading partners in Comecon because, with the exception mentioned above, they had accumulated current account deficits especially in 1989 and 1990 (cf. *Dokumentationen* 1990: 1). Since German currency union they had moved to hard currency accounts which, because of their lack of such currency, would only seem to balance out if there were guaranteed sales of goods. But this solution comes up against the difficulties mentioned above, ranging from the unwillingness of insecure managements to draw up contracts and make purchases to the changing consumer behaviour of the population.

The shift in foreign trade to world market conditions is also influenced by factors which have had only a secondary role up until now, i.e. general factors of competition, the financial situation of trading partners and their debts. The opening up of these countries has led to growing competition from suppliers in the developed industrial countries. The result is a fall in imports from the Comecon area. The technical level of numerous domestic firms and producers in other Comecon countries, the range and the structure of supplies, reliability and flexibility in delivery, pricing and customer service are all proving to be uncompetitive. Thus, in Hungary, for example, the former GDR has already lost its market position in computer technology, electronic components, audiovisual electrical goods and other electrical household goods. This trend has become worse since imports were opened up more fully and since the final shift to trading at current world market prices and hard currency payments started on 1 January 1991. Thus, nearly all sectors of production have been exposed to direct competition with supplies from western industrial nations.

In this respect the GDR is very lucky and has many advantages because of its special position. And these advantages are such that they do not have a particularly favourable effect on the competitiveness and export capacity of other countries in Comecon. As regards the former GDR, even in the future exports will be heavily subsidised and supported for both social and economic reasons as well as geopolitical considerations. The Soviet–German Protocol on Trade of September 1990 is a clear example of such geopolitical considerations. Under the terms of this protocol, foodstuffs from the GDR will be exported to the Soviet Union at a cost of one billion Deutschmarks. The farmers in the GDR will receive a subsidy to make up the difference to the 1.5 billion costs of production ('Nahrungsgüter' 1990: 1). The other countries in eastern Europe can scarcely afford such measures as they do not have rich western brothers.

A specific feature of this process is that the transformation of the economic structures in the former GDR and other Comecon states is not occurring everywhere at the same rate. Compared to its neighbours, the changes in the GDR since November 1989 have proven more dynamic. Thus 85 to 90 per cent of Czechoslovakia's foreign trade was still allotted to Czech export firms in July 1990. At that time only twenty-three firms had been turned into private limited companies ('CSFR hob . . .' 1990: 2). These disparities have increased apace since economic and currency union between the two German states.

At least for the foreseeable future the Comecon countries will continue to drift apart from each other. Already there are great differences between the former socialist economies, and this trend will increase in the short term at least. In one further respect, firms in the former GDR have a clear advantage. Since structural changes are proceeding more slowly in the other Comecon countries, compared to the GDR, they will have a very limited ability to adopt the latest technology. Thus geographical proximity to and traditional links with the GDR could prove advantageous. At the moment, it is not yet possible to estimate in which sectors these advantages will prove more significant and in which they will be less important because of the factors detailed above. At the same time, it is obvious that the inclusion of the GDR in the European Community will have drastic results in reducing the flow of goods traditionally imported from the Comecon countries. ˉ

Aspects of Security Policy

For decades eastern Europe's subordination to Soviet hegemony delayed or hindered political or economic changes in this region. Up until now, 'security' in eastern Europe has meant in the final analysis guaranteeing the Soviet Union's superpower interests and the position of the ruling elites in the various countries. The GDR played a quite significant role in this security arrangement. However, for Poland the GDR had a significance which went far beyond this in security matters. In 1950, shortly after it had been founded, the GDR had, for example, recognised the Oder–Neiße line as the joint border with Poland. In the whole of the post-war period, therefore, this aspect of the GDR was seen as a positive point by Poland. As already indicated, the GDR not only constituted a military buffer against the west but also acted as a buffer against the western political system. This 'watch-tower of socialism in Europe' absorbed some of the influence from the west and took on a major part of the east's defence against those western activities which were seen by the Soviet leadership as an attempt to reduce its sphere of influence and which various communist leaderships classed as efforts to undermine socialist society.

The GDR's importance in guaranteeing existing relations within the 'socialist community' was just as significant as its role had been in the changes which swept eastern Europe in 1989. Up to that point far-reaching changes had occurred only in Hungary and Poland. The fall of the 'First Workers' and Peasants' State on German Soil' started a domino effect. After 9 November the dominoes fell one after the other as revolutions followed in the rest of the 'socialist camp'.

The GDR's previous significance in matters of security stemming from Soviet claims to supremacy and other security concerns has vanished since the changes in eastern Europe. Poland's western border was only finally recognised by the West German government after some delay and under pressure from the allies. Additional guarantees to Poland on this matter were reached in agreements at the Two + Four talks. But this has not solved all the security issues in eastern Europe by any means. The questions of security relationships and alliances have only been settled decisively in the case of the former GDR, or Germany. The last obstacle to the GDR's inclusion in NATO was finally removed with the talks between Chancellor Kohl of West Germany and the Soviet President, Gorbachev, which took place in Shelesnowodsk in the Caucusus in August 1990. The break-up of the communist system in the other states and the decline of Soviet hegemony has resulted in the collapse of those existing economic and security structures in which they were integrated without anything new having replaced them.

The 'Zwischeneuropa' ('Europe in between') ranging from Poland to Bulgaria has suddenly become an open space. In terms of economics these countries are now dependent on whatever understanding the west can muster for its poorer neighbours. In security matters the unknown factor for the countries of eastern Europe is the fact that the end of the Warsaw Pact has not only meant the end of dictatorship and independence from another power. It has also left a vacuum behind.

The Western Alliance seems to have shown little sign of wanting to develop new security structures for the whole of Europe once the Soviet Union had agreed to the inclusion of the GDR in NATO. At the Two + Four talks Washington resisted any transfer of rights to the Conference on Security and Co-operation (CSCE) and prevented efforts to turn it into a body for European security. Czechoslovakia and, more especially, Poland had hoped that, against the background of German unification, there would be some initiative towards creating security structures for the whole of Europe (Szyndzielorz 1990). Thus, NATO remains a western military alliance, the CSCE obtains a few supervisory military functions – and eastern Europe is left hanging.

This vacuum conceals far greater dangers due to the extremely difficult social, economic and political situation in these countries. A whole series of ethnic and national conflicts within and between these countries are still unresolved. Nor can eastern Europe remain untouched by the complications associated with the break-up of the Soviet Union, especially in the Baltic states, White Russia, and the Ukraine. In these circumstances, it will be particularly (and fatefully) important for eastern Europe whether a Great Russian chauvinist or a reformer is in charge in Moscow.

These fears, which are rife not only in Poland, were probably best summed up by Wojciech Gielzynski in Solidarity's weekly paper:

The sudden change of the international situation brought about a feeling of complete disorientation in Poland. Everything has become so complicated, we were not prepared for this, we reckoned on a smooth 'return to Europe'. The Soviet Union's position has also become complicated. As long as Gorbachev stays in power and does not change course then the Warsaw Pact seems to guarantee our security. But what if some Great Russian chauvinist takes his place? Won't the 'ghost of Rapallo' return, the temptation to arrive at some sort of agreement with the Germans? Everyone knows who will pay the price for this. And if on the other hand the Soviet house should start to crumble will the Warsaw Pact still act as a shield against a possible revival of German expansionism? (Gielzynski 1990)

The unknown factors of security and political policy and, above all, the disastrous economic situation hold many risks. What will happen if the national and ethnic conflicts in eastern Europe come to a head? What happens if it comes to clashes between Russia and its east European neighbours because of border disputes and ethnic problems? What can be done if, for example, Silesia wants to break free from Poland and unite with Germany because of the economic catastrophe and loss of legitimacy in Poland? Such voices in west and south-west Poland are not yet in the majority. But the trends are worrying. In many places in the last local elections it was Poles who were electing Germans to local government in Silesia. And there are more and more people aiming to prove their German origins – ironically now that they have been freed from dictatorship and the market economy has been introduced (cf. Kleine-Brockhoff 1990: 17–22).

The crass social and economic differences between eastern and western Europe, the want of any economic concept for the whole of Europe, the imponderables of security policy along with the many fears arising from this all reinforced such tendencies. The quite understandable fear of being left behind on the social and economic front simply because you lived east of the Oder–Neiße line strengthened the desire to achieve a solution similar to that of the GDR. Moreover, confidence in Tadeusz Mazowieski's government was dwindling rapidly. In the summer of 1989, 60 per cent of the electorate went to the polls; in spring 1990 just 40 per cent turned out for the local elections. Even in the heated political atmosphere surrounding the Presidential elections in November 1990 only 55 per cent of the electorate took part.

The contradictions of the system were sharply exposed during the communist era in Poland, and the same is now true of the conditions during the transition to democracy and the market economy. Profound social and political conflicts, legal and institutional weakness, western migration, tendencies towards nationalism and authoritarianism – all these phenomena can be seen across the whole of eastern Europe.

Hopes that eastern Europe could create a new security order and a stable regional framework on its own do not look very promising. Poland made an approach to Czechoslovakia: Prague turned it down. It is not just that Poland seems to offer little in economic terms and even less in psychological terms. Germany and the European Community are far more attractive than Poland and thus there is a stronger urge to look towards the west. Any co-operation in eastern Europe today is regarded, at best, as a function of the intention to adapt to the west. Consequently, it is not just Poland which is caught between fear of Russia, a fear of being crushed once more between Germany and Russia, attempts to find a powerful economic partner in Germany, and efforts to achieve greater security by means of a closer relationship with the successors of the former Soviet Union (cf. Graczyk 1990).

The uneven balances of power and historical legacies in this very region have led to difficulties in the formation of a new autonomous security structure in eastern Europe. With 40 million inhabitants, Poland is the most densely populated and largest state in eastern Europe. Nor has it been forgotten that before the outbreak of the Second World War Warsaw pursued the idea of a 'Third Europe' for a while, in other words an alliance of countries situated between the Baltic and the Black Sea. In this respect too, Poland appears to be an unreliable partner even today, all the more so because of its declining economic power and because frustration is greater here than in any other country. Such a situation provides fertile ground for aggressive tendencies.

Precisely because of such uncertainties in eastern Europe the Baltic states are looking instead to Scandinavia or even to Germany as a means of escaping their economic, political and ethnic difficulties. And once the Ukraine and White Russia have fully achieved their independence and fought out their battles within the former Soviet Union, then, especially in Poland, the ghosts of the past will return, old claims against one another will re-emerge and memories of past injustices will resurface. This is to say nothing of the problems of stabilising the region and reaching an understanding here because of the conflicts between Hungary and Romania and possibly between Hungary and Slovakia, the Macedonian question and the severe ethnic problems in Bosnia-Herzegovina, and the numerous other political, ethnic and religious conflicts after the outbreak of the first war of the new era between Serbia and Croatia.

For the east European countries the break-up of the GDR and the end of the Warsaw Pact will result in a new geopolitical constellation even where Germany is concerned. Previously the two German states were firmly anchored to their respective alliances and restricted in their sovereignty. Their position towards their respective superpowers ultimately determined the relationship of others to them. In the bloc system which existed up until 1989 both German states were 'political pygmies'.

The new Germany recovered full sovereignty following unification. The new shape of relations between the east European countries and Germany is not simply the result of changes in their political systems: it has also to do with the fact that these countries now have to deal with what is in European terms an economic, and a future political, superpower. In view of the vacuum which has emerged in eastern Europe this fact is all the more significant.

Germany and the Soviet Union

Germany and Russia have always had particular importance in eastern Europe. Germany's traditional role in this area came to an end as a result of the Second World War unleashed by the Nazis. Once again Germany is the centre of gravity, an economic, social and political focus just as it once was. On the other hand, Soviet hegemony installed in the region after 1945 has come to an end. Yet relations between the Soviet Union (and then Russia) on the one hand and Germany on the other have assumed a new form since the tumultuous events of 1990. Even in this respect there has been an unmistakable shift in the framework of European power. Its final shape and effect on eastern Europe depends largely on developments in the former Soviet Union which cannot yet be foreseen. Nevertheless, German–Russian relations are absolutely crucial for the region.

It is hardly surprising that Poland displays particular sensitivity about this relationship in historical terms, a sensitivity which has scarcely been assuaged in recent times. A few facts may be seen as typical of the current political situation in this area from an east European point of view. They shed light on the special relationship between Germany and Russia, and on the secondary position which Poland and the other countries occupy in between the powers. A whole series of what could be classed as historical agreements between Bonn and Moscow were reached in the extremely short period between the summer and autumn of 1990 as a result of the good understanding achieved, intense negotiations and considerable concessions. Conversely, in order to get its western border recognised by the West German government, Poland felt driven to pursue bilateral and multilateral activities in the period after the radical changes in 1989/90 and during the unification of Germany. The fact that it was the western powers and not the Soviet Union who took up the Polish issue in the negotiations on German unity was quite telling.

It was also significant that the Soviet Union and Germany very quickly agreed to the withdrawal of the Red Army from the eastern half of Germany whereas, even at the start of 1991, the Soviet Union was still refusing to agree to Polish demands for the withdrawal of Soviet troops by the end of 1991. Germany and the Soviet Union had reached an agreement on the transit of the Red Army troops stationed in East Germany as if it were the most natural thing in the world, without having cleared this with the Polish authorities in advance. This became obvious in January 1991 when, for the first time, Polish border guards at Szczecin turned back a Soviet military train en route from Germany to the Ukraine. Warsaw insisted that the transit of the 370,000 Soviet soldiers to be withdrawn from the former GDR by the end of 1994 would be allowed to continue only if an agreement was reached on the withdrawal of a separate 50,000-strong contingent of Soviet soldiers from Polish territory ('Polen weist . . .' 1991: 6).

The fact that the (old) Federal Republic was able to negotiate with the Soviet Union completely independently on the question of German unity, a matter actually reserved for discussions with the allied powers, was chiefly thanks to its powerful economic and financial position. The Federal Republic had achieved an enormous political success, against which the western powers could not only not raise any objections, but which in one fell swoop had taken the German government into a leading position alongside the USA in the Western Alliance against the Soviet Union.

In this context German policy was no less logical than German–Soviet co-operation. It was not so much the process of German unification which was dependent on the attitude of the Soviets – it was more or less happening anyway – but rather the scale of external complications in this process. In such an extreme case of linkage between domestic and foreign issues as happened in the process of German unification it is beyond doubt that the scale of external complications had an effect on internal problems and difficulties. Moreover, nobody could predict how quickly the situation in the Soviet Union would change and what effect this would have on German unification. The order of the day in German foreign policy was thus to find a speedy solution with the Soviet leadership in a manner best suited to the process of German unification.

The special nature of the German problem and the Soviet Union's importance in solving it explains the Federal Government's intense search for an agreement with the Soviet leadership. Equally, the specific nature of the Soviet problem lay behind the fact that Moscow was ready to accommodate the West Germans and make the concessions and agreements now known, not least of which was the inclusion of the GDR in NATO. Against the background of Washington's general approval, Bonn had become the Soviet Union's most important point of reference in the Kremlin's efforts to master its major problems. In return for these concessions, Germany offered economic aid to the Soviet Union and then to Russia, and guaranteed German support in the west for Gorbachev's perestroika and efforts to stabilise the Soviet Union.

This Soviet offensive aimed at *rapprochement* with Germany was also certainly influenced by the fact that up until now other western countries had proven reluctant when it came to offering concrete assistance to the crumbling Soviet Union. The reasons for this are no less revealing than the difficulties determining Moscow's position. Apart from political uncertainty, there were still structures in the Soviet Union which gave rise to fears that loans and investments would be totally without effect if they were sucked into the bureaucratic whirlpool of the huge Soviet economic and state apparatus. Gorbachev was in no position to bring about changes in the Soviet Union in such a way that they would help reconstruct the economy, secure living standards that would be half-way tolerable for wide sections of the population and provide sufficient incentive for western investors and creditors so that they would get involved.

Gorbachev was faced with the serious problems of a country sinking into economic and political chaos and the start of the disintegration of a multi-national state. The Federal Republic offered assistance in return for a quick agreement on German unity under conditions which were acceptable to the west. The German–Soviet agreement was consistent: Moscow held the decisive card on the question of German unity, whilst the Federal Republic, because of its economic strength, was able to offer the Soviet Union what no other state in western Europe could or would concede. For both sides it involved more than just millions in loans. They negotiated a comprehensive 'Treaty on Co-operation', ranging from joint production ventures to the development of new technology. Even in the past the Federal Republic was the Soviet Union's most important partner in the west; this is true of the new united Germany to an even greater degree. Several factors explain this: geographical proximity, Germany's economic power and technology, Germany's willingness and interest in working with the Soviet Union and now Russia, a long tradition of co-operation over the years and not least the fact that the GDR was the Soviet Union's most important trading partner in the 'socialist community'. The new Germany was Gorbachev's and is now Yeltsin's most important ally in their intended process of modernisation.

For Gorbachev it was all a question of politics. The exclusive negotiations and special talks with the West German government all reflected Germany's growing power and anticipated current and future shifts in the balance of power in Europe. Germany is not only the most important partner at the moment when it comes to loans, but will also be so in the future when the issue on the agenda is if and how the states which have emerged from the old Soviet Union will participate in the European Community. Moreover, the EC will play a not insignificant role in Russia's future position in Europe and the world. Seen in this light, German–Soviet negotiations and the outcome of them represented nothing more than a recognition of their own interests of state by the respective countries.

In the second half of the 1980s the Soviet leadership allowed its outlook on real events and developments to be obscured less and less by old ways of thinking. This particularly applied to the process of German unification, which it realised could not be stopped and, at worst, could only be made more complicated or delayed to its own disadvantage. And it was also true of Gorbachev's vision of a 'common European house' where, as up until now, there will obviously be residents living on the better, upper storeys who will set the rules, and those living on the lower storeys who will have to abide by them. In the current restructuring of the European home the Russian leadership is clearly looking for friends and neighbours who promise to be of most use to them. Of course, this policy depends on the continuation of economic reforms and a minimum of political stability.

Old Barriers and New Walls

Pessimists are afraid that the economic and social divide between east and west could become much wider, that the west's policy of cutting itself off from the east could become more intense, and that eastern Europe will become western Europe's, and especially Germany's, Mexico. Yet the hopes tied up with the future of a united Germany are much greater than the fears. The peoples of central eastern Europe and some of their elites have been fascinated by the Federal Republic's economic, social, political, legal and institutional system for a long time.

When it comes to improving the desolate economic conditions of the countries concerned then Germany is their main hope. Their traditional foreign relations have been partly destroyed. At the same time, the breakdown of these centralised economic systems and the discovery in 1990 of the full scale of economic mismanagement have made it much clearer that the gap between them and the western nations is far wider than was previously believed in east and west. Year one post-communism has shown that the break-up of centrally administered economies does not mean that functioning economic systems have been established yet. It is recognised that they still have hard times in front of rather than behind them. And uncertainty is spreading about if and how the problems of economic reconstruction can be tackled. On all sides it is emphasised that the intended aims cannot be realised without foreign assistance.

It is obvious that these hopes are directed chiefly at the united Germany: high standards in technology, productivity and the capital strength of the German economy; geographical proximity; traditional strong economic ties. Alongside the Soviet Union the GDR was the second most important and, in terms of supplying high quality industrial goods, usually the most important foreign partner. The Federal Republic, or Germany as the case may be, has hitherto always been the most important western economic partner for the countries of eastern Europe. Even before the Second World War this was the case and this has not changed in the post-war period – despite all the limitations imposed by the 'Sovietisation' of the eastern part of Europe. Be it the GDR, Poland, Czechoslovakia or Hungary, it was the Federal Republic which held first place in their foreign trade 'with the west'.

For these reasons the greatest contacts exist with West and East Germany, and the greatest degree of joint experience has been accumulated with them, too, establishing the best developed structures for co-operation. It is expected that privatisation and the abolition of foreign trade monopolies as well as new legal regulations will attract western investors. And finally it is hoped that for geographical and political reasons Germany will show most interest in an active economic commitment to its neighbours in eastern Europe. Conversely, there is also western interest in supporting the east. The dire economic and political situation in these countries makes help and co-operation a priority of European politics, if the continent is not to fall into economic and political conflict, social hostility and nationalist confrontation.

Germany's need for stable economic and political conditions in eastern Europe underlines the case for intensive German efforts to achieve co-operation. Germany is most tangibly affected by the various political and economic conditions in the one-time 'real socialist' countries. The worse it is for the people in eastern Europe, the more they will try to reach the wealthy west – and that means Germany in the first instance. Social unrest and political disputes in neighbouring countries to the east will rebound on Germany first of all.

It remains to be seen how far these hopes will be fulfilled. Billions of Deutschmarks will be swallowed up by the costs of financing German unity, the integration of the former GDR and the needs of economic and political redistribution. It is certainly in Germany's interest that economic differences with its neighbours do not become too great, that social contradictions do not become explosive and that political structures do not become unstable in these countries. But social and political peace and economic redistribution at home come before that in neighbouring states. It is hardly surprising that the German government is pressing for aid to eastern Europe to be made a 'European task'. On its own, Germany could scarcely meet the enormous needs of eastern Europe even if the integration of the former GDR required somewhat less expense.

The European Community will certainly offer assistance. The founding of the Bank for Economic Reconstruction and Development, and an initiative co-ordinated by the European Community aimed at stabilising the balance of payments situation for the former Comecon countries are, amongst other things, some of the steps towards assistance and signs of a willingness to improve the difficult economic situation in eastern Europe. It is not only German firms and regions which will intensify their co-operation with the countries of eastern Europe in these new circumstances. Whether this will be enough to provide effective support for these washed-out post-communist economies is highly doubtful. Because of gaps in the infrastructure and other difficulties the attraction for investment on a grand scale is less than politicians had anticipated in the euphoria surrounding the 'Opening Up of the East' and the introduction of the market economy.

In addition there is the geographical and mental distance separating eastern Europe from countries like Britain, France, Spain or Italy. The west Europeans are, and feel themselves to be, less affected than the Germans by events in the eastern half of Europe.

This further increases the undeniable reluctance of western Europe to start any redistribution in favour of the former socialist countries. Even if they wanted to do this, the western governments and parties would be taking a great political risk with such a strategy. Few west Europeans are so altruistic or hold the belief that they have it so good that hundreds of billions could be transferred to the east.

In any case, to date there has been no discernible far-reaching co-operation or significant increase in exchanges between the states of eastern Europe and the western countries since the collapse of the communist systems in autumn 1989. The same is true of Germany. A large hole has been left behind by the collapse of the GDR along with the ruin of the old system in the east European countries and the new economic restrictions (rather than politically motivated ones as in the past) on both foreign and domestic trade. It is still not clear who and what should and will fill this hole.

For the GDR the problem of integration into the western economic community has already been settled. For the other east European countries the hurdles have, on the other hand, become greater still. The expansion of the EC with the former GDR as well as other 'western' countries is bound up with complications for the Community, which means that any reservations about the participation of more east European countries will certainly not diminish. On the other hand eastern Europe needs help and hope. Peter Bender writes that psychology is almost as important as the economy: where speedy changes are not possible there must at least be a credible vision. Thus the Poles, Czechs, Slovaks, Hungarians and others need an agreement guaranteeing them 'entry' to Europe. They need the certainty of obtaining the same opportunities as the Spaniards, Portuguese and Greeks did in their day (Bender 1990: 3).

What is to be feared is that the expectations of joining the prosperous and wealthy western economies as harboured by politicians, economists and by the people most of all, will be dashed as quickly as those hopes that everything would be better following the introduction of the market economy. Doubts in the west about the economic integration of the east have increased in line with the awareness of the scale of the economic calamity in the relevant countries. At a discussion in September 1990 in Vienna, Peter Glotz, the SPD's party manager, spoke of a 'great deception', if anyone were to talk about the inclusion of eastern Europe in the European Community.

Yet this will have a corresponding effect on the east–west relationship. The first signs are clear and they will undoubtedly increase. The flood of refugees from eastern Europe has not fallen back since the dictatorships have fallen and the market economy has been introduced. There is no time to wait for the reactions from the west either. One European country after another is tightening its entry restrictions for eastern Europeans. The traditional gulf dividing west and east Europe was bridged only, if at all, for a short historical moment in autumn 1989; today the gulf is as wide as ever. The walls and barbed wire fences erected by the dictatorships have fallen, ideological separation has come to an end. Economic and social division of the continent continues to exist.

Translated from the German by Gordon W. Smith.

References

Bender, P., 'Wenn auf die Freiheit nichts als Armut folgt', *Die Zeit*, 31.8.90, p. 3

'Beteiligungen – Ausweg aus ineffizienter Kooperation', *Handelsblatt*, 9.5.90

Boschek, H., 'Die deutsche Wiedervereinigung schlägt auf die alten Handelsstrukturen durch', *Handelsblatt*, 6.6.90, p. 11

'CSFR beklagt die sinkende Liefermoral von DDR-Firmen', *Handelsblatt*, 16.5.90, p. 14

'CSFR hob staatliches Außenhandelmonopol auf', *Dokumentationen zur Außenwirtschaft, DDR*, 18.7.90, p. 2

Dokumentationen zur Außenwirtschaft, DDR, 1.8.90, p. 1

'Finanzielle Hilfen für Exportverträge mit RGW-Ländern', *Dokumentationen zur Außenwirtschaft, DDR*, 11.7.90, p. 4

Gielzynski, W., 'Wariant rezerwowy', *Tygodnik Solidarnosc*, 9.3.90

Graczyk, R., 'W drodze do Europy', *Tygodnik Powszechny*, 11.2.90

'Handel DDR–Polen', *Die DDR-Wirtschaft*, 7, 1990, p. 22

'Innerdeutscher Handel und Außenhandel im 1. Halbjahr 1990', *Dokumentationen zur Außenwirtschaft, DDR*, 1.8.90

Kleine-Brockhoff, T., 'Der schleichende Anschluß', *Die Zeit*, 5.10.90, p. 17

Kulke-Fielder, C., 'Wirtschaftliche Realitäten im heutigen Europa', *IWP-Berichte*, 6, 1990, p. 18

Leicht, R., 'Von der Freiheit zur Einheit', *Die Zeit*, 28.9.90, p. 4

'Nahrungsgüter für eine Milliarde DM in die UdSSR', *Berliner Zeitung*, 11.9.90, p. 1

'Polen weist Militärzug an Grenze ab', *Süddeutsche Zeitung*, 11.1.91, p. 6
'RGW-Export nur zu 70 Prozent erfüllt', *Frankfurter Allgemeine Zeitung*, 10.9.90, p. 15
'Der Steinzeit-Handel gilt nicht mehr', *Berliner Zeitung*, 25.4.90, p. 4
Szyndzielorz, K., 'Widmo Niemiec', *Przeglad Tygodniowy*, 11.2.90
Vajda, P., 'Hogyan "szabadittuk fel" az NDK-t', *Nepszabadsag* (weekend supplement), 24.3.90
'Die Wirtschaftskrise in der DDR beschert Moskau Überschüsse im Außenhandel', *Handelsblatt*, 25.4.90

–11–

German Unification and the West

Gert-Joachim Glaeßner

When, at midnight on 2 October 1990, the national anthem rang out in front of the Reichstag in Berlin and the flag of the Federal Republic of Germany was raised, a long cherished dream became reality – if one is to believe the official statements of the politicians. A people which had for forty-five years been divided by insurmountable borders was united again in one national state. The victorious powers of the Second World War had renounced their reserve powers regarding Germany as a whole and opened the way to state unification.

As so often, so too when considering the events which led to German unity there is a recognisable tendency to lend historical developments a certain logic and inevitability; to interpret them, in other words, in the light of their final results. But such an approach is mistaken. Fundamental to the following discussion is the thesis that, until the end of 1989, none of the participants, neither the Federal Republic and the western powers nor the Soviet Union, pursued an active policy aimed at unifying Germany, even though it was evident that a lasting peace in Europe was inconceivable without a solution to the 'German problem'. In spite of all efforts to achieve 'new thinking' in international relations, fear of the consequences of ending the post-war order established by force in central Europe was greater than the knowledge that this order was already rotten from the core. It required the spontaneous force of the masses in the countries of central Europe and the GDR to demonstrate this to their contemporaries.

The contradiction between the rhetoric of reunification shared by all West German governments and the impossibility of achieving it was for decades a bone of contention between the political parties. The SPD had only with reluctance accepted the fact that the Federal

Republic's membership of NATO in 1955, which had made the prospect of reunification even more remote, was the price for the country's sovereignty. The same is true of the CDU/CSU as regards *Ostpolitik*. The *de facto* recognition of the GDR by the Federal Republic and its allies was the prerequisite for a *modus vivendi* in Europe. Given the rigidly confrontational system produced at Yalta, the political statement that the unity of Germany would have to be part of any future European order was no more than an empty formula. The uprising of the peoples of central Europe and of the citizens of the GDR against communist domination forced the politicians to change tack completely. The unification of the two German states became a matter of urgent importance – and immediately the flimsiness of the standard formulae hitherto used by each side became very obvious.

A considerable discrepancy became evident between official policy and the actual or assumed attitude of the population towards the question of reunification. It was no longer clear 'whether most West Germans would risk their current prosperity in order to achieve' German unity. 'They reluctantly pay taxes to support the weaker economies of Southern Europe and of East Germany; and recognise that any further opening to Eastern Europe would bring demands for them to pay more' (Wallace 1989).

Foreign observers saw more quickly and more clearly than the Germans themselves that the revolutionary changes in central Europe and the upheavals in the GDR represented a problem for the Federal Republic's sense of its own identity. It took the Germans a long time to recognise that the unification of the two German states had suddenly become possible. Now that unity has been achieved, it can be seen that, in the euphoria that prevailed in 1990, it had been easy to underestimate the many difficulties which will have to be overcome if the two German societies are to grow together. Politicians in the Federal Republic had acted without heed to the scepticism expressed by many intellectuals regarding the problems to be expected in uniting two entirely different states *and* societies. As early as the summer of 1989, when unification seemed only a vague possibility on the horizon, Hugh Trevor-Roper expressed doubts:

> What began as a temporary administrative expedient for the period of the military occupation prevailed, and the administrative expedient hardened into a political system. That system has now lasted 44 years. Institutions – opposite, incompatible institutions – have been planted

and have taken root on either side of the new internal frontier. Those institutions are now integrated into the life and habit of all Germans. The frontier might disappear overnight, but those institutions and those habits not. Nor would the vested interests on both sides. . . . Perhaps if controls were removed, communism in East Germany would shrivel like a scroll. But would that not be a revolution, a de-stabilisation of Europe, which for 44 years has lived in a balanced peace? . . . The only questions are, do the Germans really want it, and, if so, how can it be achieved without destroying the delicate balance of Europe which has been based on division? (Trevor-Roper 1989)

The tension between, on the one hand, the hope that communist domination in central Europe might be ended and, on the other, fear of the unpredictable consequences of such a revolutionary change accompanied the process of German unification. A European reconciliation which excluded the Germans was inconceivable, as was the continuation within a united Europe of the division of Germany into two states. Despite Bonn's 'quiet yearning' for unification (*New York Times*, 23.9.89), a single German national state as the result of *rapprochement* seemed, until the end of 1989, highly unlikely. There remained the vision of a 'reassociation' of the two German states bedded in a wider Europe. To Stephen Larrabee, who is representative of many other observers, this possibility seemed in the final analysis to make better sense than the continued existence of an unstable GDR. Every political leader 'will face growing pressures for reform and will be confronted with a nearly insoluble dilemma: Resist pressures for reform, and risk an internal explosion; accede to them, and set in motion trends that could not only sweep the party from power but undermine the very existence of East Germany' (Larrabee 1989).

Constitutional Obligation versus *Realpolitik*?
The Development of German–German Relations

The gap between wish and reality was, for decades, in no field of international politics so great as in the sphere of German–German relations. Again and again the GDR proved its anxious concern to demonstrate its sovereignty and independence of the Federal Republic. The 'BRD' was much maligned by the SED leadership but admired by a largely uncritical population as the attractive alternative to their own reality. In the Federal Republic every government emphasised the duty imposed on it by the Basic Law to strive for the unity of Germany in freedom. In its preamble the Basic Law states:

> The German people . . .
> Animated by the resolve to preserve their national and political unity and to serve the peace of the world as an equal partner in a united Europe, Desiring to give a new order to political life for a transitional period, . . . have also acted on behalf of those Germans to whom participation was denied.
> The entire German people are called upon to achieve in free self-determination the unity and freedom of Germany.

Given the world situation, however, all political forces in the country were obliged by the exigencies of *Realpolitik* to have dealings with those who stood in the way of this aim, the leadership of the Soviet Union and their lieutenants in the GDR. At the same time everyday life in the Federal Republic developed its own momentum without any need for the GDR. People generally thought of West Germany as 'Germany' and of the GDR as a largely unknown and even uninteresting country. Despite the constitutional obligation contained in the Basic Law and the determination of all political parties not to give up the aim of German unity, ordinary West Germans, unlike their compatriots in the East, would have been quite happy to accept the status quo.

As the division of Germany into two states and two societies continued, it appeared less and less likely that the aim of German–German politics embodied in the preamble to the Basic Law could ever be achieved, particularly since the formulation of this aim was never linked by either side with the possibility of giving up the norms which were fundamental to its own state and society. All political efforts were now concentrated on realising the best possible conditions for making the division into two states as bearable as possible and for contributing as far as one could to improving the situation of people living in the GDR. Neither the SPD–FDP coalition nor its successor, the coalition of CDU/CSU and FDP, was able to disguise the ambivalence inherent in such a policy: in the circumstances of the Cold War, the aim of unification on the one hand and insistence on the Federal Republic's legal right to act on behalf of all Germans on the other were mutually exclusive. The policy of détente, which found expression in international law in the CSCE Helsinki Treaty of 1975, did not in fact represent an end to the Cold War. *Ostpolitik* was based rather on a realistic analysis of the constellation of forces in world politics which made the end of the blocs conceivable at best as a goal for the distant future, once the Cold War was over.

The revolutionary processes in the Soviet Union and in central Europe rapidly demonstrated the inconsistencies and fractures in the Federal Republic's policy. The Germans themselves scarcely noticed this. The increased concern shown by their western neighbours and their allies was all the greater. Long before German reunification was placed on the official agenda of world politics at the start of 1990, fear was rife that the Germans might go it alone and opt for a German–Soviet alliance on the lines of Rapallo (the German–Soviet Pact of 16 April 1922).

Events in the GDR brought to the surface deep-seated fears even in neighbouring countries, such as France, which for decades had enjoyed close and friendly relations with the Federal Republic. Thus Alain Peyrefitte wrote in *Le Figaro* on 11 November 1989 that Germany would again become a nation of 80,000,000 people, by far the most efficient and powerful in Europe. It would develop into the most powerful partner of the Soviet Union, which urgently needed such a partnership. The balance between France and Germany, which had been established from the outset during the construction of Europe and which, despite all trials and tribulations, it had been possible to maintain ever since, would now disintegrate. The former Prime Minister, Michel Debré, expressed himself in similar vein in *Le Monde* on 14 November 1989 when he remarked that, against the background of current events and in particular of the end of the Berlin Wall, France should recognise the future which was now opening up and that this was a new Rapallo.

Consequences of *Ostpolitik*

Until the beginning of 1990 there was broad agreement in the Federal Republic that (re)unification would be a long time coming. This was the background to Willy Brandt's statement that the search for reunification was a sham and the Federal Republic's 'life-lie' (*Lebenslüge*) (Brandt 1988). This led the Editor-in-Chief of the weekly newspaper *Die Zeit* to state in the summer of 1989 that the idea of Germany's unity should be given up in favour of the freedom of Germans living in the GDR (Sommer 1989). The former Federal Chancellor Helmut Schmidt protested vehemently against this view. His argument was that no European neighbour would believe that the Germans had given up this aim because they regarded 'their own national unity and self-determination as natural' (Schmidt 1989).

Not a great deal separated Sommer and Schmidt in their analysis of the situation. Both saw the unification of Germany in one nation-state as a distant prospect. In Helmut Schmidt's view no patent remedies for the German question were in sight. He drew the Germans' attention to the example of Poland which had been divided for more than a century, had then been broken up once again in the twentieth century, and yet had re-emerged as a nation-state. 'I am confident that *in the course of the next century* [my emphasis: G.-J. G.] there will be a common roof over the German nation which will guarantee freedom' (Schmidt 1989).

There was also remarkable agreement among (West) German politicians that the unity of Germany as a nation-state was not the first priority of *Ostpolitik* and of policy on Germany (*Deutschland-politik*). The main aim was to improve the situation of people in whose countries the regime, it was believed, could not be removed. This was the central concern of the policy of 'change through *rapprochement*' and was at the heart of the CSCE process. 'Is it really reunification', asked Franz Josef Strauß in 1985, 'which above all else moves, torments, depresses and drives us? Surely it is less unification in the sense of the re-establishment of the unity of Germany as a state; surely it is more the cherished wish to restore in this region conditions which are democratic and worthy of man.' Since November 1989 there has been no further sign of the kind of prioritisation which Strauß and other conservative politicians had repeatedly argued for during the 1980s. Historical events have made such long-term views of the problem redundant.

Even for the CDU/CSU and the federal government which they led the unification of the two German states was not a pressing issue. Indeed, at the beginning of 1988 consideration was given, in a draft of the CDU's new party programme, to the possibility of dropping reunification as the aim of *Deutschlandpolitik*. The CDU's draft programme focused on the European dimension of the German question. The aim of unity could only be achieved 'with the agreement and support' of neighbouring states in east and west. This meant implicitly that the legal position which had always been invoked, particularly as regards the Oder–Neiße border, was no longer tenable. An end to the division of Europe and therefore of Germany presupposed an end to the east–west conflict: 'A solution to the German question therefore cannot be achieved at present'

(Christlich-demokratische Perspektiven 1988: 4). The responsibility of the Germans consisted in doing whatever was currently possible to temper the east–west conflict in Germany and in Europe.

The CDU/CSU's *Deutschlandpolitik* had long been characterised by a growing contradiction between its official programme and the realities of practical politics. This stretched back to the 1960s. The *Ostpolitik* and *Deutschlandpolitik* of the social-liberal coalition formed by SPD and FDP in 1969–82 brought a lasting improvement in Germany's relations with her eastern neighbours, but at first was vehemently opposed by the CDU/CSU. The CSCE conference, which in 1975 concluded in Helsinki with a final accord which became a kind of 'Magna Carta' for the opposition movements in communist countries, had also been rejected by the opposition.

Domestically, the eastern treaties acted as catalyst for a polarisation in public opinion and between the parties such as the Federal Republic had not known since its early years. The passion with which they were debated indicates that more was at stake than a foreign policy decision. Not unlike the situation after November 1989, what was at issue was the way the Federal Republic saw itself as an integral component of the western community. For decades Germany had formed 'the front-line in the battle between democracy and communism', and this contrast had left its indelible mark on political thinking in both German states. 'What for other countries amounted to tensions in foreign policy became for the Federal Republic and the GDR a political civil war,' (Bender 1986: 9).

Ostpolitik had undertaken the attempt to bring to an end this civil war. The continuation of this policy, bedded though it was in the general détente between east and west and in the CSCE process, was seriously endangered at the end of the 1970s and beginning of the 1980s. At this time conditions in Germany were anything but favourable for a policy directed towards conciliation and co-operation in practical questions. The high expectations invested in the Helsinki final accord had been disappointed. In reviewing relations between European states after the final CSCE conference in 1975, it is above all the problematic events which stand out: NATO's decision to deploy new medium-range nuclear missiles in Europe, the invasion of Afghanistan by Soviet troops in December 1979, the Polish crisis which led to the imposition of martial law in December 1981, and, overshadowed by these events, the visit of the Federal German Chancellor, Helmut Schmidt, to the GDR.

In spite of this and many other strains, the relationship between the two German states remained remarkably stable. In some measure, this led to irritation in both east and west about the reliability of their respective allies. Both German governments were concerned not to increase tensions but, on the contrary, to contribute to détente at the point of intersection between the two systems by further developing existing treaties. The 'policy of small steps' was continued, a precondition for which being that any going back on the results of the social-liberal *Ostpolitik* and *Deutschlandpolitik* was out of the question.

Beyond any doubt the visit of Erich Honecker to the Federal Republic (7 to 11 August 1987) was an important milestone not only in German–German relations but also along the path leading to full international recognition of the GDR. It is clear in retrospect that the visit marked a turning point in German–German relations. The internal prestige which the GDR had acquired and which was later further reinforced by a state visit to France doubtless contributed to the fact that the GDR's political leadership ignored clear symptoms of a social crisis and rejected the idea of reform.

In spite of the – on the whole – positive results of *Deutschlandpolitik*, it became evident after Erich Honecker's visit to Bonn and the ensuing hardening of positions within the SED leadership that the Federal government's policy basically lacked any forward-looking rationale. Its main components – pragmatism, revisionism, the insistence on legalistic argument, and a very few new ideas for the future – proved uneasy bedfellows. This was particularly clear once the wider framework within which this policy operated became the subject of increasingly dynamic change.

A fundamental dilemma at the heart of *Deutschlandpolitik* is apparent here. The parties of government and the SPD opposition failed to recognise that there was a remarkable contradiction within their policy, a contradiction which had become increasingly sharp during the 1980s. The initial concept underpinning the *Ostpolitik* and *Deutschlandpolitik* which Egon Bahr had conceived as early as 1963 – the idea of 'change through *rapprochement*' – was no longer valid. While the policy of balancing out each side's interests still led to change in the GDR, that is to improvements in everyday life there, it also led increasingly to an unintended consolidation of the orthodox regime. A similar observation can be made regarding policy towards both the Soviet Union before Gorbachev's accession (possibly also for the period following his abandonment of perestroika and glasnost in January 1991) and also towards central Europe.

The expectation that the GDR would open itself to the outside world and display a greater disposition towards tolerance domestically (Gasteyger 1976: 174) was not fulfilled. On the contrary, as the crisis grew more acute, the old leadership in the politburo developed a bunker mentality which wasted any chance of a timely change of course and ended with the disintegration and collapse of the SED's power.

Like the Social Democrats, though for different reasons, the government ran into difficulties with its policy (which concentrated on finding solutions to 'human problems') because the social framework and fabric of the socialist countries began to change. Neither government nor opposition had any conception of how it might respond to the process by which GDR society was emancipating itself from the party-state without at the same time terminating its pact with those in power. (With their clear support of the opposition and of the citizens' movements which were springing up, the Greens did not face this problem, but they also, of course, did not have the problem of having to pursue *Realpolitik*.)

The opposition in the GDR was a negligible factor as far as its active membership is concerned. It played a very minor part in the calculations of western politicians, who therefore overlooked that these few courageous men and women articulated what so oppressed the great majority of the population. This is the only explanation for the fact that, within a very few weeks, they became the focal point of the revolt against the rule of the SED. As Timothy Garton Ash has pointed out, 'this East German rising was not contemplated in Bonn's Deutschlandpolitik. Those in the GDR who contributed most to Germany's peaceful October revolution . . . had benefited least from the Federal Republic's governmental policy towards the GDR. Bonn politicians now actually celebrate the "peaceful revolution". Two years ago most of those politicians would have described it as "dangerous destabilisation"' (Garton Ash 1990: 11).

In 1987/88 no-one could have foreseen the collapse of the socialist systems. The fact that they were in (latent) crisis could not be overlooked, however. Moreover, the framework of *Deutschlandpolitik* clearly began to change after Gorbachev's accession to power in 1985. The Federal government and the largest opposition party reacted to the new situation to the extent that they declared their support for Gorbachev's policy, but they clearly distanced themselves from the growing protest movements in the socialist countries. Government and opposition reacted in the usual fashion even towards the turmoil in the GDR. They demanded a more liberal approach from the GDR and, beyond that, declared themselves ready to sit down with party and state leaders 'in the interests of the people'. However, they had no clear idea of how to deal with the opposition groups, opting for a kind of symbolic politics by praising their noble ideals but otherwise avoiding them. They were later praised all the more loudly for having initiated the 'peaceful revolution'. This basic approach was only changed – and then within a few days – in December 1989.

The visit to Dresden by Chancellor Kohl on 19 December 1989 made it dramatically clear that the determination of the people of the GDR to bring about reunification could no longer be denied. On 8 November 1989 the Chancellor had declared in his report on the state of the nation: 'However difficult it may be for us and above all for our compatriots in the GDR, let us continue with patient perseverance to trust in the path of *evolutionary change* [my emphasis: G.-J. G.] at the end of which must stand full respect for human rights and the free self-determination of all Germans' ('Bericht der Bundesregierung' 1989: 1059). On 28 November 1989 the Chancellor had drawn up a long-term 'Ten Points Programme' which provided for contractual structures and confederative structures between the two German states as a first step and was intended ultimately to lead via a federation to the unification of Germany. No timetable was attached to these proposals: 'No-one knows today what a unified Germany will finally look like' (*Neues Deutschland*, 1.12.89, p. 6).

On 30 January 1990 Hans Modrow, then Minister President of the GDR, travelled to Moscow to consult the Soviet government on the future of the GDR. It could be foreseen at the time that the unification of the two German states would inevitably take place in a relatively short time; people were on the streets categorically demanding nothing less. After his visit to Moscow, Modrow suggested, to the evident discomfort of his own party (now renamed as the SED-PDS), that Germany should again become, in the words of the GDR's own national anthem, the united fatherland (*einig Vaterland*) of all citizens of the German nation. In so doing he took up the demand which had been voiced with increasing fervour at the weekly mass demonstrations which the SED-PDS still rejected at this point as an expression of growing nationalistic and chauvinistic tendencies.

Europe is entering a new phase in its development. The post-war chapter is coming to a close. The prerequisites for peaceful and neighbourly co-operation among all peoples are taking shape. The unification of both German states is moving on to the agenda . . . A definitive solution of the German problem can only be achieved through the free self-determination of the Germans in both German states, in co-operation with the four powers and taking into account the interests of all European states. It must promote the European process, the aim of which is to free our continent once and for all from military dangers. The *rapprochement* of both German states and their subsequent unification should be seen by no-one as a threat. (*DDR Journal 2*, 1990: 72)

Thus Modrow was ahead of his party in bidding farewell to one of the greatest illusions of the Honecker era, the idea that a socialist nation could be artificially created in the GDR. An official account of Modrow's period in office has him expressing the following view: 'I am fed up of stalling the will of more and more Germans and in the end trying to catch up with events. At some point these could take off on their own, and if the streets take over the German question, it won't be the demonstrations of October and November 1989 any more with their call for "no violence!" ' (Arnold 1990: 97). In the following weeks and months this question came to predominate over all others. All the politicians were trying, with varying success, to catch up with events.

Modrow returned with the Soviet Union's agreement that it would not oppose such a development. What only two months before had appeared as a possibility on the distant horizon was now the pressing issue of the day. However, the Soviet Union still appeared set on the neutralisation of Germany.

Developments received a push from the results of the elections to the *Volkskammer* on 18 March 1990. These demonstrated that the population did not share with the citizens' movements and many intellectuals the dream of a renewed, human socialism in the GDR. The majority wanted the rapid unification of Germany, in the hope that this would bring the solution to their problems.

Still undecided was the future status of Germany in the alliances. The Federal government had left no doubt that it did not support neutrality, indeed regarded it in the long term as highly problematical and even dangerous. However, this hurdle too was surmounted during the Chancellor's visit to the Soviet Union in the summer of 1990. The stage was now set for a successful conclusion to the Two + Four negotiations.

The German Question and the Western Alliance

The unmistakable differences within the eastern camp were matched by no less significant differences in the west. If, in the words of Churchill's military adviser and the first Secretary General of NATO Lord Ismay, the rationale of the Western Alliance was 'to keep the Americans in, to keep the Russians out, and to keep the Germans down', the question for western observers of Federal German politics in 1989 was whether and how this formula required to be changed. 'That strategy, however, only made sense as long as the Soviet Union continued to play its allotted role as master of the evil empire. The Russian threat justified the need for Nato, while Nato's strength stopped the Germans from having ideas above their station. Suddenly everything looks different' (Kellner 1989). The new motto, Kellner adds, should now be 'to help the Russians up and to keep the Germans in'.

Similar ideas informed discussions within the American administration. The Bush administration was reviewing American policy towards East Germany, seeking a balanced way of encouraging democratisation there 'without fostering a pell-mell movement toward reunification of Germany that would threaten both Moscow and America's Nato allies' (*New York Times*, 20.10.89, p. A13). A high official within the administration was quoted as saying: 'With Poland and Hungary we can encourage reform and self-expression without feeling it is in any way inconsistent with American interests. But when we support the same things in East Germany you are knowingly accelerating a process which would make the ultimate reunification of Germany more possible' (*New York Times*, 20.10.89, p. A13).

In an article on the end of the Cold War, Nigel Hawkes, Diplomatic Editor of the *Observer*, named what, in the view of many in Britain, was the decisive aspect of all the discussions about the dissolution of the blocs and the democratisation of eastern Europe: fear of a Germany-dominated Europe, which had never been a recipe for peace and stability. Discussion about Germany's membership of NATO should be seen against this background. The geopolitical position of Germany represents a problem for all her neighbours. As long as the Cold War determined the climate in Europe, the Germans were firmly anchored in the Western Alliance. When, given the internal and external changes to the Soviet Union as the leading power in the east, a far-reaching transformation of the European political landscape began to take shape, a measure of uncertainty ensued about the future direction of Germany. Even before November 1989 there were signs of uncertainty in American public life. These had to do with the fact that the old certainties were crumbling, the old image of the enemy had to be revised and new political strategies had to be found. A new assessment was required of the constellations of political power in Europe, of the new role of the Soviet Union, and of the position of Germany in the 'European house'.

Unease, not to say fear, that the Germans might ventilate new geopolitical options were widespread in the period immediately prior to the German unification process. In the Federal Republic more and more voices were raised in favour of what amounted to a rehash of the old ideas of neutrality, thereby feeding fears in the west that Germany might choose to go it alone. That these fears were widespread is evident from a variety of commentaries in the press in 1989/90. For example, writing in the *Independent* in the summer of 1989, Peter Kellner remarked in an article tellingly entitled 'Keeping the Germans on a Leash': 'If West Germany is not tethered effectively to the wider international community, the long-term pressures inside the country towards "Alleingang" – going it alone, and dragging Austria and East Germany into its orbit – could prove hard to resist.' These tendencies could turn into a dangerous and irresistible force in the politics of the Federal Republic: 'A new leash is needed' (Kellner 1989). This is all the more the case, given that the unification of the two German states brings a new factor into European politics: 'Germany will seek to regain the power to determine the fate of Europe. The only way to reduce the risk inherent in that situation is to wrap the Bonn government even tighter into the community of free nations. As economic bonds replace military alliances, that means that the European Community will become more important than NATO' (Broder 1989). Peter Torner, the president of the Council on Foreign Relations, even noted a 'bizarre nostalgia' for the Cold War (Tarnoff 1989). Henry Kissinger spoke of 'a sudden nostalgia [that] has developed for the status quo' (Kissinger 1989: 22). Lawrence Eagleburger was quoted as saying that the Cold War had produced a remarkable set of stable and calculable relationships between the great powers. Uncertainty about Gorbachev's prospects of success also contributed towards consolidating old positions (Zumwalt and Bagley 1989; Pipes 1989). Even the provincial press was alarmed. There was talk of the 'good old days' when the division between East and West had still been clear ('Good Riddance to Cold War',

The Hartford Courant, 24.9.89). The changes in Europe – of that there was and is no doubt – prescribe a leading role for Germany in Europe, or, as George F. Will put it in a commentary, 'Germany Will Be the Head of the European House' (*International Herald Tribune*, 1.12.89). The question is which role the expanded Federal Republic will in future play in the Western Alliance and in the European Community, how the relationship of the Federal Republic to the Soviet Union will develop with a unified Germany remaining a member of the western community. The position of both the government and the largest opposition party on this complex of issues is quite clear.

Bubbling Under the Surface. Can the Germans be Trusted?

'Who are these people we see on our television', asked Mary McGrory in the *Washington Post* on 15 October 1989,

> these people who sing 'We shall overcome', carry candles and sass their police? They are East Germans, we are told. But they are not Germans we remember from a generation past. They are not the goose-stepping, Heil-Hitlering, authority-loving people who followed a mad leader to a war that devoured the world and decimated a generation, who acquiesced in – or at least made sure they didn't know much about – the extermination of 6 million Jews. (McGrory 1989)

The autumn of 1989 changed the image of 'the' Germans. For the first time in their history they risked an uprising against a dictatorship and fought for democracy and human rights. The question remains whether these events will leave a lasting imprint on the future image of the Germans.

'Don't trust the Germans' – thus the title given by Roger Scruton, a leading conservative thinker in Great Britain, to an article he published in the *Sunday Telegraph* in June 1989, on the eve of a NATO summit and at the height of a debate on the stationing of new, short-range nuclear missiles in Europe. The West Germans, he asserted, were no longer of a mind to support the policy of the west. They were flirting with the idea of neutrality and unilateral disarmament. This endangered the Western Alliance and supported the long-term aim of Soviet policy to drive the Americans out of Europe. The result of this process would not be peace and lasting détente, nor a common European house: 'The iron curtain will be raised, but only to fall again in the Atlantic. West Germany has now taken a decisive turn away from the Western Alliance' (Scruton 1989). Scruton offers his readers a scathing reminder of a historical tendency in German politics to derive Germany's claim to a position of leadership from her central location in Europe. Yet, as a leading article in the *Independent* (25.5.89) put it, 'very few people, least of all most West Germans, want a restoration of German hegemony in Europe'.

It was the Federal Republic of Germany which had first decided to adopt the political ideals of western democracies. Yet many critical intellectuals question whether and to what extent this decision will last and whether it was not reached above all for ideological reasons – to establish clear demarcation (*Abgrenzung*) *vis-à-vis* communism and to set up a western-style free democracy as a counter-model to totalitarian dictatorship in the GDR. In the history of the Federal Republic, the image of communism as the enemy served the needs both of foreign policy and of German–German policy. It ensured the 'preservation of a power structure which cannot do without deterrence' and made criticism of that power structure taboo (Frisch 1977: 16). Whether the western orientation of the Federal Republic was in fact more than just a signpost in the east–west conflict would become evident in the process of upheaval in Europe.

There was an obvious lack of clarity and firmness in some areas. The population of a country which was only forty years old had not developed a sense of national identity. German history was broader and more painful than that of the geographically and culturally more limited Federal Republic.

> The West Germans sought redemption first in hard work and then in being good Europeans, thus making a crucial contribution both to Europe's economic revival and to the creation of the European Economic Community. Material success inevitably failed to satisfy the spiritual needs of a people long inclined to abstract yearnings; and the West Europeanism was soon complemented by Willy Brandt's Ostpolitik. The federal system and the absence of a true capital favoured strong regional development and cultural decentralisation, but did nothing to foster a sense of identity. (Independent, 25.5.89, p. 24)

It was generally recognised, however, that in its western part Germany has developed into a consolidated democracy. 'It's emergence as much the most properous, democratic and civilised state to have flourished on German soil is a tribute to the hard work and good sense of a people chastened by the horrors of war; and also to the wisdom of the western allies who shaped the Basic Law, or constitution, on which it was founded' (*Independent*, 25.5.89, p. 24).

Nevertheless: can the Germans be trusted? Many commentators in recent years have raised doubts on the issue. It seems to me, however, that there is a remarkable discrepancy between the opinions of leading intellectuals in the western countries and the man in the street, a contradiction which also runs through German society. While well-known intellectuals such as Günter Grass and Jürgen Habermas spoke of 'a bargain called Germany' and of 'DM-nationalism', the overwhelming majority of citizens welcomed the unity of Germany. Admittedly, they also stated in all the opinion polls that the unification process was taking place at too great a speed. Opinion polls in neighbouring European countries present a differentiated picture. In February 1990 a prestigious French opinion research institute (Sofres) produced results showing that 58 per cent of the French reacted positively when asked whether they were in favour of reunification; 28 per cent favoured the retention of two German states; 43 per cent expressed the view that reunification would make more difficult the political integration of Germany; and 37 per cent were afraid that the position of France would be weakened by German unification (Grosser 1990: 148). At the end of 1990 a study by the same institute showed that 58 per cent took a positive view of German reunification, 9 per cent were against it, and 28 per cent answered 'don't care' ('Das Profil,' 1991: 27). A year earlier, at the beginning of 1990, a poll by *The Economist* and the *Los Angeles Times* had been conducted in Great Britain, France, Poland and the United States (see Table 11.1). A poll by a French institute, CSA, which had also been conducted at the beginning of 1990 in the Federal Republic, Spain, France, Great Britain, Italy, Hungary, Poland and the Soviet Union, produced results such as those given in Table 11.2.

All the poll results show that the unification of Germany mobilised a variety of deep-seated feelings, expectations and fears, or, in the words used by Claude Cheysson in a BBC interview on 28 May 1989: 'Before the Germans were tempted by the wind of the East, our Germans were fully integrated' – and now it was important to ensure that things stayed that way.

It is the fear that Germany might become too powerful which, above all else, dominates public opinion in Poland, the country

Table 11.1 'Do you favour or oppose the unification of Germany?'
(figures in %)

	Britain	France	Poland	America
Favour	45	61	41	61
Oppose	30	15	44	13
Neither	19	19	14	9
Don't know	6	5	1	17

(*Source: The Economist*, 27.1.90, pp. 29–34)

Table 11.2 'Do you personally take a positive or negative view of
German reunification?' (figures in %)

	FRG	Spain	France	Britain	Italy	Hungary	Poland	USSR
Very positive	31	48	17	21	41	23	9	17
Rather positive	49	25	51	40	37	45	17	34
Rather negative	15	4	17	15	8	16	26	17
Very negative	2	2	6	12	5	6	38	13
Don't know	3	21	9	12	9	10	10	19

(*Source: Frankfurter Rundschau*, 19.2.90, p. 16)

which suffered most under Germany during the Second World
War, and to a lesser extent in France (despite thirty years' official
partnership) and in Great Britain. As might be expected, the
reasons for this are complex. Underlying it is the historical experience of these countries with 'the Germans', which is intimately
connected with the question of the German nation-state and its role
in the middle of Europe. And there is the old fear of German
romanticism, irrationalism and nationalism. Western reactions to
the events of 1989 and 1990 demonstrate that, despite all official
pronouncements, attitudes to the Germans are reserved, cautious
and sometimes coloured by suspicion. Occasionally there is even a
touch of the bizarre, as when, for example, Roger Scruton describes Germany as a vacuum in the heart of Europe, as

a tomb in which the remnants of Prussia once were buried, and in which
the ghost of a stricken people constantly reappears, calling for vengeance
and redemption . . . The Germans now wish to throw their arms away;
their longing is based on guilt . . . We should recognise in these things
something of the exorbitant spirit which spoke through Hitler: the desire
to transcend the patient work of politics, into a state of unity and grace.
(Scruton 1989)

Heleno Saña expresses similar ideas derived from historical memory. In his book *The Fourth Reich. Germany's Late Victory*, he sees the Germans as having two political options: 'Some want to dominate Europe from the outside, the rest from within. The first option is the more primitive, the second the more subtle, both hold out the promise of nothing good. For neither the one nor the other would bring about the de-Germanicisation which the world and not least the Germans themselves need in order to free themselves of their megalomaniac obsessions' (Saña 1990: 267). And, finally, a French source: Georges Valance, Editor-in-Chief of *L'Express*. Like Zbigniev Brzezinski who, in an interview with *Le Figaro* (18 July 1990), noted that 'the end of the Cold War would leave two victors: the United States and Germany. And two losers: the USSR and France', Valance sees France as losing out after German unification: 'German reunification constitutes a tremendous challenge to France. Since the war France has been lucky, very lucky . . . The German economic giant is being transformed before our eyes into a political giant. The centre of Europe is moving towards Berlin as Paris takes on the aspect of a southern city. The future of the continent is dealt with in Bonn, Moscow or Washington. Paris is just kept informed' (Valance 1990: 9).

In spite of the positive attitude which their neighbours in east and west have taken towards the Germans' wish to be reunited, there remain doubts about the steadfastness and political reliability of the Germans. A reunified Germany has still to prove that it is in a position to preserve the Federal Republic's forty-year-old democratic tradition despite its increased size and the threat of social and political conflicts.

In 1949, at a celebration to mark the birth two hundred years earlier of Johann Wolfgang von Goethe, Thomas Mann regretted that the ideals of European democracy had never enjoyed prestige or political power in Germany. Politicians in the Federal Republic subsequently adopted all the more readily Thomas Mann's hope and demand, expressed at the time with considerable pathos, that a European Germany should grow which was a good place to live and to which the world could respond positively rather than with fear 'because it has a part in the democratic religion of mankind' (Mann 1968: 214).

Translated from the German by Ian Wallace.

References

Arnold, Karl-Heinz, *Die ersten hundert Tage des Hans Modrow*, Dietz: Berlin, 1990

Bahr, Egon, 'Das Gebot staatlicher Einheit und das Ziel Europa im Widerspruch', *Frankfurter Rundschau* ('Dokumentation'), 13.12.88, p. 10

Bender, Peter, *Neue Ostpolitik. Vom Mauerbau zum Moskauer Vertrag*, dtv: Munich, 1986

'Bericht der Bundesregierung zur politischen Lage der Nation im geteilten Deutschland', in Presse- und Informationsamt der Bundesregierung (ed.), *Bulletin*, 123, 9.11.89, pp. 1059ff.

'The Best Germany We Have Had', *Independent*, 25.5.89, p. 24

Brandt, Willy, 'Deutsche Wegmarken', *Tagesspiegel*, 13.9.88, p. 9

Broder, David S., 'Start Planning for a New Era and a New Germany', *International Herald Tribune*, 15.11.89

Bruns, Wilhelm, *Von der Deutschlandpolitik zur DDR-Politik? Prämissen, Probleme, Perspektiven*, Leske & Budrich: Opladen, 1989

'Christlich-demokratische Perspektiven zur Außen-, Sicherheits-, Europa- und Deutschlandpolitik', *Frankfurter Allgemeine Zeitung*, 19.2.88, p. 4.

DDR Journal 2, Die Wende der Wende. Januar bis März 1990. Von der Öffnung des Brandenburger Tores zur Öffnung der Wahlurnen, ed. Tageszeitung, Berlin, 1990

Frisch, Max, 'Wir hoffen', in Frank Grube and Gerhard Richter (eds), *Der SPD-Staat*, Piper: Munich, 1977, pp. 14–21

Garton Ash, Timothy, 'Germany Unbound', *New York Review of Books*, 22.11.90

Gasteyger, Curt, *Die beiden deutschen Staaten in der Weltpolitik*, Piper: Munich, 1976

Glaeßner, Gert-Joachim, 'Die Ost- und Deutschlandpolitik', in Gert-Joachim Glaeßner, Jürgen Holz, and Thomas Schlüter (eds), *Die Bundesrepublik in den siebziger Jahren, Versuch einer Bilanz*, Westdeutscher Verlag: Opladen, 1984, pp. 237ff.

——, 'The Fall of "True Socialism" and the Meaning of German Democracy', in *The Oxford International Review*, 1 (1), 1990, pp. 4f.

Grosser, Alfred, 'Es könnte doch viel schlimmer werden . . . Eine kritische Betrachtung aus Paris', in Ulrich Wickert (ed.), *Angst vor Deutschland*, Hoffmann & Campe: Hamburg, 1990, pp. 141–52

Hawkes, Nigel, 'Fatherland in Display of Maternal Instinct', *Observer*, 18.6.89

Kellner, Peter, 'Keeping the Germans on a Leash', *Independent*, 12.6.89

Kissinger, Henry, 'Living with the Inevitable', *Newsweek*, 4.12.89, pp. 22–5

Larrabee, F. Stephen, 'The Unavoidable "German Question"', *New York Times*, 21.9.89

Mann, Thomas, 'Goethe und die Demokratie', *Politische Schriften und Reden*, vol. 3, Fischer: Frankfurt a.M., 1968, pp. 212–33

McGrory, Mary, 'Have the Germans Really Changed?' *Washington Post*, 15.10.89, pp. B1–B5

'One Germany: Bonn's Quiet Yearning', *New York Times*, 23.9.89

Pipes, Richard, 'The Russians Are Still Coming', *New York Times*, 6.10.89

'Das Profil der Deutschen. Was sie vereint, was sie trennt', *Spiegel Spezial*, 1, 1991

Saña, Heleno, *Das vierte Reich. Deutschlands später Sieg*, Rasch und Röhring: Hamburg, 1990

Schmidt, Helmut, 'Einer unserer Brüder. Zum Besuch Erich Honeckers', *Die Zeit*, 31, 24.7.87, p. 3

——, 'Was ist der Deutschen Vaterland? Ein endgültiger Verzicht auf die Einheit würde nur das Mißtrauen unserer Nachbarn in Ost und West verstärken', *Die Zeit*, 29, 14.7.89, p. 4

Scruton, Roger, 'Don't Trust the Germans. Far from offering the greatest hope for the future of Europe, West Germany's eagerness for detente with the Soviet Union poses a serious threat to our security', *Sunday Telegraph*, 21.6.89

Sommer, Theo, 'Quo vadis Germania? Eine Standortbestimmung der Bundesrepublik nach den Besuchen von Bush und Gorbatschow', *Die Zeit*, 26, 23.6.89, p. 3

Strauß, Franz Josef, 'Die moralische Substanz der Nation bleibt erhalten. Beitrag von Franz Josef Strauß beim Münchner Podium 84 "Reden über das eigene Land: Deutschland"', *Frankfurter Rundschau* ('Dokumentation'), 2.1.85, p. 16

Tarnoff, Peter, 'A Bizarre Nostalgia for the Cold War', *New York Times*, 19.9.89

Trevor-Roper, Hugh, 'On the Unification of Germany', *The Independent Magazine*, 17.6.89

Valance, Georges, *France Allemagne. Le retour des Bismarck*, Flammarion: Paris, 1990

Wallace, William, 'Germany Is the Key as Europe Emerges from the Post-War Ice', *Independent*, 14.6.89, p. 24

Zumwalt, Elmo, and Bagley, Worth, 'When Will Mikhail Run out of Steam?' *The Washington Times*, 11.10.89

Notes on Contributors

Mike **Dennis** is Senior Lecturer in Contemporary History and Interdisciplinary Studies at Wolverhampton Polytechnic. He is the author of *German Democratic Republic. Politics, Economics and Society* and edited a special GDR issue for *East Central Europe*.

Gert-Joachim **Glaeßner** is Professor of Political Science at the Humboldt University and the Institute for Social Science Research in Berlin. He has written numerous works on comparative communism and the GDR, most recently *Der schwierige Weg zur Demokratie. Vom Ende der DDR zur deutschen Einheit* and, as editor, *Eine deutsche Revolution. Der Umbruch in der DDR, seine Ursachen und Folgen*.

Henry **Krisch** is Professor of Political Science at the University of Connecticut in Storrs and President of the GDR Studies Association of the USA. His publications include books on *German Politics under Soviet Occupation* and *The German Democratic Republic. The Search for Identity*.

Manfred **Lötsch** was Professor of Sociology at the Academy of Social Sciences in the former GDR. An acknowledged expert in the analysis of social structure, he has published widely on this topic and on the scientific and technical revolution.

Martin **McCauley** is Senior Lecturer in Soviet and East European Studies at the School of Soviet and East European Studies, University of London. He has worked on the GDR for over 20 years and among his publications are *Marxism-Leninism in the GDR: Socialist Unity Party (SED)* and *The German Democratic Republic since 1945*.

Sigrid **Meuschel** is a *Privatdozentin* at the Free University of Berlin. Her recent book, *Legitimation und Parteiherrschaft. Zum Paradox von Stabilität und Revolution in der DDR 1945–1989*, deals with German political culture and the impact of the national question on the GDR.

August **Pradetto** is Senior Research Fellow at the Institute for International and Regional Studies at the Free University of Berlin. His most recent publications are *Techno-bürokratischer Sozialismus in Polen in der Ära Gierek (1970–1980)*, a book on Poland during the Gierek era, and *Bürokratische Anarchie. Der Niedergang des polnischen 'Realsozialismus'*.

Rolf **Reißig** is Director of the Berlin-based Institute of Studies in the Social Sciences. Previously, he was the last Director of the Academy of Social Sciences in the former GDR. With Gert-Joachim Glaeßner he co-edited the book *Das Ende eines Experiments. Umbruch in der DDR und deutsche Einheit*.

John **Sandford** is Professor of German at the University of Reading. His main research interests lie in the fields of post-war German politics (in particular the politics of dissent in the GDR), the German mass media, and the German cinema.

Ian **Wallace** is Professor of German at the University of Bath. He is founder/editor of *German Monitor* (formerly *GDR Monitor*), has published widely on GDR cultural affairs, and is currently working on a book on Anna Seghers.

Index

Index

Of Related Interest

Europe and German Unification

By Renata Fritsch-Bournazel

The unforeseen end to the postwar period in Europe confronted both the Germans themselves and their neighbors and allies with the need to rethink existing positions and reformulate the relationship between Germany and Europe as a whole. The author of the highly successful *Confronting the German Question* has completely rewritten and updated her material for this new assessment of the situation at the beginning of the 1990s.

It is well documented throughout and uses a broad selection of assessments and statements by both protagonists and commentators to probe this central question of our times.

Renata Fritsch-Bournazel is Senior Fellow of the Centre for International Relations of the Fondation Nationale des Sciences Politiques and Professor of Politics at the Institute d'Etudes Politiques, Paris.

January 1992
272 pp.
bibliography, index
0 85496 979 9
0 85496 684 6 (paperback)

Uniting Germany: The Unexpected Challenge

Edited by Dieter Grosser

German unification came as a surprise. Nobody in West Germany had expected the collapse of the German Democratic Republic so soon. What were the causes of the breakdown of the Communist system in East Germany? How did the Federal Republic and the Four Powers react when unification first became possible, then inevitable? Was there an alternative to the currency union? How does German unification affect the European Community and the international system? These are some of the fundamental questions examined in this volume by distinguished German political scientists.

Dieter Grosser is at the Geschwister-Scholl Institute of Political Science, Munich.

July 1992
ca. 200 pp.
bibliography, index
0 85496 752 4
German Historical Perspectives Vol. VII